SOMETHING'S IN THE AIR

America's drug laws have always exerted an unequal and unfair toll on Blacks and Latinos, who are arrested more often than Whites for the possession of illegal drugs and given harsher sentences. In this volume, contributors ask: how would marijuana legalization affect communities of color? Is legalization of marijuana necessary to safeguard minority families from a lifetime of hardship and inequality? Who in minority communities favors legalization and why, and do these minority opinions differ from the opinions held by White Americans?

This volume also includes analyses of the policy debate by a range of scholars addressing economic, health, and empowerment issues. Comparative lessons are drawn from other countries as well.

Katherine Tate is Professor of Political Science at the University of California, Irvine. She is the author and coauthor of several books, including most recently, *What's Going On? Political Incorporation and the Transformation of Black Public Opinion.*

James Lance Taylor is Associate Professor and Chair of the Department of Politics at the University of San Francisco. Taylor is the author of *Black Nationalism in the United States: From Malcolm X to Barack Obama.*

Mark Q. Sawyer is Professor of African American Studies and Political Science at UCLA. He is the author of the award winning book, *Racial Politics in Post Revolutionary Cuba*, and co-editor of *Just Neighbors?: Research on African Americans and Latino Relations in the United States.*

SOMETHING'S IN THE AIR

Race, Crime, and the Legalization of Marijuana

*Edited by Katherine Tate, James Lance Taylor,
and Mark Q. Sawyer*

Routledge
Taylor & Francis Group

NEW YORK AND LONDON

First published 2014
by Routledge
711 Third Avenue, New York, NY 10017

Simultaneously published in the UK
by Routledge
2 Park Square, Milton Park, Abingdont Oxon OX14 4RN

*Routledge is an imprint of the Taylor & Francis Group,
an informa business*

Library of Congress Cataloging-in-Publication Data

Something's in the air : race, crime, and the legalization of marijuana / edited
    by Katherine Tate, James Lance Taylor, and Mark Q. Sawyer.
        pages cm
    Includes bibliographical references.
    1. Drug legalization—Social aspects—United States.   2. Marijuana—
United States.   3. African Americans—Drug use.   4. Hispanic Americans—
Drug use.   5. Discrimination in criminal justice administration—United
States.   6. Minorities—United States—Social conditions.   I. Tate,
Katherine.   II. Taylor, James Lance.   III. Sawyer, Mark Q., 1972–
        HV5825.S58424 2013
        362.29'50973—dc23
        2012051299

ISBN: 978-0-415-84239-6 (hbk)
ISBN: 978-0-415-84240-2 (pbk)
ISBN: 978-0-203-75838-0 (ebk)

Typeset in Bembo
by Apex CoVantage, LLC

Printed and bound in the United States of America by Publishers Graphics,
LLC on sustainably sourced paper.

CONTENTS

List of Figures and Tables   vii

Editors' Introduction: Ending a War or Just California Dreamin'?   1
Katherine Tate, James Lance Taylor, and Mark Q. Sawyer

1   Criminal Justice Costs of Prohibiting Marijuana in California   13
Jonathan P. Caulkins and Beau Kilmer

2   Public-Health Considerations in the Legalization Debate   31
Chyvette T. Williams and Thomas Lyons

3   The Paths Not (Yet) Taken: Lower Risk Alternatives to
Full-Market Legalization of Cannabis   40
Robert J. MacCoun

4   Why Did Proposition 19 Fail?   54
J. Andrew Sinclair, Jaclyn R. Kimble, and R. Michael Alvarez

5   Winds of Change: Black Opinion on Legalizing Marijuana   65
Katherine Tate

6   The Highs and Lows of Support for Marijuana Legalization
Among White Americans   79
Paul Musgrave and Clyde Wilcox

7 Building Minority Community Power Through Legalization   92
James Lance Taylor

8 The Latino Politics of Proposition 19: Criminal Justice
and Immigration   115
Melissa R. Michelson and Joe Tafoya

9 No Half-Measures: Mexico's Quixotic Policy on California's
Proposition 19   126
Nathan Jones

10 The "Chronic" and Coercion: Exploring How Legalizing
Marijuana Might Get the U.S. Government off the Backs
and Throats of Americans (or, Not)   139
Christian Davenport

References   *155*
List of Contributors   *171*
Index   *177*

FIGURES AND TABLES

Figures

1.1 Distribution of Criminal Justice Costs, by Category   27
3.1 Ratio of Past-month Drug Use Rates in Alaska vs. the Entire
     USA, 2003–2009   44
3.2 Trends in Lifetime Cannabis Prevalence 1985–1995,
     for Australian States and Territories   45
3.3 Changes in Cannabis Prices Relative to 1990 South
     Australia Levels   46
4.1 Distribution of Votes by County. (Statewide average is
     47 percent.)   62
4.2 The Darker the County, the Higher the Vote for Prop. 19   63
5.1 Support for Legalization of Marijuana by Race, 1973–2010   68
6.1 Support among Whites for Legalization by Generation   83
6.2 Support for Marijuana Compared to Other Issues among
     Whites   84
6.3 Estimated Effect and Standard Error of Membership in Social
     and Political Group on White Support for Legalization
     from 1975 to 2010   85
6.4 Probability of Supporting Marijuana Legalization by Party
     and Age in 2010   89

Tables

1.1 Criminal Justice Unit Costs for Drug Offenders in
     Six California Jurisdictions (US$ 2004)   18

1.2   2010 Marijuana Arrests in California, by Age and Level   18
1.3   Time Needed by California Judicial Officers to Resolve
      Cases in an Efficient and Effective Manner and
      Corresponding Cost at $18 per Minute   20
A1.1 Carey et al.'s (2005) Estimate of Time Needed for
      a Typical Court Case (in Minutes)   20
1.4   Marijuana Offenders in California Prisons,
      by Controlling Offense   21
1.5   Criminal Justice Costs of Prohibiting Marijuana for
      Those Aged 21 and Older in California   26
1.6   Sensitivity Analysis: Incremental Effect on Total Cost   27
2.1   Illinois Felony Cannabis Arrests, 2005   34
3.1   Patterns of Cannabis Prevalence in South Australia vs. Other
      Australian States and Territories   45
3.2   Assessing the Models   52
4.1   Survey Response Data. Who Favors Proposition 19?   57
4.2   Political Variables: Oppose, Don't Know, or Support for
      Proposition 19   58
4.3   Demographic Variables: Oppose, Don't Know, or Support for
      Proposition 19   59
4.4   Ordered Logistic Regression: 0 = Oppose, 1 = Don't Know,
      2 = Support. N = 2,811 California Registered Voters   61
5.1   2010 Poll on the Legalization of Marijuana and State
      Adoption of Medical Marijuana by Race (Weighted Data)   69
5.2   African American Opinions about Blacks and
      Special Favors, Spanking Children, Premarital Sex,
      and Courts and Criminals   72
5.3   Logistic Regression of Support for Legalization of Marijuana
      among African Americans, 2000–2010   75
8.1   White and Latino Marijuana Possession Arrest Rates
      in 33 California Cities, 2006–2008   119
9.1   Timeline of Calderón's Statements on Proposition 19   132

EDITORS' INTRODUCTION

Ending a War, or Just California Dreamin'?

Katherine Tate, James Lance Taylor, and Mark Q. Sawyer

America's drug laws have always exerted an unequal and unfair toll on racial and ethnic communities. Blacks, Latinos, and American Indians are arrested more often than Whites for the possession of illegal drugs, and courts also impose harsher sentences on minority drug offenders. In 2009, based on the U.S. Department of Justice statistics, 1.7 million adults were arrested for drug-abuse violations, and 46 percent of those arrests were for possession of marijuana. That is why when pro-marijuana advocates were able to get Proposition 19, an initiative to legalize marijuana for personal consumption by persons 21 and older, on the November 2010 ballot in California, the head of the state's NAACP chapter endorsed it. Proposition 19 also won the endorsement of Dr. Joycelyn Elders, the nation's first Black U.S. surgeon general, who served in the Clinton administration. Legalization of some drugs, like marijuana, Clarence Lusane writes, "would resolve some of the biggest problems of the current drug crisis and drug war" (1991, 214). The drug crisis and war on drugs disproportionately impact minority Americans (Alexander 2010; Lusane 1991; Provine 2007).

California, in 1996, was the first state to legalize the use of marijuana for medicinal purposes. By 2012, 16 states, including Washington, D.C., now permit its use with a medical prescription. In 2010, a majority-minority city, Oakland, California, became the first city in the nation to license factories (four of them) to grow and sell marijuana for medical use. Oakland's city council backed issuing pot licenses as a way to create new jobs. Advocates for legalizing marijuana contend that it should be a vehicle for the state to collect new revenues, treating it, therefore, like alcohol and taxing for revenue-collection proposes. It will save the state revenues from the cost of maintaining its overflowing drug courts and prisons. A main reason for the legalization of marijuana is that it will eliminate the illegal market and close off a long and terrible pipeline leading toward the mass incarceration of minority youth.

Yet there is also strong opposition to the legalization of marijuana under Proposition 19. Black churches have expressed opposition to Proposition 19. Most Democrats in California have opposed it. Governor Jerry Brown, the then-Democratic candidate in 2010, said he was against Proposition 19 because the state would lose revenue from the federal government if it passed. Democratic U.S. Senator Dianne Feinstein has said that Prop 19 would contribute to rising crime rates and violence. Kamala D. Harris, the Democratic candidate for California's state attorney general in 2010, said that the proposition would encourage "driving while high" and drug use at work. Public-health advocates argue that the taxes collected from the sale of marijuana won't cover the spike in health costs related to its use; in this way, too, it is like tobacco and alcohol. In general, some policy experts contend that Proposition 19 is a fantasy since federal legislation is required for the legalization of marijuana in the states (Kleiman 2010).

Marijuana for medicinal purposes was legalized first in 1996, but now, nearly 20 years later, little research exists in public policy on how new drug policies affect communities of color. As minority politics and race scholars, we feel a responsibility to communities of color in addressing current and controversial topics, and organized this volume to address the question of whether the legalization of marijuana would help or hurt the Black, Latino, and mixed-race communities. This type of research can contribute to a brighter future for minority citizens. America's rules have been harshly unfair to Blacks and minorities, and thus, we ask whether legalization of marijuana might be necessary to safeguard minority families from a lifetime of hardship and inequality. Some of us say yes and others say no, while some have yet to take a side in this debate. Who in minority communities favors legalization and why, and do these minority opinions differ from the opinions held by White Americans?

While we enter into the debate over the legalization of marijuana as it pertains to the improving or worsening conditions for minorities in this country, we have invited a range of scholars to join this debate because it raises racial, economic, social, health, and criminal justice issues. The issue is also worth exploring in both a national and cross-national comparative framework. The drug trade is international, and U.S. drug policies will have global effects. While some see the drug war in Latin America as contributing to violent lawlessness and extending U.S. influence into the region, others believe decriminalizing marijuana or other drugs will only lead to more resources for violent drug cartels. Thus, we take on this question broadly, asking what explains this new drive for legalization in states, and what are the economic advantages and disadvantages of legalization for Americans generally? Is legalization feasible, practical, even inevitable? In addition to its use as a textbook in minority-politics courses as a new social policy matter, we see this volume as having wide appeal for courses on American government, law, public policy, criminal justice, urban politics, and public health.

In the next section, we present both sides of this debate from a minority-politics perspective.[1] A minority perspective reflects the legal and political constraints facing communities still disadvantaged by poverty, unemployment, lower levels of education, and social stigma. While the style of the section may be different from the style in other essays, it represents a useful view into the debate that launched this volume. This perspective also considers prospects for minority advancement in light of changing racial attitudes and political trends in this country. We then conclude with an outline of the organization of this volume.

This Is Our Exit Strategy: The Case for Legalization

Since the 1980s, the number of people under correctional supervision, either in prison, on probation, or on parole, has increased significantly, from 1.8 million in 1980 to 7.3 million, based on statistics reported by the Bureau of Justice Statistics of the U.S. Department of Justice. Blacks make up nearly half of the state and federal prison populations, even though they represent only about 12 percent of the U.S. population (Bell 2006; Mauer 1999). The process starts with the young. The Sentencing Project found that one in four Black males 20 to 29 years old were under criminal justice supervision in 1989 (Mauer 1999). In 1997, 9 percent of the Black population was in jail or had been jailed compared to 2 percent of the White population, based on government statistics. Young offenders are taken from their families and sent to prison, and then these minority young adults are released with criminal records, unable to find a job. For Black women, an increase in their rates of incarceration also occurred between 1985 and 1995. Drug convictions can carry felony charges, and thus, some ex-offenders are barred for life from ever voting.

Recreational drug use remains high; prison time does not reduce rates of addiction. Some policymakers think the best approach is to decriminalize soft drug use, like marijuana. Increasingly, analysts think marijuana use at home is not harmful, and yet millions are arrested each year for its use. African American House Representative Charles Rangel (D-NY), once the chair of the powerful Ways and Means Committee, thinks the country should decriminalize pot instead of wasting more resources on preventing its trafficking and use. At a House Judiciary subcommittee meeting, he stated, "There's no question that with the limited resources . . . that we put on law enforcement, that we ought to decriminalize it" (Katel 2009). Ten states reduced penalties for marijuana possession so first-time offenders receive no jail time. Furthermore, at this time, marijuana use for medicinal purposes is legal in 14 American states. The federal government in the Obama administration decided to drop its opposition to states having medical pot–dispensaries (Katel 2009), but later vigorously ratcheted up drug law enforcement against such dispensaries.

For increasing numbers of Americans, legalization of personal-use marijuana is the *only* alternative to draconian laws drawn up in the "war on drugs" regime of the past three decades. It is well established that concern and paranoia over petty "crack" cocaine arrests for sales, possession, and use drove the mass warehousing of California's prisons and jail populations to become the largest in the United States (Lusane 1991; Provine 2007; Reinerman and Levine 1997; Weatherspoon 1998; Weaver 2007). Miller (2008) contends that the U.S. federal system of crime control has left minority citizens less able to challenge unfair sentencing laws.

Noting that marijuana possession constituted nearly 8 of 10 drug-related *arrests* in the 1990s, Michelle Alexander (2010) insists that this period of "unprecedented punitiveness" resulted "in prison sentences (rather than dismissal, community service, or probation)" to the degree that "in two short decades, between 1980 and 2000, the number of people incarcerated in our nation's prisons and jails soared from roughly 300,000 to more than 2 million. By the end of 2007, more than 7 million Americans—or one in every 31 adults—were behind bars, on probation, or parole" (Alexander 2010, 59). Pushed by drug prosecutions, the rising rate of incarceration reached unprecedented levels in the 1990s. Today's movement toward more prisons, mandatory minimums, and reinstatement of the death penalty logically followed the racially exploitative "law and order" campaigns of the 1960s and 1970s (Murakawa 2008). Conservative American politicians use the mythical Black or Hispanic male drug dealer, like the Black female welfare queen, to drum up votes.

A widespread consensus in reported government statistics, advocacy studies, and policy think tanks suggests that African Americans bear the brunt of law-and-order management of U.S. marijuana laws because of how marijuana use is *racialized*. Political scientist Doris Provine contends that the U.S. government increased its punitive response toward drug use as a response to racial fears and stereotypes. She writes: "[d]rugs remain, symbolically, a menace to white, middle-class values" (2007, 89). Both politicians and media have used this issue to construct a crisis and sustain punitive state drug laws. The war on drugs, she concludes, has greatly harmed minority citizens through their imprisonment, contributing to deep inequalities in education, housing, health care, and equal opportunities to advance economically.

The facts of use, sales, and possession, confirmed by academic and critical legal studies literature, are strikingly different from how the national and local media choose to present them. One study focusing on marijuana initiate found "among Blacks, the annual incidence rate (per 1,000 potential new users) increased from 8.0 in 1966 to 16.7 in 1968, reached a peak at about the same time as "Whites" (19.4 in 1976), then remained high throughout the late 1970s. Following the low rates in the 1980s, rates among Blacks rose again in the early 1990s, reached a peak in 1997 and 1998 (19.2 and 19.1, respectively), then dropped to 14.0 in 1999. Similar to the general pattern for Whites and Blacks, Hispanics' annual incidence rate rose during late 1970s and 1990s, with a peak in 1998 (17.8)" (National Survey on Drug Use 1999).

Individuals and groups in civil society, advocacy communities, and state legislatures must put forth a serious struggle among activists and potential coalition partners who can understand the need for reform as a matter of civil rights and justice, and not the morality of marijuana consumption. Supporting decriminalization potentially can be the training ground for a new generation of leadership in addressing the larger problem of mass incarceration and social and political isolation associated with it. For Black people and their allies who long for the days—against all odds—of political education, voter mobilization, legal reform, group solidarity, challenge to the political parties, and political empowerment, expressed in the modern civil rights movement, the matter of decriminalization is ripe for galvanizing a collaboration at the grassroots. Too many Blacks have assumed that the "War on Drugs" ended with the dissipation of the "crack" emergency, when, in sum, marijuana's criminalization—rather than incarceration—of Black people has been more perennial.

If Michelle Alexander (2010) is correct in arguing that mass incarceration has effectively reasserted Jim Crow second-class citizenship (or no citizenship) rights on African American people, then they must get off the sidelines of the legalization of cannabis or decriminalization struggle and stop allowing others to fight what is essentially their battle. This has long been the case in the challenge to the crushing "prison industrial complex." Whites and others, for the most part, have been the leaders in reform efforts concerning such things as mandatory minimums, the old 100:1 gram of cocaine-to-crack formula, and health care for geriatric or HIV/AIDS patients in prisons, while we have seen Calvin "Snoop-Dogg" Broadus become more influential than the congressional Black Caucus to our young. When ordinary people change their thinking and consciousness and begin to demystify small, personal-use marijuana, then the leaders will eventually come around without reticence or fear. The marijuana debate needs to be reframed to remove all penalties against its use (Scherlen 2012). This is our exit strategy; decriminalization reform is the only path to reversing the dismal trends minorities face in America.

California Dreamin': The Case against Cannabis

Proposition 19 lost, but its supporters in California still dream of a win and have pledged to put it back to a public vote again. In 2012, pro-marijuana groups in Colorado and Washington State had enough signatures to place legalization measures on their November 2012 ballots, and their initiatives passed in the November elections. The federal government may very well sue states that legalize marijuana for personal use because federal laws trump state laws in this matter. In lawsuits, the federal courts would likely agree with the federal government's argument that it cannot successfully defend its ban on the drug if some states legalize a substance that the government considers neither medicine nor safe. The U.S. Supreme Court ruled 6–3 in *Gonzalez v. Raich* in 2005 that, under the Commerce Clause, the federal government has the right to prosecute those growing cannabis for home use, even in states where it is legal for medical use.

The Food and Drug Administration (FDA) has not approved marijuana use for any condition or disease. Marijuana has passive smoking effects on the health of children and elderly, just like cigarettes do. The new policy environment in states permitting its use for therapeutic purposes overshadows the clear research establishing that marijuana use has unwanted side effects, triggering asthma and causing lung cancer. It also impairs memory and motor skills, robbing the user of the ability to think clearly as well as operate a vehicle. Yet its long-term effect on the brain is unclear, making this mood-altering drug dangerous for people, especially the immature brains of children. The federal government contends marijuana use is often a precursor to use of other illegal substances, such as cocaine, methamphetamine, and acid. Domestic and sexual violence is correlated with marijuana use, as well.

First, the case against legal cannabis starts with the position that legalization won't end the racism in the criminal justice system. The California chapter of the American Civil Liberties Union (ACLU) endorsed Proposition 19 as a rational response to ending a costly and failing drug war. The state ACLU position suggests that legalization might reduce the extreme racial disparities in criminal arrests. Legalization will not end the nightmare that Blacks and Latinos face daily in the American criminal justice system. Racism will still mean that racial disparities in prosecution and sentencing will continue since the underage will still be targeted. Racial profiling will persist, and unlawful police abuse of minority citizens will continue. The police will continue to stop and frisk minorities more than Whites, and senseless police violence leading to the deaths of minority suspects will continue. Furthermore, calculating politicians will remain hostile to minorities and will continue to criminalize, even if marijuana becomes legal. Legalization might only harden the racial disparities in arrests, reducing the penalties White youth suffer from being caught, but not reducing them for Black and Latino youth. Marijuana legalization cannot be made into a "civil rights" issue. Greater efforts need to be spent on challenging the racism broadly in the American legal system.

Second, the establishment of pot dispensaries and marijuana farms in California won't help the problem of unemployment and underemployment in minority communities. The Indian casino example is important since casino gambling emerged during a time when the federal government was determined to reduce levels of federal assistance to American Indians, who, after a century of hostile and misguided federal policies, were experiencing high rates of poverty, under education, crime, and health issues. American Blacks and Latinos also lack the protections and sovereignty American Indians have to ensure that revenues from gaming are distributed fairly and widely to American Indians. Meanwhile, American Indians continue to lag behind Americans in terms of poverty rates and educational attainment. In 2008, 30 percent of American Indians lived below the poverty line, double the national average. Gaming did not reduce the group's high poverty rate. Gaming, however, did lead to significant wealth for some tribes in the 1990s, but some Indians have expressed concerns about the long-term costs of casinos to

Indians and some Indians have mixed feelings about casinos (Wilkins 2007). The politics of "self-sufficiency" efforts for American Indians also deflects responsibility for the social and economic conditions they face from the federal government's policies of assimilation and termination, as well as from discrimination in their states. It plays into a neoliberal agenda that supports market forces as a better way to achieve better outcomes for disadvantaged minorities. It feeds fantastical beliefs that minorities on their own, without government assistance, can improve their grim economic job prospects and economically disadvantaged schools, and close down the opportunistic businesses that tend to spring up in their segregated communities.

Racial advocates need to sustain efforts toward group reparations for Blacks who have been tragic victims of America's laws and policies (Walters 2008). Latinos need sane immigration laws to protect their communities from continued exploitation and despair. Without these political efforts, denial of America's racist and exploitative past will remain strong under a rising tide of American conservatism. We need to reject the self-help economic framework behind the push for legalization. Legalization is no panacea for unemployment, poverty, and homelessness among Blacks, Latinos, and American Indians. While advocates of legalization like to claim that increases in social services to poor and minority community would accompany legalization, there is no indication that state and federal governments, in fact, would couple legalization with increased spending on anti-drug-abuse public health programs.

Drug legalization will increase consumption. Most of all, illegal drugs will continue to be heavily marketed and sold in poor and minority communities. Thus, minority communities face severe social costs in legalizing pot. There is a strong correlation with drug use, crime, and violence. Furthermore, studies establish that students who use drugs such as marijuana do not perform in school as well as students who abstain. Blacks and Latinos suffer already from extremely high school-dropout rates relative to Whites and Asian Americans. An illegal drug trade also will likely still flourish, and it will continue, for many reasons, including that nations supplying illegal drugs such as marijuana will continue to ban them, and their poor will continue to be pulled into violent and socially destructive drug wars. With the continuation of illegal international distributors, it will be impossible to end illicit drug trafficking.

Legalization of pot will legitimate illegal lifestyles, where young minorities will continue to pulled into the illegal trade that will exist under tightly regulated and geographically limited markets. Proposition 19 carries tough penalties for those distributing marijuana to minors, and thus, the young will remain at risk for incarceration, even where marijuana is legalized for wealthy adult users. Once it is legal, young children will be exposed to drugs in their homes more and also at risk of being compelled to participate in drug use by other relatives. One scholar of Black politics, Cathy J. Cohen (2010), points out that young Blacks lack the agency or the freedom to make a better life for themselves. Her survey

work reveals that most young Blacks want middle-class conventionality for themselves and their future families, but the lives that they actually live are interpreted
as collective defiance instead of understood as rooted in a negative-opportunity
structure. Legalization will continue to limit the options minorities have to keep
drugs and a dangerous drug culture away from their kids.

Furthermore, legalization of this drug will erode the moral fabric of the
community. This is old-fashioned rhetoric in light of the marijuana advocates'
longstanding civil-liberties argument for its legalization. Thus, this case against
legalization sounds like the sentiment of the "preacher" liking "the cold" in the
song "California Dreamin'" by the Mamas & Papas.[2] Pro-marijuana groups,
including social libertarians, see the government's ban on cannabis as a violation
of one's civil liberties protected under the Constitution, in addition to having
contributed to the significant rise in incarceration in this country. Others have
likened it to being denied personal freedoms such as the right to an abortion and
same-sex marriage.

The analogies are unfair because pregnancies and homosexuality are not personal choices for women, gays, and lesbians but are rooted in biology. The correct
analogy for the legalization of marijuana is the legalization of prostitution, since
both have serious negative group externalities, especially for women and children.
Feminists, however, are deeply divided over the matter of prostitution. Legalization
of prostitution, proponents claim, would eliminate the stigma and social construction of sex workers as deviants, leading to greater equality and freedom for marginal members of society. Still, Julia O'Connell Davidson (1998) in her discussion
of this debate writes that while she is sympathetic to feminist calls for prostitutes
to have "the same legal and political rights and protections" other citizens have, she
says the data from her research on prostitution makes her not want to "celebrate
the existence of a market for commoditized sex." The feminist debate over prostitution generally lacks references to the huge gulf between rich and poor countries,
and that the yoke of prostitution generally goes to these poor nations. "Burma,"
she writes, "with a capita GPD of just U.S. $69, exports an estimated 20,000 to
30,000 women and girls to work in prostitution in Thailand, while several thousand more cross the border into China to sell sex" (2002, 94).

Feminists opposed to the legalization of prostitution argue that proponents
tend to gloss over the fact that we have a world bent on exploiting women, girls,
and minorities. The Western idea of "individual freedom," where citizens can be
set free from state oppression, fails to recognize that freedom is contingent upon a
set of economic, social, and political relations. The world's strongly race, gendered,
classed, and legal recognition of sex work won't change that. The same applies to
the legalization of marijuana in the United States.

Therefore, the destructive path of drug addiction, and sometimes even casual
use, won't magically go away through legalization. The uneven toll it takes on
the lives of poor minority families won't disappear through legalization, either.
Because minorities see the daily damage on families and communities caused

by drug use, drug addiction, and drug trafficking, many will remain opposed to legalization. Just as some (often minority women and the young) are forced into the sex trade, some will be forced into the drug market (often minority men and the young).

Finally, legalization represents a dream carrying dangerous, long-term, and chilling political costs. These are the kinds of costs to a Black civil rights agenda that Derrick Bell (2004) passionately argues came with the landmark 1954 *Brown* decision, outlawing *de jure* segregation in public schools. *Brown,* he argues, "dismisses *Plessy*," the 1896 ruling upholding separate-but-equal, "without dismantling it." After *Brown,* he points out, the massive continuing problem of segregation leading to the unequal education of minority school children now was widely seen as rooted in things such income inequality or other cultural factors, not in American racism. Legalization of marijuana, therefore, could do the same, silencing further claims about this unfairness since the "only" unfairness left now in the criminal justice system under legal pot is punishing "drug trafficking" and "criminal-minded" minors or "dangerous" and "violent" minority drunks. Bell theorizes that *Plessy* was struck down because it served the long-term interests of White Americans. The benefits of *Brown* to Blacks, he contends, were nil.

Thus, Bell concludes that we can't fix American racism with American law. American law operates under a silent covenant, or the understanding by elites that the racial order will be the same. Furthermore, like *Brown,* legalization will reduce public responsibility and a public response to a legacy of racism and discrimination in the criminal justice system against minority citizens. Arguments that racism continues to inflict serious harm on minorities and their families will be dismissed in the same manner that concerns over segregation in public schools are dismissed. In the end, under legalization, many will argue that problems continue to exist in the minority community only because this community has a higher percentage of individuals who *abuse* drugs.

Legalization demands today appear especially elitist, and literally so, because legalization may really only benefit America's economic and social elites. In fact, medical marijuana profoundly illustrates the way laws protect wealth and "Whiteness" over the poor Black and Latino communities. Wealthy Americans use this legal route over the poor, who can only gain access to the drug through illegal means. Legalization of one banned substance for social use will not kill the disease of racism in America, as supporters claim. While some proponents of legalization talk about keeping the price of the drug high to generate higher taxes and keeping its use low, others point out that this strategy will not eliminate then the black market (Pacula 2009; quoted in Scherlen 2012).

Legalization of marijuana won't free the black and brown prisoners, and high rates of incarceration for minorities may continue unabated in states where pot is legal. Minorities must understand that laws and policies may not apply to them equally. Furthermore, "law abiding" and "decent" Americans will still seek to blame Blacks and Latinos for the social ills involved in drug use; minorities will continue to be punished for it, and a racial disparity in sentencing for drug use will persist. In the end, legalization won't result in any collective benefits for Blacks, Latinos and other minority groups, only punishing social costs combined with the enormous political cost of adopting a policy to kill racism in the American legal system and society when it won't.

The Chapters in This Volume

The legalization debate continues to heat up. This issue is not likely to go away. We asked several scholars and policy experts to write chapters addressing key issues in the debate. In the first section of this volume, we present chapters that broadly examine the question of legalization; scholars engaged in the drug policy and public health fields wrote these. What are the costs and benefits of legalization to the state, and to the nation? Who is paying for the War on Drugs, and can we more fruitfully walk away from it through the legalization of marijuana? Some believe that states should legalize marijuana. State legalization would not only save taxpayer dollars, it also would increase state revenues as a new "sin tax." Legalization, therefore, would serve as a new state lottery program. In Chapter 1, Jonathan P. Caulkins and Beau Kilmer investigate such claims. While estimates range from up to \$2 billion to prosecute illegal marijuana use, they find the savings to the state are much lower. Still, the fact that the state is poised to save money through legalization remains an important reason why increasing numbers of Americans now support legalization.

Some contend that marijuana in small quantities is no more harmful than beer. Others insist that marijuana is substantially more dangerous. What are the public health costs involved in legalization? In Chapter 2, Chyvette T. Williams and Thomas Lyons contend that criminalizing marijuana has actually increased health costs in the United States where American minorities suffer widening disparities in health because drug laws and enforcement disproportionately affect them. These costs accrue to the public through Medicare. Thus, again, the financial toll the criminalization of marijuana use has on the public sector merits careful further study. The criminalization of marijuana may be too costly for Americans to continue to bear.

Chapter 3 of the volume, by Robert J. MacCoun, explores further the economic components behind the push for legalization. Proposition 19 was flawed, some contend, because as a full-market approach, it doesn't provide a real solution to the lines of conflict between federal and state government in drug enforcement. The federal government has sought to prosecute those growing marijuana for personal consumption, something Proposition 19 would permit. An ongoing conflict between the federal government and the state of California has flared up over the state's medical-pot dispensaries. The best public policy on marijuana, MacCoun writes, would permit legal access yet reduce consumption. Clearly, such a policy would yield better levels of support because it would attract those on the field who want to continue its prohibition but don't like the high enforcement costs. MacCoun provides an analysis outlining the potential strengths and weakness of several paths toward legalization, such as home cultivation, cannabis coffee shops, or recreational cannabis clubs.

We also address the question of what explains the rising push for legalization in California. In 1972, California voters rejected a proposition to legalize marijuana. When they went to the polls again in 2010, some political analysts noted that since many California voters were undecided, Proposition 19 might actually pass. Instead, it lost by a margin of 46.5 to 53.5 percent. In Chapter 4, J. Andrew Sinclair, Jaclyn R. Kimble, and R. Michael Alvarez analyze opinion data from the fall of 2010, and they tell us why Proposition 19 lost. One important finding in their analysis is that while some Black leaders backed legalization of marijuana in 2010, the Blacks in the state who voted in the 2010 mid-term elections were conservative-minded on the matter, rejecting it by a significantly higher margin than White mid-term voters did. Timing this for an election year yielding a higher turnout and winning high-level Democratic or Republican Party support for the legalization of marijuana might help the advocates of legalization. Elite opinion on this matter, however, remains crucial in this debate.

In Chapters 5 and 6, we examine public opinion on this legalization issue using national opinion surveys. We include separate chapters on public opinion trends on legalization among African Americans and Whites. Who supports the legalization of marijuana, and why? Katherine Tate in Chapter 5 shows that opposition to legalization in the Black community is based on Black racial conservatism. Blacks who hold negative opinions of Blacks oppose legalization. For both groups, gender is important since Latinas and African American women are generally more opposed to legalization than Latinos and African American men. In Chapter 6, Paul Musgrave and Clyde Wilcox show that the increased support among Whites for legalization was not simply due to generational change. They contend a more favorable policy environment emerged, especially once medical marijuana became legal in some states. Thus, Whites, they contend, are very sensitive to the political frame in the debate. Framed negatively, White support for legalization could easily plummet.

In the remaining chapters, we return again to the issue of race and marijuana and what it means for minority communities, Mexico, and the United States. In Chapter 7, James Lance Taylor argues that the incarceration of Blacks for marijuana possession functions like slavery, the sharecropping system, lynching, and segregation in keeping African Americans from advancing in society. He writes, "Marijuana and other drug laws are effectively the 'Black codes' of the 21st century," and thus, they must be eradicated as part of a civil rights agenda. In Chapter 8, Melissa R. Michelson and Joe Tafoya contend that the criminalization of marijuana has served to criminalize Latinos since many Latino men are often seen as active in the illegal drug trade. Efforts to create pathways for citizenship for the undocumented are hotly opposed in the United States because of the negative stereotypes Americans have about this group. Decriminalization of marijuana would benefit Latinos in reducing these negative stereotypes and likely unblock the immigration policy-making process.

Legalization of marijuana affects not only minorities caught up in the prosecution of drug offenders in the United States, but also global citizens engaged in drug trafficking. In Chapter 9, Nathan Jones assesses the impact of California's Proposition 19 on Mexico, finding it beneficial for Mexican citizens. It changed the debate about the drug war in Mexico. While President Felipe Calderón opposed the measure and underscored his commitment to continue the national war against Mexican drug-trafficking organizations, he expressed his willingness to discuss legalization at the international level. Seeing this question as also an international one is important; the politics and status of U.S. minorities are also dependent on the laws governing the status of racial and ethnic groups abroad. We expect to see further studies extending the findings Jones reports here.

In Chapter 10, Christian Davenport explores under what conditions the legalization of marijuana would reduce the frequency and severity of government coercive behavior against African Americans. He writes that while legalization might serve as a mechanism of reducing police violence and discrimination against minorities, legalization also might lead to greater mistreatment of minorities by the state. Legalization, he believes, represents a partial solution to the race problem in the United States. In analyzing this question uniquely from a minority-politics perspective, Davenport hopes that legalization policies address squarely the strong concerns minorities have about their safety from state prosecution and social and physical well-being. Thus, it is not a simple question of whether or not marijuana should be legalized for minority Americans, but a question of how should it be legalized. Will drug legalization, in fact, keep minorities from continued state prosecution? Will it keep minorities and their children safe, improve their life chances, and reduce racial stigma? These types of questions should be sitting front and center in the legalization debate.

Notes

1 A minority perspective, however, still languishes generally at the margins of social science disciplines (Wilson and Frasure 2007; Walton and Smith 2007).
2 Queen Latifah (Dana Owens) also has a version of this song on one of her albums.

1

CRIMINAL JUSTICE COSTS OF PROHIBITING MARIJUANA IN CALIFORNIA

Jonathan P. Caulkins and Beau Kilmer[1]

A common argument for legalizing marijuana is that it would save the criminal justice system time and resources. Indeed, estimates of the cost of enforcing California's marijuana laws featured prominently in the debate about Proposition 19. Some advocates cited research claiming that legalization would save California $1 billion in criminal justice expenditures.[2] This chapter finds that such estimates are too high by at least a factor of five. Also, although these figures are sometimes presented as a potential savings to taxpayers, it may be more realistic to think in terms of allowing these resources to be redirected toward other types of crime.

Estimating marijuana-enforcement costs is not easy, especially for California. For example, most arrests are for misdemeanors, not felonies, and the literature contains little information describing how burdensome misdemeanor arrests are for police or courts. And, even before California SB 1449 went into effect in January 2011, possession of less than one ounce already was usually treated as a special type of "citable" misdemeanor that typically only led to the equivalent of a traffic ticket. Such nuances help explain why existing estimates differ by a factor of 10.

This chapter assesses previous efforts and generates improved estimates. Since most legalization proposals keep marijuana illegal for those under 21 (a group that accounts for roughly 45 percent of all marijuana arrests in California), we only estimate costs associated with prohibiting marijuana for those 21 and older.

Existing Estimates of the Cost Marijuana Prohibition Imposes on California

This section summarizes past studies' estimates. The figures presented are those in the original publications; they have not been adjusted for inflation.

Miron (2005): $981 Million. Miron's (2005) approach involves prorating historical costs. For example, if the total expenditures on an activity (such as making arrests) is $100 million per year and 10 percent of those actions involve marijuana offenders, then the estimate of that component of enforcing marijuana prohibition is $10 million per year.

Miron concludes that the United States spends $7.7 billion per year enforcing laws against marijuana production, distribution, and possession, including $5.3 billion by state and local governments and $2.4 billion at the federal level. Miron's paper included state-specific figures; for California, the estimate was $981 million (in 2003 dollars).

Miron (2005) breaks down the criminal justice process into three components: police, judicial, and corrections. Policing expenditures on marijuana enforcement are estimated as the total budget for policing services multiplied by the proportion of arrests for marijuana offenses, after making an adjustment for the possibility that some marijuana arrests are incidental to other enforcement action.

The particular numbers for California in Miron (2005) are $8.7 billion spent on police services × (0.9 percent of arrests being for marijuana sales/manufacture + 0.5 × 1.8 percent of arrests being for marijuana possession) = $228 million.

These calculations have limitations, of which we mention two. First, not all arrests are equally burdensome on police. Investigating a homicide typically involves greater time and effort than does making a marijuana arrest, which may in turn be more work than making some other arrests (e.g., for loitering). By prorating the entire police budget in proportion to arrests, Miron is assuming that all arrests are equally burdensome, including, implicitly, that equal amounts of investigative effort precede all arrests.

Another more important limitation of Miron's approach is that police do much more than just arrest people. They also do traffic enforcement, emergency response, crime prevention other than via deterrence (e.g., via community policing and education interventions), and a host of other functions. It is very hard to prorate police budgets across these functions. The problem is analogous to figuring out how much of a Coast Guard cutter's cost to attribute to drug interdiction as opposed to interdicting other goods, enforcing fishing regulations, and performing other Coast Guard roles (Murphy 1994). However, it is not even safe to assume that the majority of a police department's budget should be prorated across arresting activities.

For judicial costs, Miron (2005) multiplies the total judicial budget ($6.255 billion for California) by an assumed national fraction of felony convictions for marijuana in state courts (10.9 percent).[3] This raises three concerns. First, just as police do more than arrest, courts likewise do more than adjudicate criminal cases. Second, not all felony convictions consume the same amount of judicial resources; nationally, the proportion of drug convictions obtained by guilty pleas (which are cheaper than trials) is somewhat higher than it is for other offenses, particularly violent offense (Sourcebook of Criminal Justice Statistics, Table 5.46).

Third, the national 10.9 percent figure may be too high for California. Marijuana offenses accounted for only 3.7 percent of felonies where the prosecutors sought a complaint in 2009 (14,105/381,390; California Attorney General [CA AG] 2010). These concerns are important because judicial costs account for 70 percent of Miron's (2005) estimate of the total cost of marijuana enforcement in California ($682 out of $981 million).

Finally, Miron estimates corrections costs as the California corrections budget ($7.17 billion) multiplied by 1 percent, where 1 percent is the weighted average of the proportion of prisoners incarcerated on marijuana charges in five states. California is one of those five states, and its proportion (0.8 percent) is lower than the weighted average (Miron 2005). This alone would make 1 percent of $7.17 billion an overestimate by 25 percent.

Gieringer (2009): $204 Million. Gieringer (2009) takes a bottom-up approach that uses unit costing of all the units of an activity involved in marijuana enforcement. This approach is not as different as it sounds because estimates of the cost per unit often come from dividing total budgets by total activity levels, in which case, the two approaches reduce to the same thing. However, in the case of policing, where resources serve multiple purposes simultaneously, the differences can be significant.

Gieringer's approach is (primarily) a straightforward summing of numbers of marijuana-related enforcement activities times the unit cost of each activity, for the following activities: misdemeanor arrests, misdemeanor court cases, felony arrests, felony prosecutions, and offenders in state prison. The exceptions are jail (estimated simply as 40 percent of the prison cost) and the California Marijuana Suppression Program, which is listed as $3.8 million, perhaps based on a budget line item. Also, Gieringer assumes that fines are sufficient to offset the cost of misdemeanor arrests (which he would otherwise have counted as $300 per arrest).

The striking difference between Gieringer's and Miron's estimates is Gieringer's much lower average cost per arrest. Gieringer's figures are 17,000 felony arrests at $732 per arrest. There were roughly 61,000 misdemeanor arrests. If we cost them at $300 per arrest, that implies an average cost per arrest of $395 [(17,000 × $732 + 61,000 × $300)/(17,00+61,000)]. In contrast, dividing Miron's (2005) estimated policing cost of $280 million (the inflation adjustment of $228 million, which was in 2000 dollars) by 78,000 arrests would imply an average cost per arrest of $3,600, or about nine times as much per arrest.

Gieringer's estimate of average cost per arrest rests on an inflation update of a study that dates to 1977; however, Gieringer's source is marijuana specific. We found nothing more recent that was marijuana specific. But much has changed since 1977 besides inflation, so in our judgment, basing arrest costs on more recent studies is better, even if they were not marijuana specific.

Miron (2010): $1.87 Billion. A recent update (Miron 2010) increased the national estimate from $7.7 billion to $13.7 billion and the California-specific estimate to $1.87 billion. This update imputes a much higher cost of marijuana-related incarceration because he prorates all drug-related incarceration across drugs in proportion to the fraction of sales/manufacturing arrests by drug. However, marijuana offenders are less likely to be prosecuted and they receive shorter sentences if they are prosecuted, so this approach assigns far too much of the drug-related incarceration costs to marijuana.

California Legislative Analyst's Office. The California Legislative Analyst's Office (LAO) assessed the impact that Proposition 19's passage would have on taxpayers and, concerning corrections costs, stated (California Legislative Analyst's Office [CA LAO] 2010):

> The measure could result in savings to the state and local governments by reducing the number of marijuana offenders incarcerated in state prisons and county jails, as well as the number placed under county probation or state parole supervision. These savings could reach several tens of millions of dollars annually. The county jail savings would be offset to the extent that jail beds no longer needed for marijuana offenders were used for other criminals who are now being released early because of a lack of jail space.

> With respect to court and law enforcement costs, the LAO noted:

> The measure would result in a reduction in state and local costs for enforcement of marijuana-related offenses and the handling of related criminal cases in the court system. However, it is likely that the state and local governments would redirect their resources to other law enforcement and court activities.

Calculating the Costs for 2010

Our Approach. Similar to Gieringer (2009), we combine official estimates of numbers of activities (e.g., arrests) with unit-cost estimates from the literature. When possible, we use figures for 2010, but in many cases, we must rely on values from 2008 and 2009. Prosecution and imprisonment are the big-ticket items, somewhat overshadowing the costs of policing, probation, and parole, so we offer more detailed analysis of uncertainty for them. Indeed, the main sources of uncertainty can be stated even more precisely: uncertainty about the number of marijuana offenders in jail and whether it is better to use the average or the marginal cost per cell-year in prison.

When discussing unit costs, we quote values as reported in the studies cited, not yet adjusted for inflation to make it easier for readers to replicate and improve our analysis. The final table in this section converts these unit costs to 2010 dollars.

When possible, we use figures from state agencies to generate unit cost estimates; but for many values, California does not collect this information. For those, we rely on a drug-court cost-benefit analysis funded by the California Judicial Council, the rule-making arm of the California court system (Carey, Crumpton, Finigan, & Waller 2005).

Carey et al. (2005) used a transactional and institutional cost analysis to generate unit-cost estimates for arrest (excluding booking), booking (excluding jail), court (with and without trial), jail, and probation from the taxpayer perspective. This information was obtained from a number of sources (20):

> The costs for each transaction should include both direct and indirect costs. However, there is some flexibility regarding the source of the information gathered. These sources include budgets, interviews, calculations performed by agency staff as well as information from previous studies.
>
> In the majority of cases, the cost of these activities was gathered in three forms: (1) The hourly direct cost (generally labor cost, such as staff salaries, including benefits) associated with the agency staff involved in each transaction; (2) Support cost (usually as a percentage of direct cost) in the form of the agency or department overhead; and (3) Jurisdictional overhead cost (also as a percentage of direct cost). The research staff combined the direct transactional cost with the support and overhead costs to generate total per hour, per activity, and per transactions costs.

Carey et al. (2005) reported these costs for six jurisdictions in California chosen "with the intent of including a diverse set of drug court types in terms of size, location and participant demographics" (4).

Table 1.1 summarizes the cost information provided in Carey et al.'s (2005) methodological report. These figures represent the criminal justice processing costs for the drug court "control group," which looked reasonably similar to costs for those who entered the drug court in each jurisdiction (see Carey et al., 2005, for more details). Our assumption is that the typical person arrested for a marijuana offense has a less-severe criminal justice history than the typical person who would be eligible for drug court (who usually has a long history of abuse and dependence of hard drugs), which may bias our cost estimates upward.

Arrests. We distinguish between misdemeanor and felony arrests. Numbers of each are available from official California statistics. In 2010, 16,585 felony and 54,849 misdemeanor marijuana arrests took place in California (Harris, 2011). Table 1.2 presents the arrests by the age categories published by the California attorney general's office. We want to group ages slightly differently, combining 20 year olds with others too young to be directly affected by legalization, as the proposals are usually written. The last two columns present two different estimates for the number of marijuana arrests for those under 21: the low figure assumes that arrests for 20–29 year olds are evenly distributed by age; the high calculation assumes that arrests for 20 year olds is 0.5 × (arrests for those who are 18–19). These approaches suggest that between 43.6 percent and 48.1 percent of marijuana arrests involve those under the age of 21. For our best estimates, we multiply one minus the midpoint of these figures by the total number of arrests. This gives us 27,375 adult misdemeanor arrests and 11,301 adult felony arrests for 2010.

TABLE 1.1 Criminal Justice Unit Costs for Drug Offenders in Six California Jurisdictions (US$ 2004)

Jurisdiction	Arrest	Police Booking*	Court (No trial)	Court (with trial)	Jail Day	Probation Day
Los Angeles (El Monte)	$243	$177	$1,869	$3,344	$75	$4.08
Monterey	$291	$205	$2,026	$3,574	$66	$1.09
Orange (Laguna Niguel)	$174	$179	$2,157	$3,876	$79	$3.85
Orange (Santa Ana)	$240					
San Joaquin	$138	$140	$2,085	$3,708	$95	$0.76
Stanislaus	$103	$115	$1,966	$3,479	$60	$1.51
Median	**$207**	**$177**	**$2,026**	**$3,575**	**$75**	**$1.51**
Mean	**$198**	**$163**	**$2,021**	**$3,596**	**$75**	**$2.26**

Source: Carey et al., 2005, rounded to the nearest dollar (except for probation day). Notes: The mean and median are based on unrounded figures. The costs reported for Santa Ana are the same as those reported for Laguna Niguel, except for arrest. We do not repeat them since we wanted to make it clear that they are not included in the median and mean calculations. *For some jurisdictions, the booking costs for both the police and sheriff department were reported; here, we report the larger of the two values.

TABLE 1.2 2010 Marijuana Arrests in California, by Age and Level

	Total	Under 18	18-19	20-29	30+	<21 Low*	<21 High*
Misde-meanor	54,849	14,991 (27.3 percent)	9,587 (17.5 percent)	19,989 (36.4 percent)	10,282 (18.7 percent)	26,077 (47.5 percent)	28,872 (52.6 percent)
Felony	16,585	2,206 (13.3 percent)	2,188 (13.2 percent)	6,860 (41.4 percent)	5,331 (32.1 percent)	5,080 (30.6 percent)	5,488 (33.1 percent)
Total	**71,434**					**31,157 (43.6 percent)**	**34,360 (48.1 percent)**

Source: California Department of Justice, "Crime in California, 2010" Kamala Harris (2011). *Low calculates arrests for 20 year olds by assuming arrests for those 20–29 are evenly distributed by age. The high calculation assumes that arrests for 20 year olds are 0.5* (arrests for those 18–19).

The next question is what share of marijuana arrests lead to a booking (which is not the same as incarceration since individuals can be taken to the station, booked, and then immediately released). Those arrested for a felony are almost always booked. However, the proportion of misdemeanants booked is likely to be small since those caught possessing less than an ounce were typically not booked if they had proper identification and gave a written promise that they would come to court. Thus, we assume that all felony arrests but just 5 percent of misdemeanor arrests lead to booking. In the sensitivity analysis, we explore alternate values.

Table 1.2 reports the arrest costs for six California jurisdictions, including both urban and rural areas. For these six jurisdictions, the cost of arresting and booking someone ranges from $217 to nearly $500, with the median and mean equaling $384 and $362, respectively.[4] In a later publication, Carey and Waller (2008) conducted a similar exercise for Sacramento and reported that the combined cost of arresting and booking an offender was $311.

For arrest without booking, the median value is $207, which is in the same ballpark as the figure Gieringer implied for a misdemeanor ($300). Gieringer used a unit cost of $732 for a felony marijuana arrest, and we consider this figure in our sensitivity analysis.

Adjudication. In 2009, the prosecution dropped only 4 percent of felony marijuana arrests; the figure for misdemeanor arrests was 2 percent (CA AG 2010). From a cost perspective, an important question is whether the case actually went to trial since court cases that go to trial cost roughly 75 percent more than those that do not (Casey et al. 2005).

However, most cases are settled with a plea bargain. Data from the Bureau of Justice's *State Court Processing Statistics* finds that only 5.7 percent of prosecuted cases went to trial in 2006 (Bureau of Justice Statistics [BJS] 2010). This figure could be even lower for drug offenses, since drugs are often confiscated in these cases, making their resolution routine. But absent information specific to marijuana offenses, we use this 5.7 percent figure.

To understand the resources required to adjudicate these cases, we turn to a study conducted by National Center for State Courts for the California Administrative Office of the Courts (National Center for State Courts 2002) to determine the number of judicial officers needed in California.[5] The goal was to "accurately determine the amount of time required by judges to resolve different types of cases," including preliminary proceedings, arraignments, pleas; bench trials; jury trials; sentencing; post-judgment activities; and case-related administration for 23 case types. The judicial officers in four counties tracked their time for all cases over a two-month period in 2000. These time-use estimates were then adjusted for quality through a Delphi process with judges and court administrators in these four jurisdictions and seven other counties. The processing time in judicial-officer minutes for selected offenses related to marijuana is included in Table 1.3 overleaf. The results are not surprising. Felonies require much more time than misdemeanors, and misdemeanors require more time than infractions.

To convert time into dollar costs, we need an estimate of the average total adjudication cost per judicial officer minute. This sort of cost factor is not commonly reported, but combining the information in Table 1.1 and Carey et al. (2005) provides one estimate.

TABLE 1.3 Time Needed by California Judicial Officers to Resolve Cases in an Efficient and Effective Manner and Corresponding Cost at $18 per Minute

Type of offense	Judicial officer time (in minutes)	Corresponding Cost at $18 per judicial officer minute
Homicide	2,250	$40,500
Felony: Against persons	284	$5,112
Felony: Property offenses	104	$1,872
Felony: Drug offenses	138	$2,484
Felony: Other	216	$3,888
Misdemeanor: Class A & C	43	$774
Misdemeanor: Class B & D	4	$72
Infraction	1.06	$19

Source: National Center for State Courts, 2002. Excerpted from Exhibit 6-15.

Carey et al. (2005) estimated the number of minutes it would take judicial officers, prosecutors, defense attorneys, police officers, and probation officers per court case—with and without a trial. Table A1.1 presents those figures, along with the median cost estimates pulled from Table 1.1. For cases both with and without a trial, the cost is roughly $18 per minute of the judge's time. Thus, for felonies, we use $2,026 and $3,575 ($2,026 + $1,549 for a trial) for the costs of cases without and with a trial, respectively.

It is unclear whether most marijuana misdemeanor arrests would be the more intensive Class A/C sort (versus Class B/D or infraction), but even before SB 1449, simple possession was usually only a citable misdemeanor, more like an infraction. For lack of better information, we consider the midpoint between the two types of misdemeanors as our best guess for court costs ($418, which would

TABLE A1.1 Carey et al.'s (2005) Estimate of Time Needed for a Typical Court Case (in Minutes)

	No trial	With trial
Judicial Officer	113.9	196.8
Prosecutor	113.9	196.8
Defense Attorney	276.78	478.22
Police	—	59.7
Probation	—	23.2
Median cost estimates	$2,026	$3,574
Cost per minute of Judicial Office time	$17.79	$18.16

Sources: Carey et al. 2005; personal communication with the authors, 2011.

also include the costs associated with going to trial), but we believe this estimate is probably high since many of these offenses were treated more like infractions than misdemeanors. We consider the infraction cost in the sensitivity analysis.

Prison. The California Department of Corrections and Rehabilitation (California Department of Corrections and Rehabilitation [CDCR] 2011a) estimates the number of marijuana prisoners on December 31, 2010 to be 1,332. This total is down from 1,636 inmates on December 31, 2009 (CDCR 2010) (Table 1.4). Since we don't know when these inmates were released, we assume the middle value [1,484 = (1332 + 1636)/2] best represents the average number of inmates in California prisons for marijuana offenses throughout 2010.

Most analyses would multiply the 1,484 cell-years by the *average* annual cost per prisoner, but what we really want is the marginal cost, which excludes fixed costs. The California prison system is running over capacity, so the result of shedding 1,484 prisoners would probably be the same number of prisons operating with less extreme overcrowding, not the closure of any prisons. The CDCR recently reported the marginal overcrowding rate of $20,597 per prisoner-year (CDCR 2007). That works out to roughly $57.42 day, or less than half the $129/day *average* prison cost reported by the California Legislative Analyst's Office (2009).[6] We believe marginal cost is the correct concept to apply in this analysis, but in the sensitivity analysis below, we do report the consequences of using the average cost instead.

Ideally, we would also adjust for the kind of prison. If marijuana offenders tend to be in lower- [higher-] than-average security prisons and the cost per inmate-day is higher in higher-security facilities, then our figure would be an over- [under-] estimate, but we do not have data on the distribution of marijuana offenders by prison type.

Finally, for those previously convicted of one or more *serious* felonies (e.g., those involving violence), California's three strikes law enhances the sentence for *any* future felony conviction. As of December 31, 2010, 36 adult prisoners in California had received their third strike because of a felony marijuana conviction (CDCR 2011b); they were sentenced to at least 25 years in prison. An additional 321 prisoners had received their second strike because of a felony marijuana conviction (typically resulting in a doubling of the normal sentence). These

TABLE 1.4 Marijuana Offenders in California Prisons, by Controlling Offense

Controlling Offense	12/31/2009	12/31/2010
Hashish possession	51	36
Marijuana possession for sale	922	713
Marijuana sales	513	463
Other marijuana offenses	150	120
TOTAL	1,636	1,332

Source: California Department of Corrections and Rehabilitation (CDCR), 2011a.

individuals are included in our cost calculations for 2010. As an aside, the corresponding numbers for driving under the influence were 53 and 384, respectively.

Jail. Marijuana offenders can spend time in jail both between arrest and sentencing and also after conviction, when serving a sentence of less than one year. People whose only charge is a marijuana offense likely will be offered bail on favorable terms. For example, in Riverside County (Superior Court of California County of Riverside 2009), the bond is only $5,000 for sale or transportation of quantities up to 25 pounds or growing up to 50 plants.[7] If someone is facing multiple charges, including not only marijuana but also other more serious offenses, then the legality or illegality of marijuana may not affect the judge's decision about whether to offer bail.

Jails are operated at the local level and state agencies do not publish information about the reason for incarceration. Indeed, even local jurisdictions do not generally make this information readily available. Since more marijuana offenders spend time in jail rather than prison, this compromises our ability to estimate incarceration costs; however, we can generate a rough estimate.

The attorney general of California publishes information about the average daily jail population for the entire state, and in 2009 (most recent year available), this figure was 83,023 (CA AG 2010). During the debate about Proposition 19, a reporter for PBS tracked down the number of jail inmates incarcerated for a marijuana offense in the counties with the three largest jail populations: Los Angeles, Orange, and San Diego. The reporter stated that:

> During one day in September there were about 4,300 people in San Diego County jails. Just over 200 were there for marijuana charges alone. Only one person's primary charge was possession of less than an ounce of pot. And that person was likely in custody because of something like an outstanding warrant. That was the case with all 10 people in custody in Los Angeles for possessing less than an ounce of marijuana on another day in September. Out of the more than 16,000 people in Los Angeles County jails that day, just over 80 had primary charges related to marijuana.

This suggests that less than 5 percent of those jailed in San Diego were there only for marijuana, and the comparable figure for Los Angeles is 0.5 percent (Calvert 2010).

A reporter in Northern California (Richman 2010) conducted a similar analysis and also found that very few individuals were in jail for marijuana offenses in Alameda County (which includes Oakland and Berkeley; Richman 2010).[8]

Sgt. J. D. Nelson, the Alameda County sheriff's office spokesman, said the office's data system isn't set up to search the inmate population by offense to determine how many people are in the county's jail for minor marijuana offenses. "But I can probably tell you how many there are: zero," he said. "For possession of marijuana, zero. Maybe some for cultivation . . . but very, very few."

Given that San Diego is known for being conservative relative to other heavily populated coastal counties (and thus may be more likely to hold someone in jail for marijuana), and Los Angeles is notorious for not having enough jail space for serious offenders, these values may be toward the high and low ends of the range, respectively, for all counties in California, although apparently Alameda County's rate is even lower. Together, these three counties' roughly 25,000 inmates account for more than one-quarter of California's jail inmates, and if they had a total of 300 marijuana inmates between them, that would be about 1.2 percent of their inmates.

Of course, these three counties are not a random or representative sample of the entire state. So, although we do not have a better point estimate than 1.2 percent, as a sensitivity analysis, we consider low and high estimates that differ by a factor of two (i.e., 0.6 percent to 2.4 percent) in recognition of the limitations of newspaper accounts and convenience samples.

These estimates of jail days was then multiplied by an estimated cost per jail day of $75 (or $27,375 per year), which was the mean estimate calculated by Carey et al. (2005) in the study summarized in Table 1.1.[9]

Community Corrections

Parole. There were 1,839 parolees with a marijuana-related commitment offense on December 31, 2009. This figure increased to 2,057 by December 31, 2010. We average these two figures to estimate the mean number of parolees being super-vised each day in 2010 (1,948 parolees). A report prepared for the CDCR stated that the daily parole costs were $9.99 in 2008 (Farabee, Yang, Sikangwan, Bennett, & Warda, 2008).

Probation. There were 311,728 individuals on probation in California on Janu-ary 1, 2010, and 292,874 on December 31, 2010 (BJS 2011). Once again, we average these two figures to estimate the mean number of probationers being supervised each day in 2010 (302,301). Very little information is available on the characteristics of probationers in California, so figuring out what share of these probationers were being supervised only because of marijuana is difficult. How-ever, a few relevant facts are:

- In 2008, the LAO surveyed every probation department and found that in those counties that responded, 41 percent of probationers were under super-vision because of a drug conviction (CA LAO 2009a).[10] This is much higher than the national average (26 percent; BJS 2011).
- Roughly 80 percent of probationers are supervised for a felony offense (CA LAO 2009a).
- Of all felony drug arrests where the prosecutor sought a complaint in 2009, 13.2 percent were for marijuana (CA AG 2010).
- Of all misdemeanor drug arrests where the prosecutor sought a complaint in 2009, 40 percent were for marijuana (CA AG, 2010).

For lack of better information, we assume a total of 124,000 drug probationers (roughly 41 percent of the 302,301 total), split 80 percent/20 percent between felons and misdemeanants (similar to the full probation population); we also assume that marijuana's share among probationers is the same as among arrestees, suggesting that there were 124,000 × (80 percent × 13.2 percent + 20 percent × 40 percent) or about 23,000 people on probation for marijuana violations.

The median probation cost estimate from Carey et al. (2005) was $1.51 per day for 2005, with the average being 50 percent higher at $2.26. Based on information from 31 counties, the LAO (2009a) report put the cost of county probation at $3/day in 2007. Probation supervision costs for marijuana possession offenses may be especially low since low-level offenders tend to be put on "banked" caseloads that simply require a phone call or a visit to a kiosk every few months (LAO 2009a).[11] For our calculations, we use $2 as our best guess for the daily probation cost for a marijuana offender and consider the LAO's $3 estimate in our sensitivity analysis.

The breadth of this range means that we have a highly imprecise estimate of the probation costs for marijuana offenders. Likewise, we didn't have marginal costs for either probation or parole. Nor did we subtract costs for probationers and parolees who were under 21. But these limitations are not terribly troubling with respect to the estimate of total criminal justice costs associated with marijuana prohibition because probation and parole costs are such a minor proportion of that total.

Other Costs

Fines and Seizures. We do not attempt an independent estimate of net revenues (or costs) from collection of fines and seizures. Miron (2005, 2010) incorporates them via a savings offset, but finds them to be small, and our sense is that is right. The DEA reports seizing $12.4 million in assets in California associated with its domestic marijuana eradication efforts (BJS 2007, Table 4.38.2007). However, apparently the total value of assets forfeited in California in 2004 was only $22.5 million for all types of offenses (California Department of Justice 2005), and it often costs as much if not more to collect fines (Piehl & Williams 2010).

Technical Violations. A potentially more serious concern is failing to account for how marijuana legalization could affect technical violations for parolees and probationers whose controlling offense is not related to marijuana. Neither Miron (2005, 2010) nor Gieringer (2009) included this possibility, but this does not mean it is not important.

After legalization, abstaining from marijuana might or might not remain a condition of probation and parole. Since parole violators are such a large part of the prison population, this could be an important consideration. However, some claim the numbers of violations are small; corrections spokesman Paul Verke cited 256 as the number found to have technical violations in California last year solely for failing a marijuana test (Capitol Weekly 2009). Given that 66,185 parolees were returned to prison on their original charge for a parole violation in 2009 (i.e., excluding new offenses that go through the courts), this would put the marijuana return rate below 0.005; however, this does not include those revoked for possessing marijuana, but not charged with a new possession offense (CDCR 2010). So, exploring possible effects of marijuana legalization on the "revolving door" of parolees being recommitted (and probationers having their probation revoked) would be a fruitful area for further inquiry.

Results

Table 1.5 presents our estimates of the criminal justice costs of enforcing marijuana prohibition for adults in California in 2010. For each category, the subtotal is presented based on the cost figures described in the text, and the following row includes the subtotal after converting the costs to 2010 dollars using the Bureau of Labor Statistics' inflation calculator (Bureau of Labor Statistics 2010). Table 1.5 reports estimates to the dollar, but that is done only to allow readers to more easily reproduce the arithmetic. All of these estimates are rough and should be thought of as being good only to the nearest $10 million.

Our approach suggests that the *direct* criminal justice system cost of prohibiting marijuana for adults in California in 2010 was approximately $150 million. More than 45 percent of the costs ($70 million) are attributable to incarceration, with jail and prison roughly similar (about $35 million each). After incarceration, prosecution ($40 million) and probation and parole combined ($30 million) are the next largest cost items. Figure 1.1 presents a pie chart that presents how the $150 million in costs are distributed. By contrast, marijuana prohibition appears to place a relatively modest burden on police ($10 million per year). That is a striking result; the easy availability and sheer magnitude of the figure for the number of marijuana arrests attracts attention, but the unit costs are so low in California that marijuana arrest and booking appear not to be a major drain on law enforcement resources.

We stress the word *direct*. Prohibiting marijuana can have indirect effects that have ramifications for offending and, hence, criminal justice costs. For example, arrest and conviction for a marijuana offense might be a barrier to gaining legal employment, and on the margin, push someone to commit income-generating crimes that they would not otherwise have committed.

Table 1.6 presents sensitivity analysis showing how the total cost estimate changes using different figures and assumptions, reported to the nearest $1 million. We highlight the two that would have the largest impact on the result. First, while we believe it is appropriate to use the *marginal* cost of imprisonment since the California system is running over capacity and reducing 1,484 prisoners would not lead to a prison closure (which would have support using the average cost), we

TABLE 1.5 Criminal Justice Costs of Prohibiting Marijuana for Those Aged 21 and Older in California

ARREST AND BOOKING				Total	%
	Arrests	*% Booked*	*Bookings*		
Adult misdemeanors	27,375	5%	1,369		
Adult felonies	11,301	100%	11,301		
Total	38,676		12,670		
Unit cost	$207		$177		
Subtotal-Nominal	$8,005,829		$2,242,541		
Subtotal-$2010	$9,206,703		$2,578,923	$11,785,625	8.1%

PROSECUTION					
	Misdemeanors	*Felonies*	*Felony Trials*		
Arrests that are prosecuted	26,827	10,849	618		
Unit cost	$418	$2,026	$1,549		
Subtotal-Nominal	$11,213,288	$21,979,667	$957,887		
Subtotal-$2010	$12,895,281	$25,276,618	$1,101,570	$39,273,469	27.0%

INCARCERATION				
	Prison	*Jail*		
Annual number of inmates	1,484	1,245		
Annual unit cost	$20,597	$27,375		
Subtotal-Nominal	$30,565,948	$34,091,319		
Subtotal-$2010	$32,094,245	$35,795,885	$67,890,131	46.7%

COMMUNITY CORRECTIONS				
	Probation	*Parole*		
Annual number of adults supervised	23,000	1,948		
Daily unit cost	$2.00	$9.99		
Subtotal-Nominal	$16,790,000	$7,103,090		
Subtotal-$2010	$19,308,500	$7,174,121	$26,482,621	18.2%

TOTAL COSTS FOR ADULTS (US$ 2010)				$145,431,846	100%

Sources: Reported in Sections 3.1–3.5.

know that some prefer to use *average* cost figures in these calculations. Using the average cost of prison would increase the total cost from $145 million to roughly $190 million (a 28-percent increase).

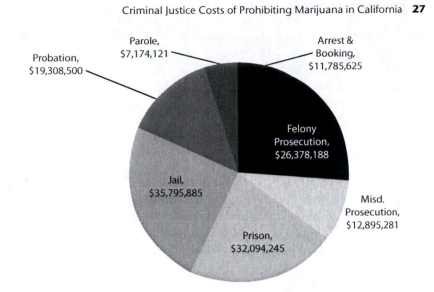

FIGURE 1.1 Distribution of Criminal Justice Costs, by Category

TABLE 1.6 Sensitivity Analysis: Incremental Effect on Total Cost

	Amount	%
Alternative assumptions that substantially affect overall estimate:		
Assume 0.6% of jail inmates are there for a marijuana offense	–$18,000,000	–12%
Assume 2.4% of jail inmates are there for a marijuana offense	$36,000,000	25%
Use the average cost for prison instead of the marginal cost	$41,000,000	28%
Alternative assumptions that *do not* substantially affect overall estimate:		
Court costs for marijuana misdemeanor offenses are similar to an infraction	–$12,000,000	–8%
Daily probation costs are $1.51 in 2004, inflated to $1.74 in $2010	–$4,730,583	–3%
Daily probation costs are $3 in 2007, inflated to $3.15 in $2010	$7,000,000	5%
Assume all misdemeanants are booked	$4,000,000	3%
Use Gieringer's $732 unit cost figure for felony marijuana arrests	$6,000,000	4%

Source: Calculated by authors.

Second, no official figures capture the number of individuals in jail for marijuana offenses. While press reports for three counties suggest this figure was low in 2010, obviously those are not official statistics. Thus, we consider lower and higher estimates that differ from our best guess of 1.2 percent by a factor of two (i.e., 0.6 percent to 2.4 percent). The low figures decreases the total costs by $18 million (minus 12 percent), and the high estimate increases costs by $36 million (25 percent).

The table also shows the implications of altering several other assumptions discussed above. None changes the total cost estimate by more than about $10 million, which is smaller than the limits of the precision on the entire exercise, so we do not discuss them further.

The bottom line is that it is possible to use alternative figures to generate a total over $200 million, but it is difficult to make enough changes to make the figure exceed $300 million (which is roughly twice our best estimate). Even if one doubles our best estimate, this is still dramatically lower than the $1 billion figure that floats around policy debates.

Discussion

Our estimates have many limitations. Some of the most obvious are also *not* the most important. For example, as noted in Section 3.6, we were not able to estimate other costs and revenues; however, we think they are small and therefore not necessary for understanding the order of magnitude of the total cost associated with keeping marijuana illegal for adults.

A greater concern is that various unit cost estimates are not marijuana specific. One might expect that to inflate the estimated costs, but only drug-specific breakdowns could confirm that hunch.

Arguably, the main difference between our estimate and Miron's concerns how fine-grained is the partition of criminal justice activities. Generally speaking, finer partitions are better because they avoid implicitly assuming homogeneity with respect to costs of all activities within one group of the partition.

Another reason why both Gieringer's (2009) and our estimates are lower than those in Miron (2005) is lower estimates of the cost of arrest and prosecution, as opposed to incarceration. Those differences occur because Miron uses an aggregate-expenditures approach, prorating entire agency budgets in proportion to arrests, whereas Gieringer and we use a bottom-up unit-costing approach, which multiplies the cost per arrest (or other activity) times the number of instances of those activities that are related to marijuana.

Nevertheless, in our judgment, the still-greater issues pertain to interpretation. Notably, the direct cost of prohibiting marijuana is not the same as the total net cost to society because there may be various indirect effects. An easy-to-understand indirect cost would be if a felony marijuana conviction blocked access to the legitimate labor market and thereby induced someone to commit other, non-drug, income-generating crimes instead. Or, conversely, if a misdemeanor marijuana arrest convinced someone it is hard to get away with crime and so deterred them from committing some other offense. A potentially much more important issue is any effect marijuana prohibition might have on alcohol consumption and associated enforcement costs (alcohol is a major driver of criminal activity). It is clear that marijuana prohibition suppresses marijuana intoxication to at least some extent and that marijuana and alcohol use are interrelated (they are both intoxicants, and heavy users of one are also more likely to use the other). But, it is not even clear whether marijuana prohibition increases or reduces alcohol consumption, let alone alcohol-related crime and criminal justice costs.

Likewise, the California state budget savings from legalization would likely be less than the current amount now being spent on marijuana prohibition because: (1) freed resources may be used for other purposes rather than being "refunded" to the taxpayer,[12] (2) most of the criminal justice resources associated with marijuana enforcement involve local and county, not state agencies, and/or (3) there would be new administrative, regulatory, and even enforcement costs of managing the legalized distribution of marijuana.

Nevertheless, prorating accounting exercises with direct costs plays a prominent role in the policy debate, so if a proportionality-based figure is going to be cited, that figure should be as accurate as possible.

This chapter finds that enforcing marijuana prohibition against adults cost the California criminal justice system approximately $150 million in 2010. With SB 1449 having gone into effect on January 1, 2011, thereby eliminating booking and trials for those caught with less than 1 ounce, these figures likely overstate the current cost of prohibiting marijuana in California.

These estimates are far below the roughly $1 billion in savings some predict from marijuana legalization in California, and as just noted, the savings—in the sense of reduced spending—could be smaller than current enforcement costs if freed resources are reallocated to enforcement against other crimes.

Notes

1. This chapter draws on work done for a class project by Carnegie Mellon University Heinz College masters students Ben Horwitz and Dawn Holmes. We thank them, as well as Jim Burgdorf for his useful comments and editorial assistance.
2. For example, see Lynch 2010 or Stateman 2009.
3. Miron (2005) generates this figure with the following calculation: "In 2000 the percent of felony convictions in state courts due to any type of trafficking violation was 22.0%. Of this total, 2.7% was due to marijuana, 5.9% was due to other drugs, and 13.4% was unspecified. This report assumes that the fraction of marijuana convictions in the unspecified category equals the fraction for those in which a specific drug is given, or 31.4% [= 2.7%/(2.7%+5.9%)]. The report also assumes that the percentage of possession convictions due to marijuana equals this same fraction. These assumptions jointly imply that the percentage of felony convictions due to marijuana equals the fraction of felony convictions due to any drug offense (34.6%) multiplied by the percentage of trafficking violations due to marijuana (31.4%). This yields 10.9% (= 34.6%*31.4%)."

4. These booking costs do not include jail (personal communication with the authors, October 2011).
5. This is the one of the sources Carey et al. (2005) used: "Non-drug-court *court* transactions were calculated somewhat differently. The identification of the cost of every court hearing outside of drug court for every subsequent court case is beyond the scope of this study (indeed, it would be a major study in itself). For this reason, the transaction of interest was determined to be the court *case* rather than a court hearing. The cost of an average court case was determined based on local budgets and interviews with local agency staff (as described above) and then was combined with information collected in several studies of time used in court process in California and other states (National Center for State Courts 2002, Carey and Finigan 2003)."
6. The text reports "it costs the state on average approximately $49,000 per year to incarcerate an offender," but later in the document, the costs are reported to be $129 per day, which generates an annual figure of $47,085. We use the first figure in our sensitivity analysis.
7. Bail can be more onerous through enhancements. For example, if the defendant has multiple prior, serious felony convictions, then the bail may be set higher, even if the present offense only involves marijuana, which might make it more difficult for the person to meet bail for the marijuana offense.
8. The average daily jail population for Alameda County is 4,371 (BJS 2011).
9. This is also very similar to the maximum amount the State of California allows local jurisdictions to bill for housing state prisoners or parolees in a jail ($77.17; CDCR 2009). Coincidentally, in an earlier version of this analysis, we used $75 since it was the rough average of the $100-per-day estimate for Orange County (Orange County Grand Jury 2007) and the $53.45 per day reported for the Los Angeles County Men's Central Jail (Premier Bail Bonds 2011).
10. "A total of 31 counties responded to at least some of the questions on our survey, including 12 of the 15 largest counties in the state. . . . In total, the counties responding to our survey represent about 85 percent of the total statewide population and supervise over 70 percent of all adult probationers in California."
11. More on banked caseloads from LAO (2009a): "About half of all probationers are placed on banked caseloads. These are offenders who are deemed by the probation department to be of low risk to public safety and, therefore, require less supervision than those on regular or specialized caseloads. For example, almost two-thirds of all *misdemeanor* probationers are on banked caseloads. Probation officers generally have infrequent contacts with probationers on banked caseloads—usually no more than once every few months. These contacts generally do not involve face-to-face meetings, but rather are done in writing, over the phone, or at an electronic kiosk stationed at a probation office. Banked caseloads typically average several hundred probationers per officer" (emphasis added).
12. As the Legislative Analyst's Office (2009b, 3) notes in its assessment of the Fiscal Impact of Legalizing Marijuana, "it is likely that some or all of such [court and law enforcement] resources would be redirected to other law enforcement and court activities, reducing or perhaps eliminating the savings that could otherwise be realized." This possibility seems particularly relevant with respect to incarceration, where the effect might not be so much reallocation to other crimes as moving from being grossly overcrowded to somewhat less grossly overcrowded institutions.

2

PUBLIC-HEALTH CONSIDERATIONS IN THE LEGALIZATION DEBATE

Chyvette T. Williams and Thomas Lyons

For the vast majority of Americans, experimentation with illegal substances begins—and ends—with marijuana. Across racial/ethnic groups, the prevalence of marijuana use is many times higher than use of any other illegal drug. The proportion of adults 12 or over who report past month marijuana use (about 6.6 percent) is more than double the proportion who have misused prescription drugs and more than 10 times higher than the proportion reporting the use of any other illegal drug.[1] The same surveys indicate that the vast majority of marijuana users do not progress to regular use of other "harder" drugs. In fact, most individuals age out of drug use altogether as they take on more adult social roles and responsibilities. Among 18–20-year olds, 22 percent had used an illicit drug in the past month (overwhelmingly, this was marijuana); by age 40, the proportion is 6 percent.[2] Some have argued that marijuana is a "gateway" to the use of other, more dangerous drugs, basing this assertion is on the fact that very few people who try drugs such as cocaine or heroin have not also tried marijuana. But, this "causal" link is merely a consequence of the much higher prevalence of marijuana use, and it is also true of the relationship between other common vs. uncommon activities. Very few people ride motorcycles who have not ridden a bicycle, yet bicycle riding does not cause motorcycle riding (Clayton & Mosher 2007). This chapter will argue that although differences in marijuana use exist by race/ethnicity, the greatest public-health impact of marijuana on communities of color is due to its status as an illegal drug. The chapter focuses on arrests and incarceration for marijuana offenses, the drug trade, and their impact on public health in inner-city urban communities.

National survey data have consistently shown that drug use among Blacks is lower than that of other racial/ethnic groups, particularly in younger age groups. The Monitoring the Future study shows that African American high school students have substantially lower rates of use of most licit and illicit drugs, including marijuana, than do Whites.[3] Past 12-month use of marijuana among high school seniors, averaged across 1976–2005, was 39.3 percent for Whites, 31.9 percent for Hispanics, and 28.6 percent for African Americans. These surveys have also shown that compared to other races, "Black youth perceive greater risk with drug use; express greater disapproval; perceive greater peer disapproval of their use; report fewer friends who used drugs; and indicate less frequent exposure to drug users" (Terry-McElrath, O'Malley & Johnston, 2009). Among individuals aged 12 and over, rates of past month use of marijuana was slightly higher among blacks (7.8 percent) than among whites (6.8 percent) in 2009, but still comparatively similar.[4]

Despite these equal or lower prevalence rates of marijuana use, Blacks are much more likely than other races to face criminal justice consequences for marijuana use. Nationally, while Blacks make up approximately 14 percent of marijuana users—and of the U.S. population—they were 30 percent of those arrested for marijuana offenses in 2005 (King and Mauer 2005). In some states and jurisdictions, such as Illinois, this disproportion was far higher. This chapter will describe the public-health consequences of the disproportionate arrest, sentencing, and incarceration of African Americans for marijuana violations.

Drugs, Drug Laws, and African Americans

African Americans are not a monolithic group, and much within-race variation exists in attitudes about marijuana and other illicit drugs; therefore, there is variation in usage. Predictors of drug use are multifactorial and multilevel, and include characteristics of the individual, social context (family, peers, school, neighborhood), socioeconomic standing, and other factors (Newcomb & Felix-Ortiz 1992, Brook et al. 2001). Thus, the unique combination of these factors, including person-environment interactions, will predict the initiation of drug use and risk for continued use, abuse, or addiction. African Americans are disproportionately disadvantaged on all factors that matter for drug use, but despite this, have lower rates of lifetime drug use when compared to Whites (Wallace 1998).

Rather than drug use per se, the real problem is the disproportionate rate of drug-related problems experienced by a subset of African Americans. Why would one race group experience more legal, health, and social problems than another race group for participating in similar rates of the same behavior? In this chapter, we will demonstrate how treating drug use and abuse as a crime, rather than a health issue, has exacerbated the already poor health and social conditions of many African Americans and perpetuates the very behaviors that the criminal justice system seeks to deter.

The fivefold increase in incarceration rates since 1980, driven largely by the War on Drugs, has disproportionately impacted African Americans and Hispanics.[5] A Justice Policy Institute report summarizes: "African Americans are disproportionately incarcerated for drug offenses in the U.S., though they use and sell drugs at similar rates to Whites." As of 2003, twice as many African Americans as whites were incarcerated for drug offenses in state prisons in the U.S. African Americans made up 13 percent of the total U.S. population, but accounted for 53 percent of sentenced drug offenders in state prisons in 2003 (Beatty, Petteruti and Ziedenberg).[6] Even though the growth of incarceration rates has leveled off, in 2009, African Americans continued to make up a disproportionate number (38 percent) of the nation's prison population.[7] This national racial disproportionality in incarceration, which has only worsened in the past decades, is particularly acute for Illinois. African American men in Illinois were, by 2005, more than 50 times more likely than White men to be sentenced to prison for a drug law violation (Whitney and Heaps 2005). Some have suggested that this disparity is largely the result of policing strategies in Chicago and elsewhere, which focus on particular neighborhoods and are demonstrably racist (Whitney and Heaps 2005).

Case Study: Marijuana Arrests in Illinois

While nationwide data show that African Americans are affected disproportionately by marijuana laws, the disproportionality in incarceration rates is most striking in certain counties and states, notably Midwestern states like Illinois. To examine the racial/ethnic composition of arrests for marijuana, the Illinois Disproportionate Justice Impact Study (DJIS) Commission obtained data on all the individuals arrested for felony drug crimes in 2005 (N = 42,297) (Lurigio et al. 2010). Note that misdemeanor arrests, which constitute more than half of marijuana arrests, were not included. Approximately 99 percent of records were coded "B" or "W" (i.e., Black or White) at the time of arrest (less than 1 percent had other codes). This designation is standard in Illinois criminal records, which do not record precise information on ethnicity or race. Therefore, in the analysis, arrestees were categorized as "white" or "nonwhite."

Table 2.1 shows the characteristics of arrestees under selected statutes of the Cannabis Control Act in 2005. Given that the population of Illinois was 75 percent White in 2000, the race of cannabis arrestees was disproportionately non-White, sometimes overwhelmingly so. For example, for cannabis sales (manufacture/delivery) on or near school property, 90 percent of arrestees were non-White.

The disproportionality in cannabis arrests is unlikely to be due to a higher rate of non-White offending. For sales of cannabis on school grounds, for instance, national data suggest that the disproportionate arrests do not reflect greater sales by non-White dealers. Nationwide, the prevalence of having been offered, sold, or given an illegal drug on school property was the same between White (23.6 percent) and Black (23.9 percent) students.[8] This fact, coupled with the fact that most youth report buying marijuana from someone of their own race, makes it unlikely that the majority of marijuana dealers are non-White in Illinois schools. In addition, the 1999 National Household Survey on Drug Abuse reported that

TABLE 2.1 Illinois Felony Cannabis Arrests, 2005

Charge	Class	Total Arrest Charges	Percent Nonwhite Arrestees
Felony cannabis possession—C	4	236	51.3 percent
Felony cannabis possession—D	4	1,685	58.6 percent
Manufacture/delivery 10–30 g cannabis	4	755	71.5 percent
Manufacture/delivery 30–500 g cannabis	3	749	43.3 percent
Manufacture/delivery of cannabis within 1000 ft of a school			
2.5 to 10 g	4	536	89.7 percent
10–30 g	3	316	91.1 percent
> 30 g*		--	

*Only charges with 10 or more arrestees in 2005 are shown.
Source: Data compiled by authors.

White youth aged 12–17 are more than a third more likely than African American youth to have stated that they sold drugs. [9]

So what accounts for the disparity? In Chicago, one factor may be patterns of policing in schools. Unlike rural or suburban schools, urban non-White schools often have a police officer stationed in the school itself; the officer helps "preserve order" but also, presumably, makes arrests for drug sales, especially marijuana sales. Like the focus on certain neighborhoods, this targeted policing in non-White urban schools produces disparity, since the same marijuana transactions in rural and suburban schools are much less likely to result in arrest.

Marijuana and the Community Justice Model

Understanding the links between drug use, crime, and incarceration, and the way they become concentrated in specific urban neighborhoods, requires an ecological perspective (Clear et al. 2001). This perspective looks not just at crime by an individual, but also at how the criminal justice response to crime affects the social ecology of the individual's neighborhood. High levels of "coerced mobility" (Clear et al. 2001)—the criminal justice system's forced transfer of neighborhood residents into and out of prisons—undermines informal social controls, which leads, in a vicious cycle, to increased crime. For instance, more than half of Illinois prisoners return to the Chicago area, and a third return to just six poor, high-crime neighborhoods out of 77 official community areas in the city (Lavigne and Mamalian 2003). Prisoners return to these neighborhoods because their families live there. In one study, nearly 80 percent of returning prisoners reported staying with their mothers upon release (Phillips 2007). It is estimated that over half of released prisoners in Illinois will be rearrested and returned to prison within three years (Illinois Department of Corrections 2004). The solution according to proponents of the ecological analysis is a community justice model, whereby interventions are aimed at strengthening vulnerable communities as a whole, not just delivering services to individuals.

Not typically considered as a variable in ecological models is the impact of the marijuana laws. Despite many local referenda and the efforts of some municipalities to reduce the criminal penalties for marijuana possession, the proportion of drug arrests that are for marijuana is growing nationally (Human Rights Watch 2009, King and Mauer 2005). For example, despite the fact that marijuana possession is officially decriminalized in parts of Cook County,[10] to be handled like a traffic ticket, up to one-quarter of all drug arrests in Chicago are for possession of less than 2.5 grams of cannabis.

A major factor in the cycle of incarceration and reincarceration may in fact be parole policies as well as drug laws (Petersilia 2003). For people under probation or parole, marijuana use is a violation that theoretically can lead to a return to prison. At the very least, use of marijuana can lead to being thrown out of a halfway house or substance-abuse treatment center, and increase the risk of return to prison. While marijuana use can be addictive and harmful, a large category of younger released prisoners on parole may have had less-severe addiction before incarceration, or their only use of illicit drugs upon release is to smoke marijuana on occasion. In ethnographic work with case managers and their clients (Lyons and Lurigio 2010), clients mentioned that they use marijuana instead of alcohol to socialize, or use marijuana on special occasions with friends. From the perspective of the case managers, some of these clients were minimizing their use of marijuana, which might have been heavier than the clients admitted. But, for many clients, the criminal justice consequences far outweighed what seemed to be minimal or unproblematic use of marijuana. The only downside from marijuana use hence becomes the possibility of getting caught.

To summarize, according to ecological theories, mass incarceration in poor neighborhoods leads to a vicious cycle that derails efforts to reintegrate prisoners when they return by undermining relations between residents and police, creating insecurity in neighborhoods, and exacerbating interpersonal problems former inmates face. An important part of this vicious cycle is the way in which returning prisoners who may not be using drugs addictively face scrutiny by parole, undergo frequent drug tests, and face the threat of returning to prison for drug law violations. The criminal justice system's focus on widespread, arguably unproblematic marijuana use makes violation even more likely. Furthermore, for those who are in rehabilitation programs, the emphasis on marijuana, if its use is benign, may undermine a message of recovery from addiction and reinforce clients' skepticism about treatment.

Other Public-Health Impacts of Criminalizing Marijuana

The precipitous increases in arrests and incarceration for marijuana possession, sale, and delivery have made the United States the leader among industrialized nations in putting its citizens behind bars (International Centre for Prison Studies 2010). While some inmates may participate in programs targeting drug use or educational attainment, imprisonment rarely solves the problems it intends, especially for low-level drug users and dealers. In fact, health and social problems are exacerbated post-release (Iguchi et al. 2002). Upon release, many inmates return to the neighborhoods and lives from which they left, and the likelihood is high of them falling back into the patterns of behavior and networks that landed them behind bars. This may be especially true for drug offenders who either have a drug use problem or sell drugs as a source of income. In addition to having a strong system of pro-social support, drug treatment for abusers and opportunities for gainful employment for dealers are critical to preventing recidivism.

The effects of criminalizing marijuana surpass localized effects on individuals who have prior contact with the penal system to broader effects on their families, their communities, and society at large. Iguchi and colleagues (2002) published a review paper delineating the numerous effects on well-being of criminalizing drug users. In short, criminalizing drug users affects children and families, access to health and housing benefits, financial aid for higher education, immigration status, voting rights, and employment prospects. Further, the authors noted that incarcerating drug users does not reduce drug use after release, but instead, exacerbates matters and perpetuates a revolving door of incarceration.

HIV and the War on Drugs. In June 2012, the Global Commission on Drug Policy published a report citing evidence for how the criminalization of drugs and drug use fuels the HIV epidemic. The report argues that scientific evidence that would otherwise protect and promote the public's health is being ignored in favor of punitive drug laws that are wholly ineffective in reducing drug use, drug trafficking, and recidivism, but that also have the unintended consequence of fueling the HIV epidemic and increasing other health and social harms. The report calls for, among many things, a scale-up of evidence-based public-health practices, such as drug decriminalization and drug treatment, which have demonstrated positive public-health results for communities.

Health Risks of Incarceration. A vast majority of incarcerations are of nonviolent drug offenders. In a recent study, Spaulding et al. (2011) showed excess mortality associated with having been incarcerated, compared to those who have not. Although patterns were not uniform across health conditions, incarcerated persons or those with a history of incarceration generally had higher rates of infectious diseases, mental illness, and some chronic diseases (Spaulding et al. 2011, Schnittker et al. 2011). It is widely acknowledged that health conditions, especially infectious diseases, among inmates were more often acquired prior to incarceration and that jails and prisons are largely containers of infection, rather than vectors. However, incarcerating nonviolent offenders, such as marijuana users and low-level dealers, in large numbers as is currently being done can amplify infectious disease spread in jails and prisons, which are closed, and often crowded, environments (Khan et al. 2005).

Violence. Violence in communities is a serious public-health problem and is strongly linked with the sale of illegal drugs (Goldstein 1985). Street gangs are usually involved in the distribution of narcotics and cocaine, but also in large-scale marijuana distribution in urban neighborhoods. Gangs are responsible for an average of 48 percent of violent crime in most jurisdictions (FBI 2011). Acts of violence in the drug trade are a function of drug prohibition. Similar to the case of alcohol, regulation of marijuana would bring its sale under the rule of law and eliminate the criminal element surrounding its sale and use.

Children and Families. In 2002, more than 2.4 million children had a parent locked in a federal, state, or local penal facility (Mumola 2006). Concomitant with the growth in marijuana incarcerations, the number of children with an imprisoned parent nearly doubled (Kjellstrand et al. 2011). An estimated over 8 million children (roughly 11 percent of the child population) have been affected by parental incarceration (Kjellstrand et al. 2011). Having a parent incarcerated has devastating effects on family relationships, both upon separation and reunion, and severely impacts children in negative ways. Research indicates that children of inmates are two times more likely to go on to experience problems with school, engage in delinquent and criminal behavior, and have mental health and substance-use problems (Murray, Farrington, Sekol & Olsen 2009; Murray & Farrington 2005; Myers, Smarsh, Amlund-Hagen, & Kennon 1999). The caretaker of children who are left behind, usually a mother, experiences additional strain both in managing the relationship across institutional walls and in raising children alone. The economic strain on the parent left behind may lead her to seek a new partner, which further complicates the relationship with the father. Reintegration of an incarcerated parent back into the relationship he left, or if the mother has re-partnered, back into his children's lives is equally complicated by the additional challenges he must face re-entering society, in general.

Employment. Socioeconomic status is a fundamental determinant of health, and having a criminal record negatively affects returning citizens' employment prospects and income. This is especially true for African Americans, who experience double jeopardy by having a criminal record and being Black. An experimental study by Pager and colleagues (2009) showed that Blacks who had a criminal record were less likely to be called back or offered a job as equally qualified Whites who had a criminal record. Further, the study found that, in fact, Blacks having no criminal background fared no better than Whites who did have a criminal history. Ex-offenders are stigmatized, and being Black compounds the disenfranchisement of ex-offenders.

For sure, African Americans who land behind bars largely are poor, lack education, and experience long and repeated periods of unemployment; but research shows that incarceration history has an added negative effect on employment and wages. Using propensity score matching, Gellar et al. (2006) assessed the independent effect of incarceration on employment and wages among demographically and psychosocially similar men. Their data revealed a 6-percent lower rate of employment among ever-incarcerated men as compared to never-incarcerated men, and wage differentials between 14 and 27 percent. Other studies are consistent with their findings.

From a public-health perspective, criminalizing marijuana creates and exacerbates existing health disparities because of the disproportionate impact of drug laws and enforcement on minorities. Further, criminalizing marijuana usurps limited resources that could be directed toward addressing prevention and treatment of drug abuse and fundamental causes of other drug-related offenses. Punitive responses to drug offenses are not effective because they do not address the root cause of drug offenses.

Conclusion

The policy debate around the legalization of marijuana has strong proponents on both sides. The very fact that marijuana is now recognized as a form of medicine and is decriminalized in some municipalities suggests that more progressive sentiments around the substance are beginning to dominate. Criminalizing marijuana has not deterred its use, but instead, has made the United States the leader in imprisoning its populace and has deepened and perpetuated racial disparities in health. African Americans have been most severely affected by drug laws, bearing a disproportionate burden of arrests and incarceration for cannabis offenses. Further, the burden has been born overwhelmingly by Black men, whose health and social conditions have reached a point of national crisis (Mauer 1990; Lichtenstein 2009). The legalization debate is more than a moral, legal, or political one. The public-health consequences and societal cost-benefit of criminalizing marijuana deserve serious consideration.

Notes

1. National Survey on Drug Use and Health 2009 *http://oas.samhsa.gov/NSDUH/2k9NSDUH/2k9ResultsP.pdf*, p. 20
2. National Survey on Drug Use and Health 2009 *http://oas.samhsa.gov/NSDUH/2k9NSDUH/2k9ResultsP.pdf*, p. 17
3. Monitoring the Future 2010 Summary *http://www.monitoringthefuture.org/pubs/monographs/mtf-overview2010.pdf*
4. Table 1.24b, National Survey on Drug Use and Health 2009 *http://oas.samhsa.gov/NSDUH/2k9NSDUH/tabs/Sect1peTabs1to46.htm#Tab1.24B*

5. Over the course of the last 35 years, the rate at which the United States places its citizens in jails and prisons has risen dramatically. For the first 70 years of the twentieth century, U.S. incarceration rates remained relatively stable at a rate of about 100 per 100,000 citizens. Since 1970, the United States has experienced a large and rapid increase in the rate at which people are housed in federal and state correctional facilities. Currently, the U.S. incarceration rate is 491 per 100,000.
6. Bureau of Justice Statistics 2009, http://bjs.ojp.usdoj.gov/index.cfm?ty = tp&tid = 132
7. MMWR Surveillance Summaries, June 9, 2006, 55(SS05); 1–108 Youth Risk Behavior Surveillance—United States, 2005 *http://www.cdc.gov/mmwr/preview/mmwrhtml/ss5505a1.htm#tab43*
8. *www.drugpolicy.org/communities/race/educationvsi/*
9. http://chicagoist.com/2009/07/22/county_board_decriminalizes_small_a.php
10. CPD, unpublished data 2008.

3

THE PATHS NOT (YET) TAKEN

Lower Risk Alternatives to Full-Market Legalization of Cannabis

Robert J. MacCoun[1]

California's 2010 Proposition 19 (and the similar AB 2254 Ammiano Bill) would have allowed local jurisdictions to legalize the production, sale, purchase, and possession of cannabis for California adults, as well as for small-scale home cultivation. Although neither measure succeeded, Prop. 19 was endorsed by over 46 percent of the electorate, and similar propositions are expected on the 2012 ballot. Other states will undoubtedly entertain related proposals in coming years. The central question in this chapter is: *if we were to permit legal access to cannabis for adults, are there better approaches than that envisioned by Proposition 19?* This chapter will not actually address whether we should legalize cannabis (see MacCoun & Reuter 2001, 2011), but rather, ask if we decide we are going to do it, how should we do it?

"Better" in this context could involve many different normative standards. Some are deontological (e.g., libertarian, religious); others are consequentialist. The latter category includes myriad public-health, public-safety, and economic factors. Assessing these consequences is complex because of considerable uncertainty about the extent to which observed associations between cannabis and harms are causal or spurious, and the extent to which any causation is due to the illegality of cannabis rather than its intrinsic effects on health and behavior factors (see MacCoun, Reuter, & Schelling 1996). This chapter will oversimplify this complexity by assuming that (1) cannabis consumption does have some harmful consequences irrespective of legal status, (2) those harms vary directly with the total quantity of cannabis that is consumed (and perhaps with the potency of the cannabis), (3) there is no substitution effect between alcohol and marijuana, and (4) marijuana's potency and quantity consumed are influenced by policy design—perhaps more so under some form of legalization than under full prohibition. From this perspective, a model is superior to Prop 19 if it permits legal access at lower risk of increased consumption.[2] This chapter does not attempt a political analysis, and indeed, public opinion data are insufficiently fine-grained, but a plausible conjecture is that a model meeting these criteria will also attract more voter support than Prop 19.

Reflections on Prop 19

Elsewhere, my colleagues and I have analyzed Proposition 19 in considerable detail (Kilmer, Caulkins, Pacula, MacCoun, & Reuter 2010), varying the assumptions of a complex simulation model of the relationships among cannabis production, prices, taxes, consumption, and revenues. We have tried to abstract insights about the design of a regime for taxed and regulated production and retail sales (Caulkins et al. 2012). For simplicity, I will simply refer to such models as *full-market models,* but the reader should bear in mind that many such models are conceivable and they may greatly differ in implementation and consequences. Here I will simply summarize some key points about market models based on our analyses (Caulkins et al. 2012, Kilmer et al. 2010).

1. Full-market models significantly reduce the risks that suppliers face. Assuming that suppliers expect to be compensated for their risks, this assertion implies that, *ceteris paribus,* prices will drop under a market model (Reuter & Kleiman 1986).
2. Market models would also facilitate production methods affording considerable economies of scale and other efficiencies; these, too, would lower prices.
3. We estimated that the combined effect of these factors could produce an 80- to 90-percent reduction in the pretax retail price of an ounce of marijuana under grow-house conditions, and possibly more under greenhouse or farm production.
4. Translating a price drop of this magnitude into a change in consumption is difficult because we know relatively little about the shape of the demand curve (e.g., linear vs. constant elasticity) and the price elasticity of demand for marijuana. But under plausible assumptions, lower prices could increase consumption by anywhere from 75 percent to 300 percent.
5. It is commonly assumed that any drop in prices under legalization could be offset by taxation. But a price drop of this magnitude would require a tax on the order of $10/gram. In contrast, excise taxes on cigarettes are about $0.10/gram—two orders of magnitude smaller. This makes it highly likely that such a legal market would fail to eliminate the black market.
6. The Prop 19 model, which devolves decisions about taxation to local governments, risks creating a "race to the bottom," where counties would opt for a much lower tax to compete for revenues.
7. Any attempt to implement a full-market model at a state or local level will be constrained by federal laws prohibiting marijuana and by federal decisions about how to enforce these laws.

This seventh point is suggested by an examination of the history of attempts to regulate tobacco and alcohol in the United States. (Humphreys 2011, MacCoun & Reuter 2001).

8.   Because of the economic stakes involved, full-market models politically empower the distribution industry in ways that make effective regulations politically difficult to implement and sustain.

If the goal is to legalize cannabis without significantly increasing consumption, other market models might fit the bill better than Prop 19. For example, a model using state rather than local taxation and regulation would avoid the "race-to-the-bottom" dynamic and would strengthen regulators' hands (see Caulkins et al. 2012). Unfortunately, by the same logic, a unified federal system would be superior to a state system, and any state that attempts to "go it alone" would attract considerable federal scrutiny and interference since such a model would conflict with various federal laws. Presumably, Prop 19's local model was in part an attempt to "fly under the radar" of federal scrutiny.

Another consideration is what to tax. Most proposals for taxing cannabis envision taxation by weight. But there are fairly compelling reasons to consider taxing by THC content, and perhaps by the THC:CBD ratio (see MacCoun 2010, Caulkins et al. 2012). Good evidence now suggests that cannabis is considerably more potent than a generation ago (e.g., McLaren et al. 2008). Circumstantial but very plausible evidence suggests that users are limited in their willingness and ability to titrate their doses, and that with increased THC consumption (and a rising THC:CBD ratio) comes increased risk of harmful health and safety consequences, including dependency (see Di Forti et al. 2009, Hall & Degenhardt 2009). Taxing by weight potentially encourages this troubling trend toward higher potency; taxing by content could help to discourage it by pushing cannabis back toward the "softer" products of earlier decades. The analogy is of course to taxes for softer vs. harder forms of alcohol. I have heard objections about the feasibility of testing and regulating by potency, but such arguments are hardly persuasive. With respect to technical feasibility, consider that cannabis-seed dealers already list THC (and sometimes CBD) levels on their online catalogues.[3] With respect to cost, testing randomly chosen samples seems a modest requirement to impose on an industry with such low production costs.

But, in the remainder of this chapter, my focus is on three plausible alternatives to the full-market approach: home cultivation (bypassing the full-market approach altogether), Dutch-style cannabis coffee shops (a partial-market approach), and buyer or grower clubs (intermediate, between home cultivation and the Dutch approach). None of these models offers the revenues that Prop 19 was purported to generate—though it is questionable whether Prop 19 would have generated them, either (Kilmer et al. 2010). But, as we shall see, these alternatives are very likely superior to Prop 19 if the goal is to permit legal adult access without risking large increases in consumption.

Home Cultivation

Prop 19 would have allowed adults to cultivate cannabis in a 5-by-5-foot plot—too small for a significant commercial operation, but probably far larger than needed for personal consumption under current technologies. This alone, without any legal sales component, would have constituted a significant change in marijuana policy.

There is no exact analogy to this proposal in other countries, but several jurisdictions (Alaska, South Australia, and Western Australia) have come close, essentially decriminalizing rather than legalizing home cultivation. Decriminalized home cultivation of cannabis for personal use but not sale is partially analogous to full-scale legalization; it increases the potential access to cannabis, reduces legal risks, and probably reduces stigma and forbidden-fruit effects. It conceivably has some effect on prices, though the effect may be modest for the small quantities permitted in the cases examined here.

Alaska. Due to a complicated string of political events and legal decisions, Alaska has had two separate periods in which home cultivation of small numbers of plants was at least decriminalized, and arguably, legalized. In May 1975, Alaska passed a law that treated possession of cannabis (an ounce or less in public, any amount in private) as a civil offense subject to a maximum $100 fine. Later that month, the Alaska Supreme Court (*Ravin v. State,* 537 P.2d 494 [Alaska 1975]), ruled that the state's constitution protected the privacy of marijuana possession and use in the home, except for amounts "indicative of intent to sell," which the legislature in 1982 established as four ounces. In 1990, a ballot initiative "recriminalized" marijuana, upgrading possession of less than eight ounces to a misdemeanor potentially punishable by 90 days of jail time. But *State v. McNeil,* a 1993 Superior Court decision, argued that "Ravin was founded in the Supreme Court's interpretation of the Alaska Constitution. The legislature—nor for that matter the people through the initiative—cannot 'fix' what it disliked in an interpretation of that document by legislation." The next decade saw considerable confusion about whether the *McNeil* ruling had in fact voided the recriminalization, and the issue was not clarified until the Alaska Supreme Court upheld a Court of Appeals decision (*Noy v. State,* 2003) reaffirming *Ravin.*

The available data are too sparse to assess the earlier period. Examining 1988 data on 12–17-year olds and high school seniors, MacCoun and Reuter (2001) noted that Alaska exceeded comparison states for cannabis prevalence, but also (to a lesser extent) for alcohol and tobacco, and (to a greater extent) for cocaine. They concluded that the data were too ambiguous to shed light on the Alaska policy.

Unfortunately, the newer post-Noy experience is similarly ambiguous. As seen in Figure 3.1, Alaska had higher rates of cannabis and other drug use prior to the late 2003 decision that re-decriminalized home cultivation. The available data show that Alaska's marijuana prevalence has fluctuated since Noy, falling from 2005 to 2007 and then rising relative to the rest of the nation from 2007 to 2009.

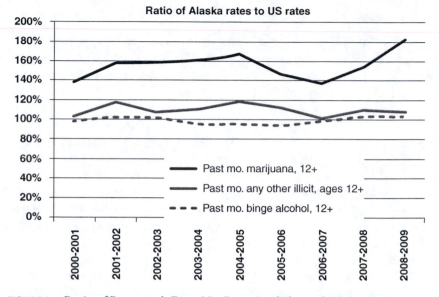

FIGURE 3.1 Ratio of Past-month Drug Use Rates in Alaska vs. the Entire USA, 2003–2009

Source: NSDUH state-level data for various years. http://www.oas.samhsa.gov.

And while Alaska's rate exceeds the national average (and, in some years, leads the nation), this was already true before the Noy decision. Thus, the data are again too ambiguous to permit any strong inferences about the effects of home.

The South Australia Cannabis Expiation Notice policy. Australia's 1987 Cannabis Expiation Notice (CEN) policy also depenalized home cultivation, although it put in place a system of modest monetary fines that rise with the quantity in possession. The initial CEN scheme allowed for up to 10 plants. This limit was later reduced to three plants in 1999 and is now down to only one plant. Although there are no stated limits on the size of the plant, a single plant is probably sufficient to supply one to three regular users for a year. Although the policy change is more subtle than the Alaska model, we know more about its effects due to a number of cross-sectional and longitudinal analyses. Analyzing survey data for 1985 to 1995, Donnelly, Hall, and Christie (1998) show that the lifetime prevalence of cannabis rose in South Australia from 26 percent to 36 percent. But they conclude that "it seems unlikely that this increase is due to the CEN system," because Victoria, Tasmania, and New South Wales showed similar increases (without adopting the legal change) and because South Australia did not differ from the rest of the country in the rate of weekly cannabis use. (See Figure 3.2.)

As shown in Table 3.1, data from the 2007 National Drug Strategy Household Survey (Australian Institute of Health and Welfare, 2008) suggest that by 2008, South Australia looked quite similar to the rest of Australia with respect to both cannabis and other illicit drug use.

Lifetime prevalence of cannabis

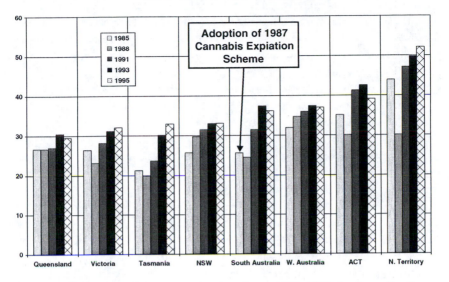

FIGURE 3.2 Trends in Lifetime Cannabis Prevalence 1985–1995, for Australian States and Territories.
Source: Data from Donnelly, Hall, & Christie (1998), Table 2.1.

TABLE 3.1 Patterns of Cannabis Prevalence in South Australia vs. Other Australian States and Territories

	South Australia	*MEAN for other states/ territories*	*MEDIAN for other states/ territories*
Past-year cannabis use (%)	10.2	10.0	9.3
Ratio of cannabis users to cocaine users	7.8	7.9	6.3
Ratio of cannabis users to ecstasy users	3.5	2.8	2.6
Recent cannabis use by 14–24 year olds	17.5	18.1	18.1
Any illicit excluding cannabis by 14–24 year olds	4.6	5.4	4.4

Source: Australian Institute of Health and Welfare (2008).

Williams (2004) analyzed data from the same household survey (for the years 1988, 1991, 1993, 1995, and 1998) using a more ambitious econometric analysis, concluding that "no evidence is found that either participation or frequency of use is sensitive to the criminal status of marijuana" in the sample as a whole. She does find that the change in law was associated with an increase in the likelihood of marijuana use among males over 25 years of age.

Thus, we see that parallel increases in cannabis use occurred throughout various parts of Australia a few years after South Australia adopted the 1987 CEN scheme, and it is possible that the scheme played some role in this effect, at least for some users. Could the parallel increases have been attributable to increases in the distribution of South Australian cannabis to other states and territories, due to increased supply and/or a decrease in price? This does seem possible. Figure 3.3 shows that from 1991 to 1992, the price of cannabis did drop in South Australia, a period that roughly coincides with the increases in use. Prices for the rest of the nation did dip soon thereafter, and their declines lagged somewhat and were smaller than the South Australia decline—two features that one would expect if the South Australian effect was diffusing to other states and territories. This was several years after the CEN policy was adopted, and if it was due to the scheme, the effect appears to have been short-lived.

Another factor to consider in interpreting the CEN experience is that, at least in the short run, it still involved considerable criminal justice sanctioning by the state. Using data on yearly CEN issuances and prosecutions, Christie and Ali (2000) show that the CEN scheme actually had a "net-widening" effect—an increase in prosecutions for minor cannabis offenses, apparently caused by the large fraction of fines that went unpaid.

Western Australia. Between 2004 and 2011, Western Australia had a similar policy. The Cannabis Infringement Notice (CIN) scheme. The Cannabis Control

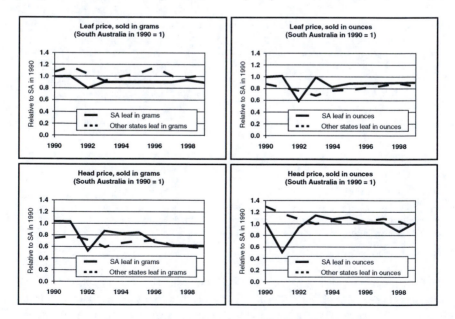

FIGURE 3.3 Changes in Cannabis Prices Relative to 1990 South Australia Levels
Source: Author calculations based on data from Clements (2010), Table 1 and 2.

Bill adopted in March 2004 established a limited fine of AU$200 for possession of up to two non-hydroponic cannabis plants (Lenton & Allsop 2010, 814). As with South Australia, the available evidence does not suggest that the policy increased consumption; indeed, between 2003 and 2007, past-year use dropped more rapidly in Western Australia than in Australia as a whole. Nevertheless, the Cannabis Law Reform Act of 2010 restored criminal sanctions for cultivation. Lenton (2011) attributes this change to the election of Colin Barnett, a vocal opponent of cannabis law reforms, as premier of Western Australia.

Assessment. The rocky history of home-cultivation policies in Alaska and Australia says more about their political fragility than about any inherent flaws in their design or implementation. The available evidence does not suggest that decriminalized home cultivation leads to increases in the prevalence of use; though consumption data are harder to come by, no clear evidence proves a significant price drop. Similarly, no evidence suggests that home cultivation in these jurisdictions has made a significant dent in the black market either. Truly legalized home cultivation could potentially lead to more dramatic effects, but it seems unlikely that it poses the risk to consumption levels of a full-market model. Caulkins et al. (2012) note that a home-cultivation allowance could undermine regulatory controls under a full-market model. But that is less a concern for home cultivation without a legal retail market. It is easy to imagine ways in which some participants could "cheat" in a home-cultivation model, but the relevant comparison is not to a perfect system but rather to the current regime, where all nonmedical growers and users are cheaters.

The Dutch Cannabis Coffee-Shop System[4]

In 1976, the Netherlands adopted a formal, written policy of nonenforcement for violations involving possession or sale of up to 30 grams of cannabis. The "gateway theory" has long been seen as an argument for being tough on cannabis, but interestingly, the Dutch saw that concept as a rationale for allowing retail outlets to sell small quantities (see MacCoun & Reuter 2001). Rather than seeing an inexorable psychopharmacological link between marijuana and hard drugs, the Dutch hypothesized that the gateway mechanism reflected social and economic networks, so that separating the markets would keep cannabis users out of contact with hard-drug users and sellers.

During the early 1980s, many coffee shops in Amsterdam and other cities began selling small quantities of cannabis. Although the numbers are currently dropping, the most recent systematic count identified around 700 retail cannabis outlets in the Netherlands—about one per 29,000 citizens (one per 3,000 in Amsterdam) (see Bieleman et al. 2009). The shops sell somewhere between 50 and 150 metric tons of cannabis at a value of perhaps 300 to 600 million euros a year.

An estimated quarter of the 4 to 5 million tourists who visit Amsterdam go to a coffee shop, and about 10 percent of them cite the legalized marijuana as a reason why they came (Amsterdam Tourist Information 2007).

The Dutch experience is challenging to characterize, because it is a moving target. In 1995, the 30-gram limit was reduced to 5 grams, and a 500-gram limit was set for coffee-shop stocks. And since the late 1970s, a set of guidelines has emerged for regulating the technically illicit retail sales in open commercial establishments. As formalized by the Public Prosecution Service, coffee-shop owners are not to be prosecuted for selling cannabis provided they comply with five rules (the so-called "AHOJ-G" rules):

1. Sales limited to 5 grams per person per day
2. No sales of other drugs
3. No advertising of cannabis
4. No nuisance to neighbors
5. No sales to minors below age 18

The shops are allowed to keep up to 500 grams of cannabis without risking arrest or prosecution (Openbaar Ministrie 2010).

In 1997, officials began closing coffee shops for noncompliance with these rules. Between 1997 and 2007, the number of retail cannabis outlets dropped 40 percent, from 1,179 to 702 (Bieleman et al. 2009).

A significant new development was the Dutch cabinet's announcement on May 27, 2011, that the coffee shops would be run as private clubs for Dutch citizens (Ministry of Security and Justice 2011). Memberships per club probably will be capped initially at 1,500, and foreign visitors (even those from the European Union [EU]) will be excluded. The cabinet cited nuisance, sales to tourists, and increases in problematic use by youth, but the rising influence of Geert Wilders's far-right party was surely a factor as well. What is striking is that the policy shift doesn't actually eliminate the "backdoor problem" that many see as an unworkable contradiction. Rather, the Dutch have essentially internalized the contradiction, accepting it for their own citizens but no longer allowing it to influence foreigners.

Are the Dutch more likely to use cannabis? MacCoun (2011) compares various data sources documenting marijuana prevalence in the Netherlands, other European nations, and the United States. Recent U.S. and Dutch rates are roughly equivalent within sampling and measurement error, and both the United States and the Netherlands rank high relative to most other nations. But in recent years, many European countries—including Italy, Belgium, Ireland, the United Kingdom, France, and Switzerland—have rates of student marijuana use that either match or exceed the Dutch rate.

By facilitating relatively easy access to high-potency cannabis, one concern is that the Dutch system might alter the intensity and duration of a cannabis-using "career," but available data do not support this idea. First, MacCoun (2011) showed that the past-month use rate among Dutch students is quite close to what we would predict knowing only their lifetime prevalence rates. And when the data include adults, the Dutch "continuation rate" is actually lower than one would predict based on similar rates in other countries. Second, MacCoun (2011) showed that Dutch users appear to "mature out" of cannabis use at a faster rate than their American counterparts. Finally, a comparison of regular users in Amsterdam and San Francisco (Reinarman, Cohen, & Kaal 2004) found quite similar rates of self-reported use.

On the other hand, MacCoun (2011) estimates that Dutch cannabis users have a higher probability of being admitted to treatment for cannabis use than is true for most countries in Europe. This could reflect a greater need for cannabis treatment in the Netherlands, but that is difficult to reconcile with their relatively modest cannabis continuation rates (relative to Europe) and quantities consumed (at least relative to San Francisco). One possibility is that the Dutch are more generous and proactive in providing treatment. Reuter (2006) estimates that the Dutch government spends about 9,200 euros per "problematic drug user" on treatment; the comparable estimate for Sweden—a country with an active coerced-treatment tradition—is about 7,600 euros. MacCoun (2011) calculates that once criminal justice referrals are excluded, there are about six admissions per 1,000 past-month users in both the United States and the Netherlands.

As noted earlier, a key part of the rationale for the Dutch coffee-shop system was the hypothesis that "separating the markets" would weaken the statistical "gateway" association between cannabis and hard-drug use. The results presented so far paint a fairly favorable picture of the Dutch model, but an important counterfactual question is: how would Dutch outcomes look if they hadn't adopted this approach? That question is difficult to answer. Peter Reuter and I (MacCoun & Reuter 1997, 2001) have suggested that the Dutch cannabis system emerged in two phases, with distinct effects—an initial "depenalization" phase with no detectable effects on cannabis use, and a second phase (roughly 1984 and 1996) in which the percentage of 18–20-year olds who had ever used cannabis rose from 15 percent to 44 percent, with past-month prevalence rising from 8.5 percent to 18.5 percent.[5] During this latter period, prevalence trends were either flat or declining in most other countries. We characterized this period as the Dutch "commercialization era," arguing that it was plausibly attributable to the rapid expansion of retail cannabis outlets, at least in Amsterdam.

This commercialization thesis has been debated in the literature (see MacCoun 2012). The available data fall well short of what contemporary methodological standards require for strong causal inference. But additional correlational support has emerged. Between 1997 and 2005, past-year use among Dutch 15–24 year olds declined from 14.3 to 11.4 percent, during a period when other European countries (Germany, Spain, Italy, and Sweden) were seeing increases. Although it is difficult to establish causation, note that the legal age for coffee-shop purchases was raised from 16 to 18 years in 1996 (Monshouwer et al. 2011), and, as noted above, this is a period in which the number of cannabis coffee shops dropped nearly 40 percent. Thus, it is plausible that the Dutch have a higher cannabis prevalence than if they had simply decriminalized possession without permitting retail sales.

Still, any effect of Dutch commercialization is probably much more muted than what one might expect under a full-market model. As discussed above, it is very likely that full-scale legalization would significantly reduce cannabis prices. But the Dutch do not have a true legalization regime; it is best characterized as "de facto" legalization, and even then, only at the retail level. Using the most rigorous estimates of US prices (Kilmer et al. 2010) and Dutch prices (Hazekamp 2006, Pijlman et al. 2005) on a purity-adjusted basis, MacCoun (2012) estimates that Dutch and US prices are roughly equivalent; at most, the Dutch prices are only slightly lower. The Dutch price data include retailer markups to cover the costs the owners incur in operating retail outlets in commercial neighborhoods. But it is also likely that prices in the Netherlands are elevated by their unusual hybrid regime that approximates legalization at the user level, but European-style prohibition at the level of the growers and traffickers—with coffee-shop owners in a gray area somewhere between these. If high-level Dutch traffickers face an enforcement risk, they presumably pass this along in higher prices down the supply chain (Reuter & Kleiman 1986). The Dutch are clearly enforcing prohibition at the higher end of the supply chain (MacCoun 2011). This presumably raises prices for consumers.

Assessment. Dutch citizens use cannabis at more modest rates than some of their neighbors do, and they don't appear to be likely to escalate their use relative to their counterparts in Europe and the United States. Moreover, signs indicate that rather than increasing "the gateway" to hard-drug use, separating the soft- and hard-drug markets possibly reduced the gateway, though it is difficult to test this argument with any rigor. But circumstantial evidence suggests that the Dutch retail system increased consumption, especially in its early years when coffee shops were spreading, open to 16 year olds, and advertised more visibly than they do today. And, if so, this increase occurred in a hybrid system in which high-level enforcement probably served to keep prices from dropping the way they might in a full-scale legalization scheme. The Dutch system is ambiguous by design and in ways that give officials leverage over prices and sales in ways that might be far harder to achieve in a full-scale legalization regime.

Cannabis Clubs and Licensing Models

In the 1990s, drug policy analysts (Kleiman 1992; MacCoun, Reuter, & Schelling 1996) discussed the notion of user licenses, somewhat analogous to driver's licenses. The idea was mostly a theoretical abstraction. But some forms of licensing have emerged as a viable policy option: buyer or grower collectives. Under this model,

a buyer (or perhaps, a grower) must join a quasi-regulated, not-for-profit organization that grows and/or provides cannabis for its members.

Cannabis social clubs have operated quasi-legally in Spain since 2002; there are
now several hundred of them (Alonso 2011). Thus far, they have withstood legal
scrutiny, though authorities haven't pressed the issue. Some are already paying
taxes. Alonso (2011, 7) wryly observes:

> By some strange legal fate, the global prohibition of drugs applied by the
> Spanish courts with the view that its goal is to protect consumers from the
> risks of drugs has given place to a strange protectionist market for cannabis,
> where there is economic activity but no profit, entrepreneurs but not busi-
> nessmen, and cooperative[s] of consumers who are associated with small
> scale cultivators, that function separately from the major distribution outlets
> and the economy.

Cannabis clubs have been under discussion in the Netherlands (Everhardt &
Reinking 2011), and such plans are likely to gain momentum as the Dutch model
moves away from a commercial model centered on tourist sales (MacCoun 2011).

In theory, cannabis clubs share many of the benefits of a licensing model, though
it is not clear whether anyone in Spain has actually "lost their license." But theoretically, cannabis clubs can scrutinize potential users, informally police existing users,
and exert peer pressure on members to keep the club in good standing. (Think of
condominium associations.) Those without a license can still seek cannabis in the
black market, but the clubs have the potential to weaken illicit supply chains.

Conclusions

At the time of writing, Colorado and Washington voters passed marijuana-reform
initiatives in November 2012. The reform proposals differ from Prop 19 in many
details, but like Prop 19, they envision a tax-and-regulate model analogous to the
current array of state tobacco and alcohol regimes. It is possible one or both will
succeed where Prop 19 failed, creating a complex political and legal conflict with
the federal government, but possibly spurring other states (including California)
to put similar measures on the 2014 ballot.

As argued in this essay, tax-and-regulate models are not the only way to permit
legal adult access to cannabis. Various partial and nonmarket models are options
as well. And even in the absence of a change in cannabis laws, signs suggest that
medical-marijuana distribution, at least in some California cities, may be evolving
away from a strict prescription model. What it is evolving toward is less clear, but
one can already see elements of home cultivation, Dutch-style cannabis coffee
shops, and recreational cannabis clubs.

In Table 3.2, I offer a tentative summary of the major strengths and weaknesses
of each model.

TABLE 3.2 Assessing the Models

MODELS	STRENGTHS	WEAKNESSES
Taxed and regulated legal market	• Provides revenue stream for the state • Taxes help to internalize the externalities • Taxing by THC:CBD content discourages higher-potency plants • Significantly curtails black market • Permits labeling and quality control	• Legal mass production will significantly decrease price • Difficult to regulate as industry gains economic and political power • High risk of state/federal legal conflict
Dutch-style de facto legalization of retail sales	• Enforcement threat limits aggressive marketing, industry political power • High-level enforcement raises prices • Significantly curtails black market	• "Backdoor problem" creates legal and political ambiguity • Uncertain state revenue stream • Moderate risk of state/federal legal conflict • Restrictions on advertising may be difficult given U.S. free-speech rights
Legal (or weakly sanctioned) home cultivation	• No promotion or advertising • Weakens black market	• Some risk of organized crime, diversion to black market • No state revenue stream
Buyer/grower clubs, licensing schemes	• No promotion or advertising • Weakens black market • Easier to monitor and enforce than home cultivation	• Some risk of organized crime, diversion to black market • No state revenue stream

Source: Compiled by author

The evidence to date is far from definitive (and almost completely lacking for cannabis clubs). And each of these models has identifiable drawbacks. But perhaps the perfect is the enemy of the good. These alternatives to the full market seem likely to permit adult cannabis use in ways that pose less risk to public health and public safety.

Arguably, it is not legalization per se but rather commercialization that poses the greatest health and safety risks. Commercialization promotes use, encourages price competition (and perhaps high-potency products), and empowers the supply industry, enabling it to resist regulatory efforts (MacCoun & Reuter 2001).

Nonmarket and partial-market alternatives limit industry power, permit regulatory controls, and can help to reduce the salience of cannabis. The catch is that they also offer less promise of revenue generation at a time of stark budget deficits.

Notes

1. I thank Keith Humphreys, Peter Reuter, Beau Kilmer, and Jon Caulkins for helpful comments on earlier drafts.
2. Marijuana legalization becomes more compelling if, in fact, people would substitute away from alcohol consumption to marijuana; the evidence on this point is mixed (see Kilmer et al. 2010 for a review).
3. e.g., *www.amsterdammarijuanaseeds.com*, *www.kindgreenbuds.com*, *www.weed-seeds.net*, *www.cannabis-seeds.co.uk*
4. This section is adapted from the more-comprehensive essay, "What Can We Learn from the Dutch Cannabis Coffeeshop System?" (MacCoun 2011), which documents in greater detail the statistical results mentioned here.
5. The timing of this jump is more notable than its magnitude; Beau Kilmer points out that while he was in high school, past-month use rose from 8.1 percent to 19 percent—without any obvious policy explanation.

4

WHY DID PROPOSITION 19 FAIL?[1]

*J. Andrew Sinclair, Jaclyn R. Kimble, and
R. Michael Alvarez*

Through the initiative process, Californians are called upon to decide the fate of
many issues in each election, and the 2010 general election was no exception. One
of nine issues on the ballot in that election was Proposition 19, which sought to
legalize marijuana use. Despite millions being spent in support of the measure,[2]
Proposition 19 was defeated by a relatively wide margin, as 4,643,592 votes were
cast for it and 5,333,230 votes were cast against it, a 46.5 percent to 53.5 percent
loss.

Earlier in the campaign season, Proposition 19's fate had been unclear; indeed,
reporters observed a notable amount of instability in the public–opinion polling.[3]
In July 2010, The Field Poll showed that voters were closely divided over Proposition 19—44 percent supported the measure, 48 percent opposed it, and 8 percent
were undecided. But, by September 2010, The Field Poll found a dramatic reversal, with 49 percent planning to vote yes, 42 percent planning to vote no, and
9 percent undecided.[4] And then in late October, right before Election Day, The
Field Poll's estimate of voter support swung back in the opposite direction, now
with 42 percent supporting legalization, 49 percent opposed, and 9 percent still
undecided.[5]

One possible reason for this last change in opinion is that the United States
Attorney General, Eric Holder, announced in mid-October that, even if California legalized marijuana under state law, the federal government would continue
enforcing federal laws against selling and distributing marijuana.[6] The "conventional wisdom" of the popular press ascribed the defeat of Proposition 19 to the
attorney general's statements, as well as the demographics of the midterm election voters and the "prospect of regulatory gridlock."[7] But each of these possible
reasons for defeat is specific to *this proposition;* they do not reflect opinions on
legalization *in general.* By using polling data from earlier in the campaign season,

we can analyze general voter attitudes toward legalization of marijuana through the initiative process.

Why did Proposition 19 ultimately fail to pass? What was it about the measure that turned voters against it in the end? To what extent can partisanship explain voters' opinions of the issue? In this chapter, we tackle these questions using data from a unique survey that we conducted in the fall of 2010 using election returns information. In the next section, we briefly present the theoretical foundations that motivate our study. We then discuss our unique survey, and from there, we examine what motivated California voters to support, or oppose, Proposition 19 in the 2010 general election.

Theoretical Foundations

How do voters make decisions? Much of the theoretical literature on voter decision-making focuses on voters who are in a relatively rich information environment. For example, in U.S. presidential and gubernatorial elections, voters have ample time to gather information because the elections are often lengthy affairs, lasting for many months and typically involving both primary and general elections. Additionally, the mass media cover these campaigns extensively, allowing voters to obtain information without a significant investment of time. With this abundance of information, voters can use many different strategies to determine which candidate to support; these include voting based on partisanship, issues, or candidate characteristics. Voters can also make inferences about the candidates based on cues, such as endorsements (Alvarez 1997, Popkin 1991).

Propositions, however, are presented to voters in a radically different context. Because propositions are not typically associated with one of the major political parties, and because propositions typically only emerge in a particular election (not repeatedly on the ballot like many candidates), voters encounter many ballot measures relatively poorly informed. Additionally, propositions often are complex, and, in many situations, they are on the same ballot with other competing issues. Thus, in this environment, information costs are high for voters, and they may not have the typical cues or heuristics readily at hand when they are asked to make a decision on a particular ballot measure (Bowler and Donovan 1998).

To analyze why Proposition 19 was defeated, we must understand the range of possible strategies that voters could be using. For the sake of brevity, we will only discuss three possible explanations for how voters decide whether to support or oppose propositions. The first possible explanation is that expressly political cues, such as partisanship or ideology, help voters make up their minds about ballot issues. To pick up on partisan cues, voters need to have the issue presented to them through the prism of partisanship or ideology. That may happen if candidates, political parties, or interest groups take opposing stands on ballot issues and actively campaign on the ballot issue (Lupia 1994). A good example of how political candidates may champion particular ballot measures and how candidates and parties might present differing positions to voters is California's Proposition 187 in 1994, a measure to deny services to undocumented immigrants. In that election, both gubernatorial candidates took opposing stands on Proposition 187, with then–Governor Pete Wilson seizing upon the issue as a vehicle for his reelection effort (Tolbert and Hero 1996). Another similar example is the case of Proposition 209, an anti-affirmative action initiative in California, on which the Democratic and Republican parties staked out clear stands on opposing sides of the issue (Chavez 1998). These examples show that when parties and candidates present voters clear and polarizing positions on a ballot measure, voters can base their decisions on partisan and ideological cues.

A second possible explanation is that nonpolitical predispositions help voters decide how to vote on ballot measures. For example, depending on the issue and how the media and politicians frame it for voters, fundamental predispositions, such as tolerance or egalitarianism, might come into play as voters debate their position on a ballot measure (Alvarez and Brehm 2002). Although theories of public opinion and voter decision-making indicate that such predispositions might factor in these choices, little evidence exists in the literature, because these factors have received little study in the context of ballot measures.[8]

Finally, self-interest may also play a role in how voters evaluate ballot measures (Downs 1957). Certain demographic groups or voters in certain regions of the state might perceive that they have much to gain (or lose) personally if a particular ballot measure passes and becomes state law. This is likely to be the case when it comes to ballot measures involving pocketbook, economic, or redistributive issues. For example, homeowners might choose to oppose property taxes, and senior citizens might oppose bond measures to fund local schools (Bali 2008). Thus, a straightforward application of rational cost and benefit calculations might help voters determine how to vote on ballot measures. Furthermore, if clear winners and losers exist for a particular ballot measure, it might be possible to find evidence of this voting strategy by looking at which demographic groups support or oppose the measure.

Thus, we have three basic types of explanations for how voters make decisions on ballot measures. Partisanship and ideology might matter for voters, especially if the political parties and candidates take clear and opposing stands on the proposition. Other predispositions, such as tolerance or egalitarianism, could also be important for voters. And, finally, some voters may vote based on self-interest, which we can investigate by asking whether certain groups, such as seniors, are more or less likely to support Proposition 19.

Our Survey

Before the 2010 general election, we surveyed 3,000 California voters. Polimetrix interviewed 1,000 registered Republicans, 1,000 registered Democrats, and 1,000 registered "decline to state" voters between September 15 and October 10. Since the survey design did not sample at random from the population (there are not equal numbers of Republicans, Democrats, and "decline to state" voters in California, and Polimetrix used respondents from its online survey panel), the data is weighted to reflect the population profile of California's electorate, with weights provided by Polimetrix.

In our particular case, the precise timing of the survey plays an important role in our analysis. All of the interviews conducted for this survey were completed at least five days *before* the attorney general gave his widely publicized statement that the federal government would continue to enforce federal antimarijuana laws in California, even if Proposition 19 passed. An article from late October in *The Christian Science Monitor* observed that, although four polls conducted in September had the measure passing, four of five polls in October suggested the measure would fail.[9] Thus, our survey was in the field during the period in which Proposition 19 appears to have been the most popular. The percent of voters that support Proposition 19 in our survey are generally consistent with other surveys conducted around the same time (see Table 4.1, below). In our sample, 56.7 percent of Californians supported the measure, while 35.0 percent opposed it.

Although many voters changed their minds by Election Day, the polling data may actually better represent underlying attitudes toward legalizing marijuana through the initiative process. The Election Day results were likely influenced by the federal government's campaign against the proposition and by concerns about the feasibility of implementation—the two issues given considerable play in the popular press in the final weeks before the election. Therefore, voters' response to these issues reflects their attitudes toward *this specific proposition* rather than their attitudes toward marijuana legalization in general.

Who favors marijuana legalization? Table 4.2, below, shows the percent of individuals who supported and opposed the law, as well as the percent who answered that they did not know, sorted by measures of political belief or information. The table clearly shows a strong partisan and ideological divide. The vast majority (76.1 percent) of the strong Democrats in the survey supported the measure, while only 14.2 percent of strong Democrats opposed it. On the other hand, only 25.6 percent of strong Republicans supported Proposition 19, while 66.5 percent opposed it. The percentages are even more lopsided when comparing across individuals that reported identifying as "very liberal" and "very conservative."

TABLE 4.1 Survey Response Data. Who Favors Proposition 19?

	Democrat	Independent or No Preference	Republican	All Voters
Oppose Prop 19	17.5	31.6	64.1	35.0
Don't Know	9.6	7.0	8.0	8.4
Support Prop 19	72.9	61.4	27.9	56.7

Source: 2010 Polimetrix survey.

TABLE 4.2 Political Variables: Oppose, Don't Know, or Support for Proposition 19

	Oppose	Don't Know	Support
Strong Democrat ID	14.2	9.7	76.1
Weak Democrat ID	26.3	9.5	64.3
Leaning Democratic ID	11.7	5.6	82.7
True Independent ID	29.2	8.4	62.5
Leaning Republican ID	51.6	6.8	41.6
Weak Republican ID	58.7	8.3	33.1
Strong Republican ID	66.5	7.9	25.6
Democratic Registration	19.7	8.7	71.6
DTS Registration	28.0	7.5	64.5
Republican Registration	60.1	8.6	31.3
Very Liberal	6.8	5.8	87.4
Somewhat Liberal	11.3	9.7	79.0
Middle of the Road	29.9	10.5	59.6
Somewhat Conservative	57.1	7.6	35.3
Very Conservative	69.8	7.2	23.0
Approve of Obama	14.4	8.7	76.9
Whitman Voter	59.6	6.7	33.7
Brown Voter	15.0	8.7	76.4
Fiorina Voter	61.6	8.1	30.2
Boxer Voter	15.1	8.2	76.7
Politicians: 0 Correct	34.7	8.5	56.9
Politicians: 4 Correct	34.6	8.7	56.7
Donate to Campaign	35.0	8.5	56.5

Source: 2010 Polimetrix survey.

Sorting respondents by candidate preference yields a similar result: supporters of Republican candidates generally opposed the measure, while supporters of Democratic candidates generally supported it. This result suggests that partisanship plays a strong role in voter opinions about legalization.

Political information and activity, however, do not appear, on the surface, to be very important for explaining attitudes on this issue (see again Table 4.2). Political knowledge was gauged by a question asking individuals to match correctly four politicians to their offices (Vice President Biden, U.S. Senator Boxer, Associate Justice of the U.S. Supreme Court Scalia, and CA State Assembly Majority Leader Calderon). Respondents with a high level of political knowledge—those who identified all of the politicians correctly—were no more or less likely to support the proposition (56.7 percent supported it, which is the same level of support as in the sample as a whole). Likewise, those having the least political knowl-edge—those who could not identify any of the politicians correctly—supported the proposition at similar levels (56.9 percent). Additionally, politically active respondents—those who donated money to any type of political campaign—supported the measure at similar levels (56.5 percent). Thus, political information and political activity do not seem to explain voter opinions on legalization.

Some nonpolitical characteristics appear to affect voter decision-making on Proposition 19, while others do not seem to matter (see Table 4.3, below). Some differences in support occur across income and gender categories, but those differences are small relative to some of the other categories. One of the more interesting results is that Whites support the measure more than Blacks or Latinos do: 58.8 percent of Whites supported the measure, while 55.9 percent of Blacks and 47.2 percent of Latinos supported it. For those who favor marijuana legalization, there is some good news: while only 45.3 percent of those born before 1950 supported the measure, 67.8 percent of those born after 1970 supported it. Thus, if voters do not change their opinions as they age, support for legalization should increase over time.

TABLE 4.3 Demographic Variables: Oppose, Don't Know, or Support for Proposition 19

	Oppose	Don't Know	Support
Born after 1970	22.8	9.4	67.8
Born 1950s/1960s	36.9	7.7	55.3
Born before 1950	46.5	8.2	45.3
Income under $40,000	31.6	9.2	59.2
Income $40,000–80,000	33.3	8.7	57.9
Income over $80,000	36.7	7.0	56.3
Female	36.1	9.6	54.3
Male	33.7	7.0	59.3
White	33.1	8.0	58.8
Black	34.2	9.9	55.9
Latino	42.2	10.6	47.2
High School or Less	40.5	7.2	52.3
Some College	35.0	8.6	56.4
College	31.5	8.1	60.4
Post Graduate	28.3	10.8	60.9
Protestant	48.1	10.5	41.4
Catholic	45.8	8.0	46.3
Agnostic	7.5	7.1	85.4
No Religion	23.7	6.5	69.8
Atheist	7.3	3.9	88.8
Other Religion	29.8	9.2	61.1

Source: 2010 Polimetrix survey.

Additionally, as Table 4.3 demonstrates, the levels of support for the measure differ by education and religious belief. Individuals with a college education tend to support the proposition (60.4 percent), as do those with some postgraduate education (60.9 percent). Those with only some college espoused less support (56.4 percent), and those with at most a high school education supported the measure the least (52.3 percent). The differences across categories of religious belief are even greater: while a mere 41.4 percent of Protestants supported the measure, 85.4 percent of agnostics and 88.8 percent of atheists supported it. Thus, religion appears to play a strong role in voter decision-making about Proposition 19.

Many of the results in the bivariate tables hold up under more rigorous analysis. Table 4.4, below, shows the results from an ordered logistic regression, for which opposing the measure was coded as 0, not being sure was coded as 1, and supporting the measure was coded as 2.[10] A positive coefficient indicates increasing probability that a respondent with that characteristic will favor the proposition. First differences are calculated for variables that are statistically significant at the .05 level. To arrive at the reported first differences, all variables were set to their median values, and the variable in question was altered from a value of 0 to a value of 1. The change in probability must equal one, so the change in the likelihood of replying "don't know" can be inferred from the reported first differences for opposing and supporting the measure.

The regression shows that partisanship clearly matters.[11] As Table 4.4 shows, changing an individual with the median characteristics in all other categories into a strong Republican increases the probability that such an individual opposes Proposition 19 by 21 percent. Changing an individual to identify as a strong Democrat has the opposite effect: the probability of supporting the proposition increases by 19 percent. Approving of President Obama's administration increased the probability an individual would support the proposition by 20 percent. Clearly, Democrats favored this proposition and Republicans did not.

Demographic variables affected the respondents, but generally to a lesser extent than did political variables (again, see Table 4.4). Respondents in the oldest age category (all individuals born before 1950) were more likely to oppose the measure than younger respondents were. Women were also less likely to support the measure than men were, although this effect is relatively small. The largest effects are reserved for Black respondents (all else held at the median, a Black voter was 22 percent more likely to oppose the measure) and a combined category of atheists and agnostics (a 23 percent increase in probability of support).

Although voters ultimately rejected this measure, the evidence from this survey suggests that voters used many of the usual political predispositions and cues to form their opinions. Party, race, religion, and gender predict support or opposition for the measure. The additional information voters received in the last month of the campaign season may have weakened some of these effects or may have altered turnout. As we will show in the next section, the election returns demonstrate that aspects of political culture certainly still played a strong role in the outcome.

TABLE 4.4 Ordered Logistic Regression: 0=Oppose, 1=Don't Know, 2=Support. N=2,811
California Registered Voters

	Coef.	Std. Err.	T–Stat.	FD: Oppose	FD: Support
Strong R.	−0.84	0.15	−5.65	0.21	−0.20
Weak R.	−0.47	0.17	−2.80	0.12	−0.12
Lean R.	−0.48	0.15	−3.11	0.12	−0.12
Lean D.	0.94	0.19	5.02	−0.19	0.22
Weak D.	0.47	0.18	2.62	−0.11	0.12
Strong D.	0.81	0.16	5.06	−0.17	0.19
Donated	−0.20	0.09	−2.23	0.05	−0.05
Approve Obama	0.84	0.13	6.70	−0.17	0.20
Politicians: 4 Correct	0.04	0.11	0.41		
Youngest	0.18	0.12	1.47		
Oldest	−0.35	0.10	−3.67	0.08	−0.08
Income under 40k	−0.06	0.12	−0.49		
Income over 80k	−0.09	0.10	−0.93		
Female	−0.20	0.09	−2.28	0.05	−0.05
Black	−0.93	0.19	−4.98	0.22	−0.21
Latino	−0.55	0.15	−3.58	0.14	−0.13
HS or Less	−0.05	0.15	−0.31		
Some College	−0.11	0.10	−1.02		
Post-Grad	−0.22	0.13	−1.69		
Catholic	−0.14	0.12	−1.19		
Other Religion	0.40	0.13	3.07	−0.09	0.10
No Religious Beliefs	0.98	0.11	8.85	−0.20	0.23

Source: 2010 Polimetrix survey.

Statewide Electoral Data

In light of the Democratic attorney general's opposition to Proposition 19, one may question whether the effect of partisanship was weakened on Election Day, but an analysis of election returns confirms the effect of partisanship. We see this effect reflected in the geographic distribution of votes for Proposition 19. Using electoral returns reported in California's *Statement of Vote,* most support for Proposition 19 clearly came from the coastal areas of California, especially the liberal Bay Area.[12] Only in 12 of California's 58 counties did a majority of voters support the measure. The counties with the highest percentages in favor are all from the Bay Area: Santa Cruz had 64 percent in favor, San Francisco had 64 percent, and Marin (just North of San Francisco) had 62 percent. Figure 4.1 shows the distribution of votes by county (as well as the state percent, in gray).

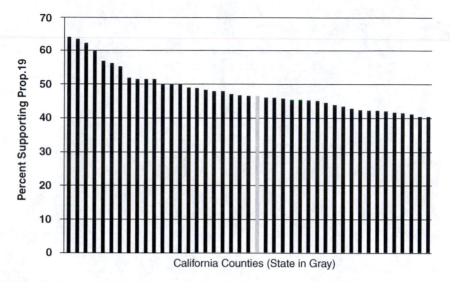

FIGURE 4.1 Distribution of Votes by County (Statewide average is 47 percent)

Proposition 19 passed in a few of the larger counties in the state: Alameda (56 percent), San Francisco (64 percent), and San Mateo (52 percent). But Proposition 19 failed to pass in the voter-rich counties of Southern California, including Los Angeles (48 percent), Orange (42 percent), San Diego (47 percent), Riverside (278,550 votes against), and San Bernardino (42 percent). Thus, something of a north-south divide occurred in the vote on Proposition 19.

The three counties with the lowest vote totals are Kings County at 33 percent (in the Central Valley), Imperial County (inland from San Diego on the Mexican Border) with 32 percent, and Colusa County (again in the Central Valley), also at 32 percent. Figure 4.2 is a state map of the county-by-county election returns. A county with a darker shade of gray in the figure received more votes in favor of Proposition 19 than a county with a lighter shade of gray. The center of the state is much lighter in color than the coast, and that the color tends to transition gradually, with few dark-gray counties next to light-gray counties.

An astute student of California politics will notice that the distribution of votes across the state shown in Figure 4.2 looks a lot like the distribution of partisanship across the state. Democrats tend to live along the coast, where Proposition 19 support was stronger, and Republicans tend to live in the interior, where support was weaker. This observation is verified when we calculate the correlation between the "yes" vote on Proposition 19 and the percentage of registered Democrats in each county—a strong 0.54. This analysis of statewide election returns confirms our individual-level results: partisanship plays an important role in the explanation for the failure of Proposition 19 in the 2010 general election.

FIGURE 4.2 The Darker the County, the Higher the Vote for Prop 19

Conclusion

We have shown that classic determinants of political culture—party, religion, race, and gender—explain voter attitudes toward the legalization of marijuana. Additionally, we have found that the geographic distribution of votes on Election Day demonstrates the role of political culture in voter decision-making on Proposition 19. Even on an issue that was not a major portion of the national discourse in the 2010 General Election, voters had enough information to place the ballot measure in their broader political context.

For those considering putting the legalization of marijuana on the ballot in other states, these results suggest three implications. First, marijuana use is less likely to be legalized in states with Republican majorities, because voters are clearly divided on the issue along party lines. Second, states in which a large fraction of the Democratic base is Latino appear to be less likely to support legalization measures, because Blacks and Whites are more supportive of the issue. Third, women and religious voters are more likely to oppose legalization. With these results, one could analyze the demographics of the states to determine which states are most likely to have a majority of voters support legalizations issue. If the issue were to appear on a ballot in the future, proponents and opponents could use these results to target their get-out-the-vote efforts.

Notes

1. Sinclair is the corresponding author. The authors thank the John Randolph Haynes Foundation for supporting the collection of the data used in this study.
2. John Hoeffel, "Money bolsters both sides of Prop. 19 debate." *The Los Angeles Times,* October 26, 2010.
3. For example, see: Daniel B. Wood, "New poll shows California tilting against legalized marijuana; the latest poll on Proposition 19, the ballot measure on legalized marijuana in California, found more opposition than previous polls. Prop. 19 backers dismiss the poll. Opponents say it is a sign." *The Christian Science Monitor,* October 6, 2010.
4. See The Field Poll, Release 2356, September 26, 2010.
5. See The Field Poll, Release 2365, October 31, 2010.
6. This was widely reported in the press at the time. For example, see: Daniel B. Wood, "Marijuana in California: Prop. 19 won't stop federal drug enforcement; Even if voters pass Proposition 19 on Nov. 2, which would legalize use of marijuana in California, the Justice Department will continue to enforce federal drug laws there, Attorney General Eric Holder said Friday." *The Christian Science Monitor,* October 15, 2010.
7. See: Daniel B. Wood, "Three Reasons Prop. 19 to legalize marijuana got the thumbs down; the federal government's opposition to legalized marijuana, midterm election voter demographics, and the prospect of regulatory gridlock may have kept California voters from passing Prop. 19." *The Christian Science Monitor,* November 4, 2010.
8. This is most likely the result of data limitations; the types of rich survey instruments that would be necessary to measure these nuanced political predispositions are usually found only in large-scale academic surveys like the American National Election Surveys or the General Social Surveys. Such predispositions are not easy to measure with aggregate election outcome data, exit polls, or other public opinion polls that are commonly used to study voting behavior and ballot measures.
9. Daniel B. Wood, "Measure to legalize marijuana trails in California, if polls are right; California's Proposition 19, which would legalize marijuana use for adults, is trailing 51 percent to 39 percent, a poll realized Friday shows. But some say polling on this issue may be problematic." *The Christian Science Monitor,* October 22, 2010.
10. A note on method selection: with an ordered logistic regression, there is only a single set of coefficients because of the assumption that it is appropriate to order the responses with an even distance between them (so, "Don't Know" is equidistant—and *between*— "Oppose" and "Support"). While it seems appropriate to place the "don't know" category between the other two alternatives, it is also reassuring that other methods (e.g., multinomial probit) achieve very similar substantive results.
11. We left out ideology because partisanship and ideology are so closely correlated. Also, note that there are seven categories of partisan identification; all of the six reported here are relative to the excluded category of "pure independent."
12. One county bordering Nevada also had a high proportion of votes in favor of Proposition 19: Alpine County. Nevertheless, Alpine County is very small: 335 voters voted in favor and 224 voted against.

5

WINDS OF CHANGE

Black Opinion on Legalizing Marijuana

Katherine Tate

In 2011, the New York City government passed a new law banning smoking in municipal parks, beaches, and plazas. The law was aimed at reducing public exposure to secondhand smoke and litter. Earlier, the New York City government also had considered banning the purchase of soda drinks using food stamps as part of a national effort to combat obesity and diabetes in children. State laws regulating and criminalizing undesirable behavior remain popular, and government claims behind such laws are that they protect citizens from immoral or dangerous behaviors. Such laws also have their share of critics. Social libertarians and groups like the American Civil Liberties Union (ALCU) have traditionally fought in court any laws regulating and criminalizing certain social practices and lifestyles. These groups argue that such laws violate the rights of Americans and are often arbitrarily enforced.

Some states had banned oral contraceptives for women until the Supreme Court ruled such laws unconstitutional in 1965 in *Griswold v. Connecticut*. States also had laws criminalizing consensual homosexual sex until the Supreme Court ruled against them in 2003 in *Lawrence v. Texas*. The 2003 ruling, in fact, reversed a 1986 decision by the High Court upholding such laws. Proponents for the legalization of marijuana would like to see courts strike down laws banning its use as being an unreasonable violation of their rights.

While social libertarians generally take a principled stand against many social laws and policies, arguing they are unconstitutional and often discriminatory, the public often takes sides incorporating other concerns. The valence attached to the group is important to the public in these debates. Since Stouffer's (1955) and McCloskey and Brill's (1983) pioneering work, research continues to find that Americans don't support the extension of rights to groups they dislike (Gibson 1988, 1992; Sullivan et al. 1982). Broadly speaking, most Americans often don't formulate policy stands based purely on their ideological principles. Rather, Paul

Sniderman, Richard Brody, and Philip Tetlock (1991) argue that Americans use affect and heuristics to form opinions in many instances. *Affect* refers to an emotional reaction to the groups public policies and laws affect. *Heuristics* are snap judgments about the world that are not full-blown ideologies.

Thus, more than making a decision based on a longstanding commitment to individual liberties and freedoms, Americans decide whether they are for gay rights, for example, based on their feelings toward gays and lesbians (affect) and judgments about whether homosexuality is good or bad for the American way of life (heuristic). Paul R. Brewer (2003) shows that rising support for gay rights is related to the new positive feelings Americans have toward gays and lesbians today. It is also because the policies of gay rights are less tied to moralistic concerns. Letting gays and lesbians lead open, public lives is not seen so much as negatively affecting American values. Affect and heuristics are why social issues cut across party and ideological lines. They are both important components of many public attitudes.

Like most Americans, Blacks are divided over laws seeking to regulate the morality and lives of citizens. While support for gay and lesbian rights has increased in the Black community, about 30 percent still object to marriage and adoption rights for gays and lesbians. Lines of disagreement in the Black community also exist on other social issues, such as the right to bear arms, smoking in public places, school prayer, stem-cell research, euthanasia, and the death penalty (Tate 2010). Blacks are also divided over the question of whether marijuana should be legal for adults to smoke in the United States. Support for its legalization, however, has grown since the 1970s. In a 2010 survey, more than half—52 percent—said they support its legalization.

While emotions play a role in their attitudes about extending rights and liberties to certain groups, African Americans generally bring different heuristics than Whites when formulating opinions. Blacks generally think about politics in group terms, pondering whether the policy is good or bad for Black America (Gurin, Hatchett, and Jackson 1989; Dawson 1994; Tate 1994). Michael Dawson (1994) refers to the use of group loyalties to formulate policy positions as a "racial utility heuristic." In addition to the significance of Blacks' social attachments to their group, in surveys, Blacks also think the world operates racially, and more unjustly, for citizens of color, than Whites do (Schuman, Steeh, and Bobo 1985; Welch and Sigelman 1991). Thus, Blacks often have strikingly different opinions than Whites on policies that invoke a racial frame.

Darren W. Davis (1995) shows that racial considerations are importantly linked to levels of political tolerance among Blacks. Blacks are significantly more threatened by their least-liked groups, typically the Ku Klux Klan, than Whites are by their least-liked group—generally Communists. Thus, more than affect, education, or psychological traits like authoritarianism, Blacks' refusal to extend to the KKK basic freedoms in the United States is a defense mechanism. Davis writes that Blacks are "certainly committed to the rules of the game," but for "terroristic and violent" groups, Blacks seek "systemic means" to control their behavior (1995, 18).

While some social policies, such as banning stem-cell research, can lack a racial frame, others, like the death penalty, are often coupled with racial concerns. Given that an American criminal justice sentence is more likely to sentence Blacks than Whites for identical crimes, Blacks think the death penalty adversely affects their community. Thus, perceptions about racial discrimination are empirically linked to Black support for affirmative action and the death penalty (Tate 2010). Finally, affect is still important because, like everybody, Blacks have different opinions of groups in society. Blacks have hot and cold opinions about illegal immigrants, welfare mothers, and evangelicals, and these different group ratings will affect opinions about policies related to amnesty, banning soda purchases for the poor, and school prayer. The logic behind the use of affect in policy-opinion formation is simple. If you don't like illegal immigrants, mothers on welfare, or preachers, why extend to members of these groups rights and privileges that will only benefit them?

Overall, this chapter theorizes that Black attitudes on the legalization of marijuana will be based on affect and racial heuristics, in addition to ideology and other background factors such as gender and religious beliefs. Affect and beliefs about racial fairness in the United States are important components of Black attitudes on the debate over legal marijuana. Some Blacks who oppose legal marijuana do so because they have negative images of Blacks today. Highly critical of Blacks in terms of their work ethic and values, they don't want to provide additional freedoms to a group they don't respect. So negative affect or racial stereotypes about Blacks will also influence Black public opinion on the legalization of marijuana.

Heuristics are also important. The legalization movement today is linked to Black demands for racial justice, since some African American leaders, such as the president of the California NAACP state chapter, support the legalization of the private use of marijuana as a way to reduce the alarmingly high incarceration of Blacks for drug possession. Data from the University of Chicago's General Social Survey (GSS) from 2000 to 2010 are pooled to develop a model determining how significant affect, racial considerations, church participation, and gender are in the debate over legal marijuana in the Black community.

Growing Support in the Black Community

The legalization of marijuana returned to the national agenda after getting washed out by the get-tough-with-crime campaigns that emerged in the late 1960s and endured through the 1990s. Support for its legalization was once low, but its group of supporters has more than doubled in size. Today, as of 2010, majority support for its legalization in the Black community exists. Furthermore, while the marijuana issue evokes racial considerations, little evidence of a racial divide exists in public opinion. African Americans, as Figure 5.1 shows, have opinions generally in line with other minority citizens and Whites. While, at times, Black support was slightly higher than support from other minority groups and Whites, the differences are not large. Thus, support for its legalization has increased for

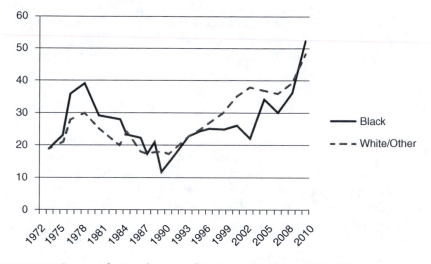

FIGURE 5.1 Support for Legalization of Marijuana by Race, 1973–2010

both groups from 19 percent in 1973, to 25 percent in 1994, to 52 and 48 percent in 2010.

Driving up support for legal marijuana in the United States was the legalization of marijuana for medical use by certain states. California was, in fact, the first state of legalize medical marijuana in 1996. Now more than a dozen states permit marijuana use when prescribed by a doctor. Public support for medical marijuana is exceptionally strong; most Americans think it should be available for medical use. When asked in a 2010 survey by the Pew Research Center whether they would support their state legalizing the use of marijuana for medical purposes if prescribed by a doctor, 73 percent said yes. Only 23 percent said no. Obviously, people tend to feel less hostility toward the beneficiaries of medical marijuana, an older and potentially terminally ill group of people. Furthermore, the involvement of the medical establishment, another group more positively received than drug dealers making a profit as a criminal enterprise, helps.

In this survey, however, Blacks were somewhat less likely than other groups to support state adoption of medical marijuana. Only 66 percent said they would support state adoption of medical marijuana. The racial group difference is small at only 7 percent, but it is also statistically significant. When asked in the same survey if they favored the legalization of marijuana, no significant race difference occurred, as evident in the GSS data set as well (see Table 5.1). Forty-one percent of Whites and 40 percent of Blacks in this 2010 Pew Research survey think marijuana should be legal to smoke.

Additional data suggest that Blacks have more polarized opinions about legal marijuana than other racial and ethnic groups. Polarized means the issue draws especially strong views from African Americans compared to other racial and

TABLE 5.1 2010 Poll on the Legalization of Marijuana and State Adoption of Medical Marijuana by Race (Weighted Data)

	White	Black	Asian	Mixed Race	Some Other Race	Refused
Q52. "Do you think the use of marijuana should be made legal or not?"						
Yes, Legal	41%	40	26	50	47	22
No, illegal	51.5	56	63	44	47	56
Don't know/refused	7	4	11	6	6	22
(Total cases)	(1115)	(172)	(35)	(16)	(144)	(18)
Q53. "Do you favor or oppose your state allowing the sale and use of marijuana for medical purposes if it is prescribed by a doctor?"★★						
Favor	73	66	80	75	75	58
Oppose	23	30	11	25	24	10.5
Don't know/refused	4	4	9	0	1	32
(Total cases)	(1115)	(172)	(35)	(16)	(144)	(19)
Q54. "Do you think that allowing medical marijuana makes it easier for people to get marijuana even if they don't have a real medical need, or doesn't it make a difference?"★★						
Yes, easier	47	48	49	25	46.5	26
Doesn't make a difference	48	46.5	43	62.5	51	32
Don't know/refused	5	6	9	12.5	2	42
(Total cases)	(1114)	(172)	(35)	(16)	(144)	(19)
Q55. For respondents who think allowing medical marijuana makes it easier to get marijuana even without a medical need, "Are you very concerned, somewhat concerned, not too concerned, or not at all concerned about this?"						
Very concerned	21	47	29	75	35	0
Somewhat concerned	31	20.5	53	0	29	40
Not too concerned	27	11	0	0	23.5	20
Not at all concerned	20	19	18	25	12	20
Don't know/refused	0	2	0	0	0	20
(Total cases)	(520)	(83)	(17)	(4)	(68)	(5)
Q56. "How concerned, if at all, would you be if a store that sold medical marijuana opened up near other stores in your area?"★★						
Very concerned	23.5	44	34	31	35	35
Somewhat concerned	20	9	29	6	9	5
Not too concerned	21.5	14	9	0	17	5

(Continued)

TABLE 5.1 *(Continued)*

	White	Black	Asian	Mixed Race	Some Other Race	Refused
Not at all concerned	34	31	23	62.5	38	20
Don't know/refused	1	2	6	0	1	35
(Total cases)	(1114)	(171)	(35)	(16)	(144)	(20)

Q57. "Keeping in mind that all of your answers in this survey are confidential, have you, yourself, ever happened to try marijuana?"

	White	Black	Asian	Mixed Race	Some Other Race	Refused
Yes	41	40	31	12.5	36	16
No	57	57	63	87.5	63	37
Don't know/refused	2	2	6	0	1	47
(Total cases)	(1115)	(171)	(35)	(16)	(145)	(19)

Source: Pew Research Center Poll: March 2010 Political Survey (Abt SRBI, Inc. Schulman, Ronca & Bucuvalas, Inc.). Pew Research Center for the People & the Press, March 10–14, 2010, telephone, 1,500 U.S. adults, downloaded from the Roper Center [USPEW2010-03POL].
**chi-square prob. <.01

ethnic groups. When asked if medical marijuana made it easier for people to obtain marijuana, there was no difference in responses. About 48 percent of Blacks, as well as Whites, Asians, and some other groups, felt that medical marijuana made it easier to access marijuana, while 48 to 43 percent said it made no difference. But, when those who felt marijuana from medicinal shops opened the door to more public marijuana use were asked how concerned they were about the matter, more Blacks than Whites felt "very concerned." As Table 5.1 shows, only 21 percent of Whites thinking medical marijuana increased access to illegal marijuana felt "very concerned," compared to 47 percent of Blacks. Also, when asked if they would feel concerned about marijuana dispensaries opening stores in their neighborhoods, more Blacks than Whites expressed deep concern. About 44 percent of Blacks said they would be "very concerned" compared to 23.5 percent of Whites. The data indicating polarization among Blacks on this issue suggests that there is little middle ground on this issue. Blacks appear to fear the legalization of marijuana for medical or social use more than other racial and ethnic groups and Whites do.

Finally, when asked confidentially in this 2010 survey if they had ever tried marijuana, matching percentages of Blacks and Whites said yes. About 40–41 percent of Blacks, Whites, and other racial groups have tried marijuana. Earlier surveys reveal that marijuana use has increased in this country. Another 2010 survey conducted by the Associated Press (AP) and CNBC found that 46 percent of the public thinks that marijuana use is harmful to one's health. Another 39 percent said marijuana had no effect on people's health.

While, clearly, its rise in use in the public is importantly linked to the increasing support for its legalization, what is vitally important is what people think of today's marijuana users. Social psychologists contend that people process information using schemas or mental representations of ideas. Thus, in addition to involving different images of marijuana users, including now those who use it for medicinal purposes, the increase in the experimentation with marijuana has pushed up support for its legalization. Fewer people associate marijuana use with hard-drug use. The same 2010 AP/CNBC poll shows that only 39 percent of the public believe marijuana is a gateway drug, leading to use of other illegal drugs. Most, in fact, believe that marijuana use has no effect on whether people use more serious drugs. Thus, the image of a marijuana user is not necessarily one of an "addict" or a "junkie." With higher reported rates of consumption, people today may think of marijuana use as having spread to people like themselves, and thus, its legalization would not necessarily benefit a class of people whom they fear and reject. Thus, the image of the marijuana user varies from clean-cut, middle-aged, and Caucasian to underaged, minority, and criminal. Furthermore, the legalization of marijuana is less tied to fears about empowering a marginal group of citizens marked by social deviancy and even poor health.

In contrast, opponents of legal marijuana continue to argue that it will increase crime. In the debate over Proposition 19, the 2010 California ballot initiative to legalize marijuana for personal use, the Democratic candidate for state attorney general, Kamala Harris, an African American, argued that she opposed Proposition 19 because it would increase crime, especially driving while intoxicated or DWIs. Some parents oppose legalization because they fear its spread among minors, who then might become difficult and delinquent. More than representing affect, these images represent schemas, or mental pictures that people carry that pop up in discussions about marijuana use. Schemas are cognitive structures that categorize and interpret objects and events (Markus and Zajonc 1985). Few people are fully able to explain what is captured in the schemas they associate with marijuana use. Determining which schemas are evoked requires experimental data not available for this study. Schemas, however, theoretically, are vitally important. They will shape opinion on the policy matter.

Explaining Black Support for the Legalization of Marijuana

One measure that potentially captures both affect and schemas in the GSS data set is one asking respondents if they hold negative views about Blacks. In general, Americans will refuse to extend additional freedoms and rights to groups they dislike, don't respect, or fear. While Blacks are less likely to hold negative opinions about Blacks than Whites and other ethnicities do, a minority of Blacks strongly agree with the statement that Blacks don't work as hard as other ethnic groups in America. Specifically, the question asks, "Do you agree or disagree with the following statement: 'Irish, Italians, Jewish and many other minorities overcame prejudice and worked their way up. Blacks should do the same without special favors.'" This measure is strongly associated with opposition to affirmative action (Kinder and Sanders 1996). It also forms part of ethnocentric attitudes, which have been shown broadly to affect American policy views from foreign aid to welfare policies (Kinder and Kam 2009).

About half of the Blacks asked this question from 2000 to 2008 agreed with this point of view, and 30 percent agreed with it strongly. In contrast, about 31 percent disagreed, while 15 percent said that they neither agreed nor disagreed. The majority of Blacks who have negative opinions about the work ethic of Blacks are expected to oppose the legalization of marijuana. This measure represents an anti-Black affect, which theoretically is linked to attitudes about marijuana. Attitudes about marijuana are racialized, and Americans who don't like minorities will not support its legalization. Table 5.2 shows Black responses to these questions.

TABLE 5.2 African American Opinions about Blacks and Special Favors, Spanking Children, Premarital Sex, and Courts and Criminals

	%	(N)
"Blacks Need to Work Without Special Favors"		
Agree strongly	29	(337)
Agree somewhat	25	(285)
Neither agree nor disagree	15	(171)
Disagree somewhat	14	(160)
Disagree strongly	17	(199)
"Need to sometimes discipline children with a good, hard spanking"		
Strongly agree	41	(484)
Agree	42	(495)
Disagree	12.5	(146)
Strongly disagree	4	(43)
"Is it wrong or not wrong if a man and woman have sexual relations before marriage?"		
Always wrong	28	(49)
Almost always wrong	14	(24)
Wrong only sometimes	11	(19)
Not wrong at all	47	(83)
"Courts in this area deal too harshly or not harshly enough with criminals?"		
Too Harshly	22	(352)
Not harshly enough	62	(982)
About right (vol.)	16	(253)

Source: General Social Surveys, Black respondents only, pooled 2000–2010, weighted by WTSSNR.

Negative attitudes toward today's young theoretically are linked to the debate on marijuana. One potential question invoked beliefs about permissiveness with the young. GSS asked if respondents believed in spanking. In the African American community, spanking is still considered a legitimate form of punishment, even as society is less tolerant of this practice. Thus, 83 percent of the Black GSS respondents agreed with the statement that "it is sometimes necessary to discipline a child with a good, hard spanking." Only 12.5 percent disagreed, with a mere 4 percent in strong disagreement. The remaining 15 percent of Black respondents put themselves in the middle on the policy of spanking children. Blacks with strict views toward children should be opposed to the legalization of marijuana. Clearly, African Americans who think that society needs to be very strict with children will oppose the legalization of marijuana as contributing to a breakdown in society's traditional cultural standards.

Another question potentially linked to Black attitudes on legal marijuana is whether premarital sex is wrong. Again, these attitudes tap into opinions about today's young. In contrast to the spanking question, Blacks are divided over the question of premarital sex. In 2008, about 42 percent of Blacks think premarital sex is always wrong or almost always wrong. The majority—58 percent—think differently, that premarital sex is wrong only sometimes or not wrong at all. Because this item was dropped in 2000 and only asked again in 2008, it could not be included in the multivariate analysis presented here. However, opinions about the lifestyles of young Americans should be tied to attitudes about the legalization of marijuana.

Beliefs about racial fairness in the criminal justice system will be tied to this debate as well. Proponents of Prop 19 have framed it as a racial-justice matter, pointing to the alarmingly high rates of incarceration of minority youth because of marijuana use. Surveys show that many Americans believe the U.S. justice system is racially discriminatory. In a 1999 Gallup Poll, 50 percent agreed with the statement that "a black person is more likely than a white person to receive the death penalty for the same crime." About 46 percent disagreed. When this percentage is broken down by race, more Blacks than Whites feel that there is discrimination in the application of the death penalty; the difference is statistically significant. Stories have surfaced about White marijuana smokers practically waving joints in the faces of police officers without arrests, while Blacks and Latinos are routinely incarcerated for marijuana use.

The GSS has one question surveyors have asked continuously from 2000 to 2010 that taps into these sentiments. Without asking about racial bias, it asks if courts deal too harshly with criminals convicted of crimes. While the question wording is loaded, since it should ask about "people suspected of crimes," not only those convicted of crimes, Americans have different opinions. Table 5.2 shows the results from 2000 to 2008 by race. As one can see, most Blacks agree with Whites and other races that the courts are too lenient on criminals. A large 62 percent of African Americans felt that the courts in their communities were not harsh enough in their dealings with criminals, compared to only 22 percent of Blacks who felt that the courts were "too harsh." Only 16 percent of Blacks felt that the courts were "about right" in their dealings with criminals. It is hypothesized that the small minority of Blacks who feel that the courts are unfair to criminals would be more likely to support the legalization of marijuana.

In addition to these attitudes, opinions about the legalization of marijuana are expected to be rooted in gender, age, education, income, partisanship, ideology, and religion. Women may be more opposed than men are to the legalization of marijuana. Women have been socialized as caregivers. Alcohol and drugs can be abused, negatively impacting the family. Men may not be as likely as women are to see this issue of legalization as being connected to the family, but rather consider it simply one about individual freedom. Similarly, families with young children may be more opposed to the legalization of marijuana than the childless or those with adult children. Experimentation and use of the drug often begins in the teen years, and although legalization is for adults only, families with small children may fear that this drug would be more available to children, if legalized like alcohol.

Older Americans who have less experience with marijuana may be more inclined to think the drug is dangerous. Older Americans may be more socially conservative than young Americans are, as well. Although social issues tend to cut across partisanship and ideology, Black Republicans and conservatives may be more opposed to the legalization of marijuana. Both groups stand for policies that promote and protect traditional conservative values in the United States, such as a ban on legal abortions and same-sex marriages. Religious Blacks may be more opposed because the Christian Black church has stood behind an agenda that opposes alcohol use, youth freedoms, and premarital sex. While some Black civil rights groups have backed the legalization of marijuana in California, some local Black church ministers have stood up in opposition to it. Finally, region and urban residency may be influential forces in this debate. Southern Blacks are thought to be more socially conservative than non-southern Blacks. Blacks living in the city, in contrast, may be more liberal.

Because the dependent measure is a dichotomous one, the logistic regression program through SPSS (PAWS Statistics 18.0) was used. The results are shown in Table 5.3. Few demographic variables are associated with opinions on the legalization of marijuana; the exceptions are gender and church attendance. As hypothesized, Black women are more opposed to the legalization of marijuana than Black men are. Because the B coefficient of a logistic regression is not easy to interpret, the Exp(B) coefficient is shown in Table 5.3. This shows the ratio-change in the odds of legalization for a one-unit change in the predictor. Thus, for Blacks who are 100 percent in favor of legalization, being female reduces the odds to only 44 percent. Gender, therefore, has a very large effect on opinions in this debate. Blacks having children under the age of 18 at home were also more likely to oppose the legalization of marijuana. The effect was less than for gender. For Blacks who are 100 percent in favor, having children reduces support by 29 percent. Blacks who

TABLE 5.3 Logistic Regression of Support for Legalization of Marijuana among African Americans, 2000-2010

Variables	B	SE	Exp (B)
Education	−.091	.117	.913
Income	.045	.041	1.046
Conservative	.004	.078	1.004
South	.042	.245	1.043
City	.173	.259	1.189
Age	.002	.009	1.002
Male	.571★	.239	1.770
Single	.458	.299	1.581
Republican	.041	.076	1.042
Family w/children	−.515#	.295	.598
Church Attendance	−.144★★	.047	.866
Courts Not Harsh Enough	−.361★★	.133	.697
Blacks Need Special Favors	.277★★	.081	1.319
Constant	−.605	.926	.546
(Total Cases)	(421)	SE	
Cox & Snell R-square	.148		
Nagelkerke R-square	.206		
Percentage Correct	72%		

Source: General Social Surveys, pooled 2000–2010, Black respondents only, unweighted.
#p<.10
★p<.05
★★p<.01

attend church regularly were significantly more likely to oppose legalization. A unit increase in church attendance reduces support for legalization by 12 percent.

Surprisingly, education, income, ideology, partisanship, and region were unrelated to opinions on this policy matter. While the coefficient for education was negative, indicating that highly educated Blacks were more likely to oppose legalization, it was not statistically significant. Blacks living outside the South or in cities were no more likely to support the legalization of marijuana than southern Blacks or those living in suburban or rural areas were.

Both attitudinal measures included in the final model turned out to be strongly related to opinions on this policy measure. The Exp(B) also reveals that these attitudinal measures have substantial effects on Black opinions. Blacks who did not agree with the view that Blacks could advance in America without "special favors" like the "Irish, Italians, Jewish and many other minorities" were more likely to favor the legalization of marijuana. The Exp(B) coefficient is 1.319, as Table 5.3 shows. A unit change in this attitude increases opposition or support by

24 percent. Thus, for Blacks whose support for legalization is 100 percent likely, switching from the strong position that Blacks need "special favors" to the strong position that Blacks "should work without special favors" reduces the likelihood of support substantially, to approximately 4 percent.

This measure, as noted earlier, measures a respondent's hostility or disapproval of African Americans. Because legalization of marijuana is a right that would be extended to groups publicly linked to marijuana because of their high incarceration rates for drug use, Americans who disapprove of Blacks will not support new or equal rights for Blacks and other minorities. While support for the legalization of marijuana has grown, many argue, because it is no longer seen as a drug used only by American minority group members, racial animus toward Blacks should be no longer linked to opinions on this debate. It still is linked, however. Racial animus or disapproval of Blacks, even among Blacks, is linked to opposition to the legalization of marijuana. Blacks who think that Blacks should not be asking for special favors in society because of their race are highly likely to be opposed to the legalization of marijuana.

Byron Orey (2004) contends that this racial resentment toward Blacks by Blacks is an important component of Black political conservatism. Some groups in the Black community remain harshly critical of the Black community, although it is not clear that the self-help messages they preach are hostile to special programs for Blacks like affirmative action. However, some Black church leaders, including those in Black nationalist churches like the Nation of Islam, condemn drug and alcohol use in the Black community, which they think is too prevalent. While there is also strong condemnation of American racism, there are sermons emphasizing Black self-reliance and abstinence as well. Malcolm X wrote, in his famous 1965 autobiography coauthored with Alex Haley, about how his conversion to Islam forced him to quit smoking marijuana, which he claimed was also linked to his criminality. Black conservative beliefs, therefore, may explain Black opposition to the legalization of marijuana.

In addition, Blacks who did not believe the criminal justice system was unfairly punitive, but who thought the opposite, that American courts were not "harsh" enough with criminals, were also opposed to the legalization of marijuana. The effect reduces or raises support by 23 percent from a unit change in this scale—from viewing the courts as too harsh, just about right, or not harsh enough. Moving from viewpoint that the courts are "too harsh" to "not harsh enough" cuts the likelihood of support for legalization to nearly half—from 100 percent to 54 percent. Again, the future suggests that while these attitudes are important today, they may become more important. In this case, if groups like the California NAACP and the ACLU make it plainer to African Americans that they are disproportionately punished for soft-drug use, it may increase support for the legalization. African Americans, representing a minority, however, who felt that the courts were "too harsh," were significantly more likely to endorse the legalization of marijuana. The fact that the criminal justice system remains so racially biased, coupled with increasing beliefs that the right is not only a benefit to the (troubled) Black community, will increase support for its legalization.

Conclusion: A New Direction in the Debate

Affect and beliefs about the criminal justice system are linked to the debate over the legalization of marijuana in the Black community. These attitudes can change in magnitude, since negative affect toward Blacks may not be so important to those considering the legalization of marijuana. Medical marijuana brings in new social groups as marijuana users, giving the cause greater social legitimacy. Furthermore, the ACLU and NAACP chapters are framing the issue differently. It is no longer seen as a pure civil liberties matter, but rather one that leads to better justice for Blacks and minorities. With new policy frames, support for the legalization of marijuana in the Black community has increased tremendously, from 19 percent in 1973 to 52 percent in 2010. The last decade, significantly, saw a large surge in support for its legalization among Blacks. Blacks remain divided, but a majority today supports legal marijuana. Some data from the Roper Center suggest that Blacks have more concerns about its legalization than other minority citizens and Whites do, fearing its spread to their communities. A large majority of Americans support the use of marijuana as a medicine, but Black Americans are somewhat less supportive than Whites, Asians, and other racial groups—a difference that was statistically significant.

Class and ideology were not relevant in the divide in Black America over the legalization of marijuana. Low-income and less-educated Blacks are just as opposed or just as supportive of its legalization as high-income and well-educated Blacks. Blacks who consider themselves "conservative" politically are not more opposed to the legalization of the marijuana than those calling themselves "liberal." As a social matter, the question of whether the ban on marijuana for adults should end cuts across partisanship as well. Black Republicans were no different from Black Democrats in their opinions about legal marijuana.

The opposition to the legalization of marijuana is rooted in gender and religion. Women are more prone to take a conservative stand over this issue because legalization may represent a threatening force to the family. Men may be less prone to seeing legalization as a family matter, but more as a personal right or freedom. Reframing legalization as a means to keep Black children from getting a criminal record over marijuana use may reduce female opposition to it (although the legalization is for adult use only). While Melissa Harris-Lacewell (2003) points to the power of the Black minister and church in the Black community in her study of Black public opinion, these leaders may bow to the civil rights community if legalization continues to evoke a racial-justice frame. However, Blacks exposed to church sermons were more likely to oppose the legalization of marijuana than Blacks who don't go to church. Religion remains especially salient for Black women. But given the shift in opinion by Black political elites on this matter, the

Black church may soften its opposition. As powerful as the roots of opposition are (gender and religion), the framing of the debate as important to keeping young Blacks safe and no longer victimized by a harsh, carceral state may eat away at these conservative roots of opposition.

The law-and-order campaign that President Richard Nixon initiated in 1968 was racial, and African Americans have always had views about crime-prevention policies that have been complicated by an unjust racial history for Blacks. Data show that Blacks, however, have moved closer to the mainstream on issues such as the rights for suspects from the 1960s to the late 1970s (Tate 2010). Furthermore, a majority of Blacks favored "three strikes" laws, imposing life sentences for those convicted of a third felony (Tate 2010), a policy linked to the dramatic surge in U.S. incarceration rates. While the congressional Black caucus attempted in the 1990s to pass legislation aimed at reducing racial disparities in sentencing, President Bill Clinton and the Democratic Party's "get-tough" agendas likely moved Blacks away from the political left on such questions.

It will take civil rights groups to push racial injustice back onto the national agenda. But Black leadership was not strongly linked to Black opinions on crime-control policies (Tate 2010). Jesse Jackson, Louis Farrakhan as the head of the Nation of Islam, and conservative Supreme Court Justice Clarence Thomas were not linked to Black opinions on the death penalty. An important development has been the easing of large-scale movement pushed by both political parties since the 1960s to increase sentencing penalties. The decline in violent crime, dropping to its lowest level in nearly 40 years in 2010, after peaking in the 1990s, has caused a reduction in a "get tough on crime" message. Furthermore, the salience of crime has declined, and new issues such as the War on Terrorism, the troubled and poor-performing economy, and the federal deficit crowd it out. This climate favors the legalization of marijuana campaign.

Blacks who oppose the legalization of marijuana now represent the minority, in a political context that favors legalization for recreational use. Partisanship has become more important force in public opinion (Carsey and Layman 2010). While the question of legal marijuana is not at all identical to that of gay and lesbian rights, the Democratic Party's move from "Defense of Marriage" to "Don't Ask, Don't Tell," to finally ending the ban on military service for gays and lesbians over the last decade, has clearly helped push up public support for gay/lesbian rights. Elite support from the Democratic Party has helped this stigmatized group's cause. Thus, if the Democratic Party, which the vast majority of Blacks identify with and support, moves toward support for legalization, it will further enlarge the new Black majority for legalization that first emerged in 2010. This will drive more Blacks into the legalization camp. Thus, there are winds of change in the air. Advocates will need to continue a campaign that elevates the matter into an important racial justice issue, not just a personal liberties concern.

6

THE HIGHS AND LOWS OF SUPPORT FOR MARIJUANA LEGALIZATION AMONG WHITE AMERICANS

Paul Musgrave and Clyde Wilcox

Popular and elite support for marijuana legalization has surged, declined, and surged again over the past four decades. In 1969, Gallup polls showed that nearly 9 in 10 Americans rejected the idea of legalizing marijuana. Support for legalization increased in the 1970s, only to plunge in the 1980s. Today, about half of Americans support legalization. What explains the highs and lows of support for legal marijuana?

In this chapter, we focus on attitudes of White Americans. We argue that the evolution of beliefs over marijuana legalization has been affected by changing frames offered by government and media. In the late 1960s and 1970s, marijuana was linked in the public mind to the "counterculture." By the early 1980s, marijuana was paired with crack cocaine in the "war on drugs" approach of antidrug activists and the Reagan–Bush administrations. By the mid-1990s, the growing movement for medical marijuana cast the drug as a palliative that could help critically ill patients, which reinforced a frame of cannabis at a harmless form of recreation.

Modern Debates over Marijuana Legalization

We begin with a capsule history of the modern era of debate over marijuana, which has proceeded through three acts. In the first act, during the 1970s, activists and officeholders in both parties assumed that antimarijuana laws would soon be overturned. In 1970, Texas Congressman George H. W. Bush endorsed the repeal of mandatory minimum sentencing rules for drug offenders (Schlosser 2003, 43). Five years later, Jack Ford publicly admitted that he had used marijuana, a choice his father, President Gerald Ford, said he disapproved of, even as he approved of his son's candor in discussing the issue (*Time,* October 20, 1975). Two years later,

Ford's successor President Jimmy Carter endorsed the decriminalization of mari-juana.[1] And, in 1981, Georgia Congressman Newt Gingrich introduced a bill to legalize the medicinal use of marijuana (Schlosser 2003, 49).

The decriminalization tide soon crested. In the second act, opposition to legal-ization grew rapidly, just as legalization activists believed they were on the cusp of victory. In the late 1970s, aspiring presidential candidate Ronald Reagan, who as governor had repeatedly vetoed legalization and decriminalization bills, used his syndicated weekly radio program to contrast his harshly antidrug marijuana views with those of President Carter (Reagan 2004, 162–163, 199–200, and 450–451). As president, Reagan proclaimed, "We're making no excuses for drugs—hard, soft, or otherwise. Drugs are bad, and we're going after them. . . . And we're going to win the war on drugs."[2] In 1988, Vice President George H. W. Bush attacked Massachusetts Governor Michael Dukakis, his opponent in the presidential race, for being soft on drugs, asserting that, "I think for a while as a nation we con-doned those things we should have condemned . . . there was talk of legalizing or decriminalizing marijuana and other drugs, and I think that's all wrong."[3] In 1996, Speaker of the House Newt Gingrich introduced legislation "demanding a life sentence or the death penalty for anyone who brought more than two ounces of marijuana into the United States" (Schlosser 2003, 49). And President Bill Clinton, an admitted former user of marijuana, chided an audience of high school students, saying, "Every single scientific study that has been done in the last several years shows alarming increases in the toxicity and the danger of using marijuana."[4]

The third act began in the mid-1990s when California voters enacted Propo-sition 215, which allowed patients to possess and cultivate marijuana for their personal medical use on the recommendation of a doctor. Since 1996, referenda in nine additional states (including the District of Columbia) have legalized medical marijuana, and four additional states have adopted medical marijuana laws through their state legislatures. By 2010, the Congressional Research Service estimated that 27 percent of the U.S. population lived in jurisdictions where state-level criminal penalties for the cultivation, possession, and use of medical marijuana had been removed (Eddy 2010). Overwhelming majorities of Americans surveyed by both academic and commercial pollsters confirmed that they wanted medical marijuana policies to be enacted in their state. Furthermore, although support for medical marijuana outpaced support for marijuana legalization across all sectors of society, support for both grew, and by 2010, approximately half of all Americans supported legalization. Public policy at the federal level and in many states did not follow this liberalizing trend, however. The amounts of marijuana seized by the DEA and the number of arrests made for marijuana offenses both sharply increased over the period from 2000 to 2010.[5]

In short, public policy has moved from a pro-legalization trajectory to a period of harsh rhetoric to an era of tolerant public attitudes and conflicted govern-ment policies. These empirical observations lead to obvious questions. Why are Americans so much more favorable to medical marijuana than marijuana legalization? Why have medical marijuana efforts been organized through the nonpartisan referendum process rather than through ordinary partisan channels? And, most important, why have the same cohorts of Americans held such strikingly different views about marijuana at different times in their lives?

Generational Explanations are Insufficient

The simplest explanation for the shift in White public support for marijuana legalization over the period 1970 to 2010 is generational. If the baby Boomers and their successor cohorts were more likely to have tried marijuana or otherwise been exposed to stimuli that made them more tolerant of marijuana than their forebears, then generational replacement should suffice to explain why opinion has shifted over time.

Qualitative evidence lends support to the idea that attitudes toward marijuana shifted after the 1960s. Prohibition had stimulated interest in marijuana among Whites during the 1920s, but the efforts of the federal government (particularly Federal Bureau of Narcotics Director Harry Anslinger) led to strict federal and state laws against the trafficking, possession, and use of marijuana during the 1930s (Schroeder 1980, 30–31; Sloman 1979; Earleywine 2002, 224; DiChiara and Galliher 1994, 44; Musto 1987, 210–229). Some state laws were particularly strict: "Selling the drug to a minor could bring the death penalty in some places during some eras" (Earleywine 2002, 244). Public opinion among Whites was accordingly strongly negative toward marijuana and cannabis users. Schroeder captures the essence of marijuana's social position: "Before the great surge in cannabis smoking in the 1960s, marijuana was largely confined to the big-city ghettos and the poor Mexican-American communities of the Southwest" (Schroeder 1980, 15).

Obviously, the counterculture movement radically reshaped these associations. During the late 1960s, marijuana quickly became one of the drugs of choice for well-educated, socially liberal White college graduates. Contemporaneous sources affirm that White Americans who came of age in the late 1960s and 1970s were more likely to be liberal in their views about, and use of, narcotics, including marijuana. Lempert (1974) postulated that decriminalization would follow when high social status individuals were identified as violators of the law. Schroeder implicitly shared that view:

> It was one thing when nationwide marijuana arrests totaled only a few thousand a year, with most of those occurring in inner-city ghettos or poverty-stricken rural areas. It was quite another when the sons and daughters or prominent citizens—governors, members of congress, military officers, doctors, and lawyers—began to show up on police blotters for marijuana offenses. And when the children of two successive American presidents turned out to be pot smokers, the epidemic seemed virtually universal (Schroeder 1980: 17).

Accordingly, the cohort hypothesis is simply that the sudden surge in the use of marijuana beginning in the late 1960s exposed the baby boomers and younger cohorts to a completely different idea of cannabis than earlier generations, whose ideas were more likely to be shaped by racial or class frames (or simply acceptance of the messages of Anslinger and others that cannabis was equally or more dangerous than heroin).

We show that this explanation fails to account for the dynamics of White public opinion over marijuana. To investigate this simple theory, we take its base prediction—that the baby boomers and other generations should be steadily more supportive of legalization than their forebears—and examine whether trends in White public opinion responses fit with that story. Our data comes from the General Social Survey (GSS) item *GRASS,* which asks respondents "Do you think the use of marijuana should be made legal or not?" We use the GSS item because it is the only survey that has asked the same question consistently throughout the period under consideration.[6] We divide GSS respondents from 1975 through 2010 into eight cohorts, basing each cohort on obvious formative influences while also keeping the cohort sizes comparable:

- *Flappers* (born 1896–1915) came of age during the Roaring Twenties and the earliest years of the Great Depression. (Due to small sample sizes, we do not report data for this cohort after 1996.)
- *Depression* respondents (born 1916–1925) came of age during the Great Depression and the earliest years of World War II. (Due to small sample sizes, we do not report data for this cohort after 2006.)
- *Postwar* respondents (born 1926–1935) came of age during the latter stages of World War II, the postwar period, and the Korean War.
- *James Dean* respondents (born 1936–1945) came of age during the era of the Beats, Dwight Eisenhower, and Sputnik.
- *Baby Boom* respondents (born 1946–1955) are the first half of the census bureau's definition of the "baby boom." They came of age from the assassination of John F. Kennedy through the end of American involvement in the Vietnam War.
- *Disco* respondents (born 1956–1965) are the second half of the census bureau's baby boom cohort; they came of age between Watergate and the bombing of the Marine barracks in Beirut.
- *Gordon Gekko* respondents (born 1966–1975) came of age between the launch of the Macintosh personal computer and the Branch Davidian standoff in Waco.
- *Clinton* respondents (born 1976–1990) came of age almost entirely during the Clinton administration.[7]

Figure 6.1 shows that the dynamics of public opinion throughout the 1970s are consistent with the expectation that generations with more marijuana users were

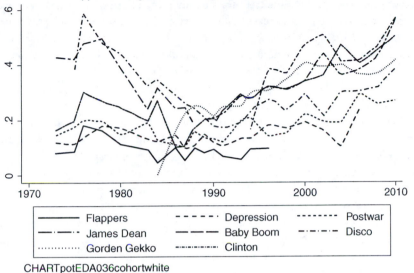

Support Among Whites for Legalization by Generation

——— Flappers	- - - - - · Depression	· · · · · · · · Postwar
—·—·· James Dean	— — — Baby Boom	—·—·—·— Disco
· · · · · · · · · · · Gorden Gekko	—··—··—·· Clinton	

CHARTpotEDA036cohortwhite

FIGURE 6.1 Support among Whites for Legalization by Generation

more likely to support marijuana legalization. But, after 1980, the generational model no longer holds. By 1990, the baby boomers and the disco generation have fallen by 30 and 40 percentage points, respectively, from their peak levels of support for marijuana legalization, and they are nearly indistinguishable from their older siblings' and parents' generations (the James Dean, postwar, and Depression cohorts). Nor is this a lifecycle effect: We observe the same compression among all generations and among parents and nonparents, and regardless of whether we view respondents sorted by age instead of generation. Contradicting the expectations of cohort theory, the experience of the baby boomers and later generations is not different from the experiences of other cohorts. Clearly, the period effect of the 1980s erased or at least suppressed generational differences in support for legal marijuana.

Putting the Marijuana Debate in Context

Why did public opinion sour on marijuana legalization in 1980s? We argue that marijuana was rhetorically associated with other narcotics as part of the War on Drugs and that this context, which went unchallenged by elite actors, changed the public's interpretation of the significance of marijuana. The historical evidence strongly suggests that activists and Republican politicians promoted new narratives about marijuana beginning in the late 1970s. In 1972, the National Commission on Marijuana and Drug Abuse had downplayed the risks of "experimental or intermittent use" of marijuana and recommended decriminalization; the commission's report later formed the basis for the advocacy efforts of Keith Stroup and his pro-cannabis group National Organization for the Reform of Marijuana Laws (NORML) (Massing 1998, 136). Indeed, the Nixon and Ford administrations were broadly in favor of treatment and other tolerant policies (Musto and Korsmeyer 2002; Massing 1998; DiChiara and Galliher 1994, 66).[8] The Carter administration was primed to follow their lead, but reversals both tactical (involving allegations of drug use among Carter White House staffers) and strategic (the mobilization of the parents' movement against marijuana, a network of conservative activists who supported zero-tolerance measures) fundamentally altered the debate (DiChiara and Galliher 1994, 66; Massing 1998, 139–148). These debates took place almost entirely within the White community, and politicians and activists such as Ronald Reagan soon seized upon the issue to mobilize and persuade voters.

Figure 6.2 highlights a different aspect of the story. These numbers suggest that for many people, homosexuality and marijuana have been redefined from vices to acceptable behaviors. The same pattern of a sharp decline followed by a sharp increase in support for legalization is present in this chart as well. Yet viewing support for legalization in the context of other salient social issues suggests a different mechanism is at work than simple generational replacement. We use the GSS survey items *XMARSEX, HOMOSEX,* and *ABPOOR* to measure support for extramarital sex, homosexual behavior, and abortion, respectively.[9] Throughout the period 1975 to 1990, support for cannabis legalization, homosexual behavior, and extramarital sex follow the same pattern and have broadly similar levels. After

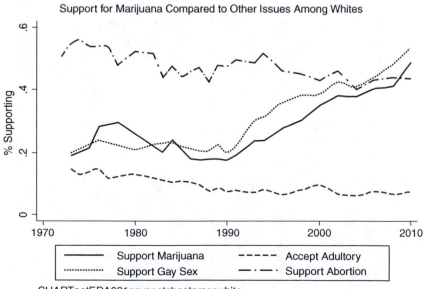

Support for Marijuana Compared to Other Issues Among Whites

CHARTpotEDA031gayspotcheatgrasswhite

FIGURE 6.2 Support for Marijuana Compared to Other Issues among Whites

1990, however, support for both cannabis and homosexual behavior tracks sharply and consistently upward, even as extramarital sex continues to trend downward. Marijuana and nontraditional sexuality have come in recent years to be seen as, at worst, victimless vices, and, for many, as acceptable behavior.

Further evidence for this position comes from the result of our multivariate logistic regressions presented in Figure 6.3. We calculate a separate logit model for White respondents in each of 18 GSS survey years that included both *GRASS* and the other covariates we display in the figure. Our dependent variable is whether the respondent supports marijuana legalization (coded as a 1) or not (coded as a 0). We display the point estimates of the logit coefficients (displayed as a dot) and the 95-percent confidence intervals for each estimate (displayed as vertical lines).

Figure 6.3 allows us to trace the long-term shifts in public opinion at a finer level than analyzing pooled GSS data. It also gives us a firmer handle on how the

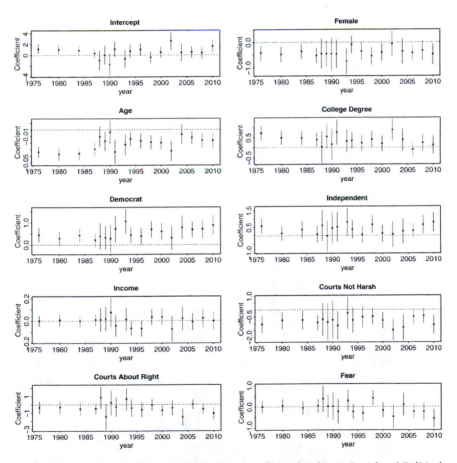

FIGURE 6.3 Estimated Effect and Standard Error of Membership in Social and Political Group on White Support for Legalization from 1975 to 2010

basis for supporting marijuana legalization has changed over time. For instance, a one-year increase in *age* has always been negatively associated with supporting marijuana legalization, but over time, the effect has substantially lessened as the flappers and depression cohorts have died off. Women have been steadily less supportive of marijuana legalization than men have. More interesting, the relationship between indicators of social status and support for legalization has shifted. In 1975, respondents who possessed a college degree made a respondent both statistically and substantively significantly more likely to support legalization. Over time, that effect has all but disappeared. With the exception of one year in the early 2000s, since the mid-1980s, college-educated respondents have been no more likely than non-college-educated respondents to support legalization.

Two sets of variables suggest the influence of different frames for marijuana legalization. The first are our variables measuring respondents' attitudes about crime and punishment. We use GSS items *FEAR* and *COURTS* for this purpose. *FEAR* asks, "Is there any area right around here—that is, within a mile—where you would be afraid to walk alone at night?" We code this variable dichotomously. *COURTS* asks, "In general, do you think the courts in this area deal too harshly or not harshly enough with criminals?" We convert the standard answers to this answer—"Too Harsh," "Not Harsh Enough," and "About Right"—to a factor variable; accordingly, the default response in our model is "Too Harsh." To our surprise, controlling for other factors, *FEAR* is almost never a significant predictor of respondents' beliefs about legalization. Unsurprisingly, however, respondents who believe that the courts are insufficiently tough on criminals are almost always less likely to support legalization. Yet note that the compression effect that we observed in the summary charts earlier is visible here as well. In the late 1980s and the early 1990s, respondents' views about the criminal justice system are not statistically significant indicators of their views about marijuana legalization, in sharp contrast to the period before and after.

A similar phenomenon occurs in our second set of political variables, which capture partisanship. Here, we evaluate the effect of being either a Democrat or an Independent compared to the excluded category, which is Republican. As Figure 6.3 shows, Democrats have been consistently more positive toward marijuana legalization than Republicans have been. Yet, although the point estimates have always been positive, these estimates have not always been statistically significant. Again, during the late 1980s and the early 1990s, the confidence intervals for Democratic respondents cross zero, making them statistically indistinguishable from a null effect. Since then (except for one survey), the coefficients for Democrat have been positive and statistically significant. Furthermore, the trend line for those estimates has sloped upward, meaning that over time, Democrats (and, recently, Independents) are growing markedly even stronger in their belief that marijuana should be legalized. Interestingly, comparing the models for GSS survey years 1975 and 2010, the estimate of the coefficient for *Democrat* has roughly doubled, while the coefficients for *age* in the same years has roughly halved.

The multivariate framework allows us to capture a shift in the public mood. What we have learned is that over time, the basis of support for marijuana legalization has changed from the young and the well-educated to the Democratic and the Independent. Views on marijuana legalization, in other words, were once strongly associated with one's social position and social views. They are now strongly associated instead with partisanship.

We turn again to qualitative evidence to discern the reasons why. What we find is that the emergence of antimarijuana messaging did not take place at the same rate in both parties. Although prominent s such as William F. Buckley and Milton Friedman espoused pro-legalization messages and stridently criticized prohibitionist policies, Republican Party candidates did not share their views (Buckley 2004; Ebenstein 2009, 226). The Republican Party instead became the home of Nancy Reagan's "Just Say No" campaign and similar attitudes. President Reagan was markedly more conservative and aggressive in his antidrug statements than his predecessors, decrying the "false glamour that surrounds drugs" and calling on parents, law enforcement, and the government to "brand drugs such as marijuana exactly for what they are—dangerous, and particularly to school-age youth."[10] A typical statement:

> Nancy and I have both taken a personal interest in the crusade for a drug free America. Like so many Americans, we watched with greater and greater apprehension during the years when too much of our media and too many of our cultural and political leaders sent out the message that using illegal drugs was okay. Well, thank God those days are over. Those days of scenes in a movie where you would get laughs out of someone who was high on marijuana . . . .—well, this conference proves that we no longer shrug off illegal drug use. Yes, Americans in all walks of life have seen the truth about drugs. Workers, employers, students, teachers are all saying no to drugs and alcohol.[11]

Both Reagan and Bush defined marijuana usage as a moral issue on par with the abuse of other, harder drugs. Numerous antidrug education and "public service" initiatives, including DARE, "Just Say No!," and the "This is your brain on drugs" commercial (1987), took place during their combined 12-year tenure in office. Among their initiatives was also the 1990 television special *Cartoon All-Stars to the Rescue,* in which the Muppets, the Smurfs, Garfield, ALF, and Alvin and the Chipmunks united to stop one teenager from using marijuana, beer, and harder drugs. The animated special was shown in April 1990, at the very nadir of drug support for marijuana legalization, on ABC, NBC, CBS, Nickelodeon, and the USA Network. The official sanction for this cartoon was unmistakable: unlike most Saturday morning cartoons, President George H.W. Bush and his wife Barbara introduced the special.[12]

By the late 1980s, the parties' messaging on drugs had grown much more similar. The 1988 Democratic Party platform called on the United States not only to "house the homeless" and "protect the environment," but in the same sentence, to "wage total war on drugs." Moreover, the platform asserted that "the legalization of illicit drugs would represent a tragic surrender in a war we intend to win."[13] Although other party platforms took a strong line against drugs, the 1988 platform is by far the strongest, and the only one to use the language of "total war" instead of crime and rehabilitation. During the same period when our quantitative evidence shows that support for legalization had collapsed, the Democratic Party had withdrawn any competing narratives supporting legalization and other more-tolerant policies—a complete reversal from both the Carter administration's support for decriminalization and the Obama administration's measured support for medical marijuana.[14] Although the reasons why the Democratic Party chose not to contest the Republican narrative about marijuana use are unclear, the fact remains that there were no competing signals to Democratic voters or Independents. In other words, shifts in elite-led messaging are associated with shifts in public opinion.

The Emergence of Medical Marijuana

Perhaps the most important shift in the context in which marijuana was considered came in the mid-1990s, when medical marijuana became a highly salient issue. California's debate over Proposition 215 and the passage of the nation's first statewide medical marijuana law ushered in a new period in which there were now two different options for de facto marijuana legalization. Since the 1990s, public opinion has been consistently in favor of medical marijuana, often by overwhelming majorities.[15]

Since the GSS has not asked survey respondents about medical marijuana, we turn to other polling sources to examine the contours of White public opinion on this issue. We use the Pew Research Center for the People and the Press March 2010 survey, which asks both the GSS question about marijuana legalization and also whether respondents favor or oppose their state legalizing the use of marijuana for medical purposes. As expected, medical marijuana is more popular than marijuana legalization. Seventy-three percent of respondents said they favored medical marijuana, whereas 23 percent opposed medical marijuana and 4 percent said they were unsure or didn't know. By comparison, marijuana legalization was supported by only 41 percent of respondents. and 52 percent opposed legalization. We created a logit model of support among White respondents for each question, using the same controls (female, college degree, age, whether the respondent had ever used marijuana before, party identification, and whether the respondent was a mainline Protestant or a born-again Christian). For each model, a positive response is coded as a 1 and a negative response as a 0. Figure 6.4 compares the predictions from these two models.

In Figure 6.4, we present the probability of supporting marijuana legalization and medical marijuana for respondents at a variety of ages (from 18 to 88) with all other covariates set at their sample means. As we expect from our earlier

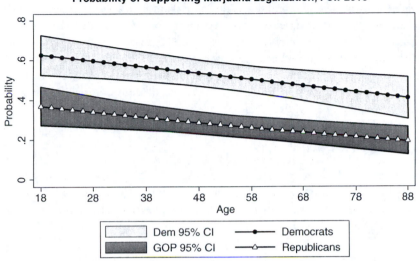

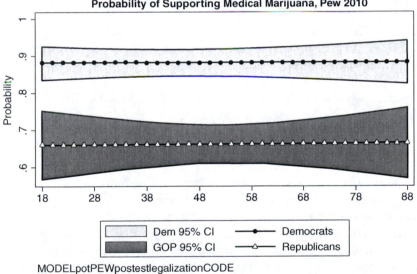

FIGURE 6.4 Probability of Supporting Marijuana Legalization by Party and Age in 2010

investigations, the probability of supporting legalization decreases with age; furthermore, Democrats are always more likely to support legalization than Republicans are. But there is no such effect for medical marijuana. The slope of the trend line is almost perfectly flat. Although Democrats remain more likely to support medical marijuana than Republicans are, no change occurs in the predicted probabilities with age. We interpret this as meaning that the introduction of the medical-marijuana context upset the long-established battle lines in the debate over legalization. Indeed, just as rising support for the legalization of marijuana in the 1970s was linked to the higher social status of that era's marijuana users compared to those in previous decades, so too does it seem plausible that medical marijuana derives much of its support from the fact that its advocates portray the issue in terms of helping those with chronic or terminal illnesses.

Conclusion and Discussion

In this chapter, we have explored the evolution of White public opinion on the issue of marijuana legalization. Before the modern era, Whites stigmatized marijuana and its users as being outside the mainstream of society. The rise of the counterculture shattered those perceptions and introduced many middle-class White youth to the drug. Although many elites believed in the 1970s that full legalization was only a matter of time, conservative activists (and then the Republican Party) successfully portrayed marijuana as both a moral failing and a threat to law and order, a move that quashed the public's incipient toleration for cannabis throughout the 1980s and the early years of the 1990s. Partisan conflict was particularly important to this shift, since the elites of the Democratic Party either chose or were forced to abandon the party's historical support for marijuana issues. Since then, levels of support for marijuana legalization have steadily increased, and viewing the issue in context suggests that marijuana is no longer stigmatized as a vice but rather is increasingly accepted as a matter for personal choice. Issue entrepreneurs have also affected the debate, in particular through the creation of medical marijuana, an overwhelmingly popular form of marijuana legalization that has made great strides in both winning public acceptance and changing public policy.

What does this suggest for the future? Should current trends continue, as older Americans die off, White public support for marijuana legalization will begin to approach the 60 percent mark. Much as Tate suggests in her chapter on Black public opinion in this volume (Chapter 5), the future of marijuana legalization seems to be one in which the issue is increasingly framed as a civil rights issue. If Whites are sympathetic to that frame, then their support for civil rights may add to their support for marijuana legalization. But that may be overly optimistic. Instead, it may well be the case that Whites will once again change their minds about marijuana legalization in response to new elite signaling. In that context, the Obama administration's subtle shift from a hands-off policy vis-à-vis California's and other states' medical marijuana policies to a much more aggressive law-enforcement attitude may portend that the federal government intends to recast medical marijuana as a law-and-order issue. Should that argument take hold, then White public opinion—and, perhaps, American public opinion as a whole—may yet take another U-turn.

Notes

1. Jimmy Carter, "Drug Abuse Remarks on Transmitting a Message to the Congress." www.presidency.ucsb.edu   http://www.presidency.ucsb.edu/ws/index.php?pid   = 7907&st = marijuana&st1 = #ixzz1IUYoipJB
2. Ronald Reagan, "Radio Address to the Nation on Federal Drug Policy." October 2, 1982. http://www.presidency.ucsb.edu/ws/index.php?pid   =   43085&st   = marijuana&st1 = #axzz1ISyiDlLK
3. George H.W. Bush, "Presidential Debate in Winston-Salem, North Carolina." September 25, 1988. www.presidency.ucsb.edu http://www.presidency.ucsb.edu/ws/index.php?pid = 29411&st = marijuana&st1 = #ixzz1IUjam1JA
4. William J. Clinton, "Remarks on Signing the Improving America's Schools Act of 1994 in Framingham, Massachusetts." October 20, 1994. http://www.presidency.ucsb.edu/ws/?pid = 49332. During his speech, Clinton had to deal with a spontaneous protest of federal policies: "There is a lot of evidence, and there is a new survey that's been put out today, saying that in a modest but very clear way, drug use is going up again among young people in America—I hope you're clapping because you agree with what I said, not because you agree that it's a good thing."
5. See "DEA Drug Seizures," http://www.justice.gov/dea/statistics.html, and "Annual Marijuana Arrests in the U.S.," http://norml.org/index.cfm?Group_ID = 7042.
6. Gallup asked an identical question during the 1970s and early 1980s, but suspended the question from the mid-1980s and only reinstated it in the late 1990s. The toplines for the Gallup item are similar to the GSS responses.
7. There are a few exceptions to this rule in the later GSS surveys, but for both the Flapper and the Clinton cohort, we simply "stretched" the cohort definition to account for the fact that there were too few respondents in the extremes of our age cohort.
8. Note the distinction between *administrations* and *presidents*. President Nixon was strongly against decriminalization, but his administration was much more liberal on this issue.
9. XMARSEX asks: "What is your opinion about a married person having sexual relations with someone other than the marriage partner—is it always wrong, almost always wrong, wrong only sometimes, or not wrong at all?"
   HOMOSEX asks: "What about sexual relations between two adults of the same sex— do you think it is always wrong, almost always wrong, wrong only sometimes, or not wrong at all?" For both, we code the responses "always wrong" and "almost always wrong" as 0 and "wrong only sometimes" and "not wrong at all" as 1.
   ABPOOR asks: "Please tell me whether or not you think it should be possible for a pregnant woman to obtain a legal abortion if the family has a very low income and cannot afford any more children?" These responses are simple: "Yes" and "No."
10. Ronald Reagan, "Remarks on Signing Executive Order 12368, Concerning Federal Drug Abuse Policy Functions." June 24, 1982. http://www.presidency.ucsb.edu/ws/index.php?pid = 42671&st = marijuana&st1 = #axzz1ISyiDlLK
11. Ronald Reagan, "Remarks at a Seminar on Substance Abuse in the Workplace in Durham, North Carolina." February 8, 1988. http:///www.presidency.ucsb.edu/ws/?pid = 35188.
12. Internet Movie Database. http://www.imdb.com/title/tt0154129/.
13. Democratic Party Platforms, "Democratic Party Platform of 1988." July 18, 1988. Online by Gerhard Peters and John T. Woolley. *The American Presidency Project.* http://www.presidency.ucsb.edu/ws/?pid = 29609.
14. "Fed crackdown on California medical marijuana: Does Obama mean it?" *Christian Science Monitor.* October 12, 2011.
15. See, for instance, Colleen McMurray, "Medicinal Marijuana: Is It What the Doctor Ordered?" Gallup.Com., December 16, 2003, in which a Gallup poll shows 75 percent support medical marijuana, or Gary Langer, "High Support for Medical Marijuana," ABCNews.Go.Com, January 18, 2010, in which 81 percent of respondents support medical marijuana.

7

BUILDING MINORITY COMMUNITY POWER THROUGH LEGALIZATION

James Lance Taylor

The focus of this chapter is twofold. First, the chapter engages the double standard theorizing of conservative scholarly and criminological perspectives that build on commonly held beliefs of Black criminal deviance while failing to account for the crime types that might result in disproportionate incarceration of American Whites, namely, offenses associated with illegal drug abuse during the War on Drugs regime. Incarcerating more Whites is not the policy solution to disproportionate incarceration of African Americans, but their underrepresentation for drug offenses contributes to significant overrepresentation of African Americans. If the criminal involvement perspective were a reliable predictor of who goes to jail and prison for imprisonable offenses, why are American Whites not disproportionately arrested and imprisoned for marijuana and other drug-related offenses? And how might legalization or decriminalization help reverse the grossly unbalanced patterns of incarceration of African Americans in the United States?

Some scholars and think-tank researchers have engaged in a selective interpretation of African American criminal involvement in violent crime that, if similarly applied to American Whites' use of illicit drugs, should deracialize the effectively discriminatory War on Drugs. These scholars have relied largely on the important early work of Alfred Blumstein (1982, 1993) and Langan (1985), which addresses disproportionate arrest and incarceration rates by race (for violent crime types), but neglects the more recent work of Blumstein (1995, 2003), which shows unexplainable patterns of arrest and incarceration of African American youth and adults (for drug-related offenses). Where this leading influence on racial disproportionality research has been a reliable scholarly witness of African American violent crime and punishment, which some conservative scholarship has justifiably touted, he is clear that War on Drug policies, especially beginning in 1985, took on a "White in lieu of Black" character that is unexplained by "the race ratio of 'offending'" (Blumstein 1993).

The debate over legalization of marijuana has broad implications for social-science research. A concern in this chapter is the manner in which racial crime statistics have been put to use to confirm conservative and reactionary "conventional wisdom" regarding race, crime, and punishment in the United States. Drug-related law enforcement, from pretextual stops and arrests to incarceration, exposes what criminologists concede is the "dark figure of crime," that is, those offenses and offenders that go unrecorded and the tendency in social-science research on race and crime to be framed in a "Black deviance-White innocence" binary (Messner 1984). For some scholars who focus mainly on Blumstein's early work and subsequent research that builds on it, disproportionate Black criminal activity accounts for disproportionate patterns and rates of incarceration. These conclusions, from the criminological research and governmental statistics claiming that petty drug-related offenses, resulting from War on Drug policies, are anomalous to serious crime-related incarcerations, serve as justifications for racial status quo, and they are, in short, very wrong conclusions.

A second goal of this chapter is to present readers with a rationale for supporting the legalization of personal-use marijuana. The War on Drugs' public policy of the past five decades has unduly fueled the mass or "*hyper* incarceration"[1] of African Americans and related groups. It seeks to inform readers and remind advocates of the racial origins of anti-cannabis laws that continue to punish African Americans discriminatorily. This situation is both untenable and unsustainable, given the use/abuse disparities between African Americans, American Whites, and others in the United States. The Sentencing Project reported 2007 national rates of incarceration at 412 per 100,000 American White residents, 2,290 for African Americans, and 742 for Hispanics (Mauer and King 2007). At the state level, this disproportionality is even more severe, with no state having a larger population of American Whites incarcerated (Oklahoma, 740 per 100,000) than the state with the lowest African American rate of incarceration (Hawaii, 850 per 100,000); this is true in every state in the union, including states with the smallest African American populations (Mauer and King 2007). The final section of this study analyzes similar disparities specifically for marijuana offenses. For African Americans, marijuana arrests are serious offenses. Particularly for African American youth and middle-aged individuals, patterns of arrest and incarceration suggest that legalization or decriminalization should be argued, not for the purpose of "getting high"—which is an indulgence for those who are not as criminalized by arrest or incarceration—but for the purpose of "getting free" from the behemoth punishment system and industry.

Black Deviance–White Innocence

Tim Wise reports some ways in which widespread anti-Black racism, stereotyping, and resentment inundate present-day society. Suffused with various levels and forms of conscious and unconscious bias, discrimination toward African Americans in both private and public sectors abound. He cites studies at MIT, the

University of Chicago, and Princeton, which show that having a definite "Black sounding name," as opposed to a definite "White sounding name," and also being a White felon compared to an African American job applicant (including college graduates) without a felony, routinely advantages American Whites (Wise 2011). Still other research points to "Afrocentric features bias," where students and law enforcement identified criminal appearance, aggressiveness, and likely criminality with more or less stereotypically African American facial appearance (Pizzi et al. 2005). Tonry and Melewski (2008) summarize this research noting, "more Black than White faces were thought to look criminal. Black faces rated above the median for strereotypicality were judged as criminal significantly more than were Black faces rated below the median. The opposite was found for White faces. The authors concluded that the police officers thought that 'the more Black,' the more criminal . . . ," even for Whites with "Afrocentric," appearance. Among other factors, race reflects powerfully on who has more or less advantage before the law and courts of the United States.

Michael K. Brown (2001) and his colleagues argue, "The experiences of white and nonwhite Americans are intimately connected. The benefits of being white are related to the costs of being nonwhite. White Americans are privileged because they benefit from the present social order. As individuals and as a group, they derive advantages from the ways in which race limits the lives of people of color, whether they know it or not." Likewise, Laura Fishman (2002) outlines the multiple "benefits of racial images of the Black criminal," to average American Whites. Most pertinent to marijuana laws is her insistence that "obsessing about the encroaching 'menace' of Black crime enables White America to deny its own criminal record which actually poses the most severe threat to the fabric of society." Moreover, she insists, "White America is the primary beneficiary of a multi-billion dollar prison industry that processes Black men and women as its basic raw material." Lastly, she argues, "the media distortion of Black involvement in drugs, crime, and violence has helped make the White American drug problem a 'Black problem' and has resulted in the War on Drugs becoming a War on Blacks."

In fact, the role of media in presenting crime coverage took a particularly "racial" turn beginning in 1965, as the civil rights movement was ending. The Black injury through official and vigilante violence, which characterized how Americans saw portrayal of racial violence, then gave way to ideological Black rage and marauding Black male criminality, thereafter. Citing the research of political scientist Velsa Mae Weaver, Glenn Loury (2008) concurs with her that "the punitive turn represented a political response to the successes of the civil rights movement." Weaver (2007) describes a process of 'frontlash' in which opponents of the civil rights revolution sought to regain the upper hand by shifting to a new issue. Rather than reacting directly to the civil rights developments, and thus continuing to fight a battle they had lost, those opponents shifted attention to *a seemingly race-neutral concern over crime."* It subsequently influenced two generations of "zero tolerance" public policy targeting the crimes of juveniles and African American individuals. In the fourth part of a series of studies conducted by the "Building Blocks for Youth" advocacy initiative between January 2000 and April 2001 in California and the United States, it was reported that:

> A qualitative analysis of all cover stories in *Time* and *Newsweek* between 1946–1995 [by M. H. Barlow] determined that the term 'young Black males' became synonymous with the word 'criminal' during the late 1960's when Blacks were struggling for equality. A March 1965 *Newsweek* article was the first to connect crime with Black crime. The first use of "young Black male" in a *Time* or *Newsweek* cover story was in 1970 when *Time* reported that 'though victims of Black crime are overwhelmingly Black, it is chiefly young Black males who commit the most common interracial crime: armed robbery.'. . . . Two years later *Newsweek* made the same connection. In later stories in the 1970's, both *Time* and *Newsweek* portrayed crime as 'largely perpetrated by 'young Black males'.' Later, Hispanic males were added to the picture. The author suggests that a combination of modern racism, media framing, and public discourse of crime as a problem of the Black urban poor has led to the racialization of crime, concluding that, as a consequence of news coverage, any discussion of crime today is essentially a discussion about race.[2]

The rationale for hyper incarceration of African Americans, even for offenses that are more commonly conducted by other segments of the population, particularly American Whites, is part of larger tendency in society where "dominant frames must *mis*represent the world (hide the fact of dominance). . . . Dominant racial frames, therefore, provide the intellectual road map used by rulers to navigate the always rocky road of domination and . . . derail the ruled from their track to freedom and equality" (Bonilla Silva 2006, 26). This is accomplished through widespread characterization of crime as a "black problem" or as *the* problem of Blacks in the United States. A typical rendition is captured in a 1987 *Chicago Tribune* report by Petersilia (1987) on criminological findings about race and crime during the drug war:

> Blacks do constitute a disproportion of the prison population, but those statistics are not evidence of racism. Males and young people are also over-represented in prison, but we do not assert discrimination because there are acceptable reasons for the differences—they commit more crime. A similar situation exists with Blacks: *Prisons are full of Blacks because Blacks are more likely to commit those crimes that get people into prisons.*[3]

Khalil Gibran Muhammad's *The Condemnation of Blackness* (2010) provides an important intervention in the "genealogy of distinct patterns of racial crime discourse," that emerged in the late nineteenth century. Focusing on nascent "racial crime statistics," Muhammad demonstrates how leading statistical research produced a pattern of data analysis and interpretation that gradually destigmatized White ethnic criminality simultaneously while "the statistical rhetoric of the 'Negro criminal' became a proxy for a national discourse on Black inferiority" (2010, 8). Most strikingly, this historical research explains how official federal data—which facilitated the "black-deviance–white innocence" rendition of racial crime discourse as follows:

> African Americans were also left behind in the federal government's new Uniform Crime Reports, a breakthrough achievement in crime reporting developed in the 1930s. The new annual federal crime reporting developed in the 1930s. The new federal crime reports became the most authoritative statistical measure of race and crime in New Deal America, superseding decennial census data. Not only did these reports breathe new life into racial crime statistics, reversing gains made by Black crime experts since the 1890s. The authors gradually removed the "Foreign Born" category from the crime tables, and by the early 1940s, 'Black' stood as the unmitigated signifier of deviation and deviance from the normative category of 'White' (2010, 13).

White ethnic immigrants, who had long been stigmatized as a problem criminal class and who were overrepresented in local jails and prisons, were aided by research that attributed ethnic White criminality to environmental factors, while the offenses of African American individuals were attributed to some racial group essence derived from their innate inferiority. Here, "White progressives often discounted crime statistics or disregarded them altogether in favor of humanizing European immigrants. . . . ." The Uniform Crime Report (UCR) may have been official, but so too was the Jim Crow milieu in which it was born. This is rarely acknowledged since criminologists and other scholars seek now, as they did then, "to shield White Americans from the charge of racism when they used Black crime statistics to support discriminatory public policies and social welfare practices" (2010, 8). Tukufu Zuberi (2001) argues, "Early in its development, social statistics was inextricably linked to the numerical analysis of human difference. Eugenic ideas were at the heart of the development of statistical logic. This statistical logic, as well as the regression-type models that the founders of social statistics employed, is the foundation on which modern statistical analysis is based. . . . Statistics as a distinct field of inquiry came into being only in the twentieth century. However, the discipline itself is much older than its institutionalized expression" (2001, 35). Beyond origins is a concern for understanding how racial statistics are used to justify racial stratification. Moreover he argues, "race as a variable must be placed within a social context" that is generative of theories concerning the meaning of race in society and research (2001, 35).

Racial crime statistics rarely, if ever, have presented African Americans in a good light, even when there are positive developments. For instance, conservative political scientist John DiIulio, Jr. (1996)—father of the Black "super-predator" fiction of the 1990s—could stridently state, "First, let's get crystal clear on the grim facts about crime, prisons, probation, and parole. Be giddy about recent drops in national crime rates if you wish, but each year Americans still suffer some 40 million criminal victimizations; about a quarter of these are violent crimes. Only about 1 in 100 crimes actually results in anyone getting caught, convicted, and sentenced to prison." For him, the "grim facts," concerning declines in reported violent crimes, which are overwhelmingly committed by young African American men against their peers, is that significant (Black) criminal activity continues unabated and insufficiently incapacitated. Tonry and Melewski find to the contrary, a consistent pattern of decline in African American involvement in serious crime, which has had no impact on decreasing disproportionality noting, "The good news is that patterns of racial involvement in serious crime as shown in the arrest data have changed. The percentage of people arrested for aggravated assault, robbery, rape, and homicide who are Black have been declining and in 2006 were much lower than in 1985. One might hope, and expect, that racial disparities in imprisonment would have fallen commensurately" (2008, 31).

DiIulio is silent on the discrepancy that enables American Whites to avoid mass criminalization for their involvement in the offenses which they do engage in more frequently—except to elsewhere claim, "The label 'drug offender' is a misnomer." As the [National Institute of Justice] study notes, the term implies "a degree of specialization not supported [by a body of research] on individual offending patterns," which shows plainly that drug offenders "commonly commit other types of crime, most notably robbery, burglary, and violent offenses" (1996, 38). The body of research on drug-crime disparities today is as vast as the violent crime literature, precisely because the continuing rates of incarceration of drug offenses are not exponential or otherwise jibe with violent crime rates at the state level. The next section addresses this literature. But here, DiIulio's inversion collapses offenders "on drugs," during the commission of violent offenses, for drug *offenses* (e.g., marijuana possession) to emphasize the former. It is akin to linking rape with drunken-driving offenses because of a pattern of rapists who drive drunk before their assaults, and conclude, "Drunken driving offenses are a misnomer." At any rate, nowhere in his initial statement on underreported criminality is there a hint of concern with nonviolent drug offenses, which all research shows are committed more commonly by American Whites—but unduly drive African American incarceration. There are important intersections in African American and American White criminal involvement in illegal drugs. Indeed, forms of White criminality today dwarf the well-chronicled and more public street crimes committed by segments of the African American population and Latinos, but these patterns tend to be individuated and deracialized. They also tend to avoid the social paranoia of crime "waves," "epidemics," "plagues," and

"crises" (Parenti 1999, 57). Tonry and Melewski note, "It is not completely cyni-
cal to wonder why soaring arrest rates for nonwhite kids in the 1980s did not
provoke the kinds of reactions that Blumstein attributes to soaring arrest rates of
white kids in the 1970s, and a comparable policy adjustment. Racially differenti-
ated effects of American drugs and sentencing policies have been starkly evident
for a quarter century."

Racial discrimination in arrests, incarceration, and imprisonment have been
most detectable precisely in areas of law that allow law enforcement some flexibil-
ity when compared to the draconian truth in sentencing, mandatory minimums,
and "three strikes" type statutory mandates that drove the vast African American
incarceration rates of the past two decades. Several pertinent researchers have
identified "the liberation hypothesis" as a phenomenon where juries, sentencing
judges, and arresting officers tend to be free to discriminate in less serious offenses
(Spohn and Cederblom 1991, 323; Sorenson et al. 2002; Garland et al. 2008, 18).
For homicide, Blumstein found only 2.8 percent were unexplainable, while for
drug offenses, barely half were explainable. Absent mandatory-minimum-styled
laws, liberation hypothesis is strongest when measuring differential treatment for
drug offenses. One study found in Miami that "Blacks and ethnic minorities may
be sentenced to prison while White defendants with the same court case may
be placed on probation" (1988, 75; see also Cassia Spohn and Jerry Cederblom
1991, 102).

Critical criminological and sociological research has long pointed to the many
problems with the Uniform Crime Reports (UCR) and National Crime Victimization Survey (NCVS) (Coleman and Moynihan 1996; Biderman and Reiss 1967)
in terms of accurately measuring incidence of criminality. Given their limitations,
scholars and researchers have employed methodological techniques to account for
measures of offending (Langan 1985). They generally do not represent an accurate
measure of the most criminally involved population in marijuana and other drug
offenses (e.g., methamphetamine; "crystal meth," "ice," or "club drugs"). Tonry and
Melewski insist, for example, that as recently as 2005 and 2006, "larger percentages
of Whites reported using alcohol, cocaine (including crack), and hallucinogens,
and the differences are large . . . one conclusion is clear: the reason so many more
Blacks than Whites are arrested or imprisoned for drug crimes is not that they
used drugs much more extensively than Whites do" (25). We know for certain
that the social construction of laws, crime, and criminals tends to underestimate
"white collar" crimes, crimes of women, crimes of the affluent, and crimes of the
dominant racial group (Coleman and Moynihan 1996). Ironically, the "*dark* figure
of crime," fails to detect criminal activity most common among American Whites
and middle-class individuals.

Adolph Reed, Jr. (2000) addresses this tendency in "underclass" studies, as
they reiterate . . . an ensemble of racial and class prejudices that lurk beneath an
apparently innocuous, certainly stupid tendency to reduce the social world to
aggregates of good people and bad people. Simply, good people are people like

'us'; bad people are not, and the same behavior is assessed differently depending on the category into which the perpetrator falls" (98). The drug war has exacerbated the problems confronting African American communities. Its damage is likely permanent as Tonry and Melewski report, "The U.S. Census estimates that 38.34 million U.S. residents in 2006 were Black. If the imprisonment rate were halved, the Black rate would fall from 26,613 per million to 13,306. That means that over 500,000 fewer Black Americans would be in prison or jail. Returning to the 1980s imprisonment rate would mean 702,400 fewer Black Americans behind bars. By contrast, eliminating all effects of bias and stereotyping would free at the most 101,900 Black Americans" (36) of the roughly 900,000 presently incarcerated. While it is unlikely that such widespread reform of state, county, and national level punishment policy is forthcoming in the present political and carceral milieu, liberalization of marijuana laws may provide a much-needed breakthrough in the War on Drugs.

The Blumstein Effect: The Problem with Race Disproportionality and the War on Drugs

In his seminal work on serious crimes, *On the Racial Disproportionality of the United States' Prison Populations* (1982), Blumstein was concerned with the fairness of the criminal justice system in light of emergent patterns of hyper incarceration of African Americans. The data for the first study came from a 1974 Department of Justice survey of state prison inmates and the 1974 UCR. The reasoning Blumstein employed noted, "if Blacks are relatively more involved in crimes as compared to Whites, and if this difference is most pronounced in the more serious crimes as compared to Whites, and if this difference is most pronounced in the more serious crimes of homicide and robbery, then it is important to discern how much of the differential incarceration is attributable to this differential involvement."

His original work was replete with terms and phrases characterizing this development as "most distressing and troublesome," of "deep concern," "a serious moral challenge," and "troubled race relations." Nowhere in his early or later research is there a hint of ideological animus toward particular African American communities or criminal offenders (e.g., the "underclass," drug abusers, or Black male youth) to which some subsequent polemical works have resorted. His study relied on the percentage of African American arrestees on a given day and compared it with the African American prison population to answer the question of whether racial discrimination on the part of state prison systems or "differential [crime] involvement" on the part of African Americans best explained the racial composition of U.S. incarceration. His work should be received with full knowledge that much of the same ground was covered by early-twentieth-century African American researchers and advocacy groups (such as the NAACP and National Urban League) using available statistical data to demonstrate problems in the relationship between police misconduct and disproportionality; as Muhammad notes,

"Police misconduct, corruption, and brutality, they argued, helped to produce disproportionately high Black arrest rates, the starting point for high juvenile delinquency commitments and adult prison rates . . . [they] used statistical evidence of racial disparities in the northern criminal justice system as evidence that racial crime statistics were an unreliable index of Black behavior. . . . " (2010, 12).

What made his work particularly useful was that he developed a method for calculating bias by determining any discrepancy between statistically explainable and unexplainable dis-proportionality in arrests. The difference between the two forms of disproportionality that is not explainable is where potential discrimination in incarceration may exist. The hypotheses of his study were twofold:

- [I]f the percentage of Black arrests were as high as that of the prison population, differential involvement alone might fully explain the racial composition of prisons;
- [I]f the percentage of Black arrests were lower than that of the prison population, racial discrimination in the administration of justice might account for the high percentage of prisoners who are Black (Langan 1985, 668).

In the case of the first, Blumstein assumes that if police or other law enforcement engage in racially discriminatory policing, then every subsequent stage of the criminal justice system would prevent significant numbers of innocent African Americans from actually being incarcerated (Garland et al. 2008). His claim that "racial differences in arrests alone account for the bulk of the racial differences in incarceration" assumes, wrongly (in the second case), that evidence of discrimination at every stage *after* arrest demonstrates the absence of discrimination up to and throughout a given arrest. Recent, well-publicized police scandals in Atlanta, Georgia, New York City, New Orleans, Louisiana, Chicago, Illinois, and Brooklyn, New York, ranging from underreporting incidence of crime to manipulating favorable crime statistics, to torture, homicide, and the practice of planting evidence on innocent citizens undermine such confidence in the validity of arrests and arrest data. Glenn Loury insists that during the decades between 1980 and 2001, imprisonment due to arrests doubled from 13 to 28 percent, while at the same time, no appreciable increase in the number of arrests occurred (2010, 7–8). Arrests, as an independent variable, lose some explanatory value in light of widespread practices by local law enforcement, such as false arrests or "driving while black or brown" (DWB) racial profiling in states like New Jersey, California, and Florida (Mann and Zatz 2002; Tonry and Melewski 2008). Moreover, scholars have analyzed arrest rates by residential neighborhood and police precinct and found that incarceration was highest in the city's poorest neighborhoods, out of proportion with their relatively low crime rates.

In the second case, Blumstein theorizes that if police do not discriminate at the point of arrest, then the system itself seeks to punish racial minorities on a more harsh and discriminatory basis, leading to disproportionate incarceration of minority group individuals. The hyper incarceration of African Americans, it follows, actually betrays arrests for differential involvement for commonly committed offenses. Here, Blumstein assumes innocence in law enforcement that is inconsistent with the early studies that argued that racial statistics were unreliable precisely due to official discrimination (see Muhammad 2010). Crutchfield et al. make the important points that "within a single jurisdiction, racial differences in treatment may be pronounced at one stage (e.g., filing of charges for pretrial diversion) and small at another (e.g., conviction and sentencing). Further, the point at which differential treatment occurs actually varies across jurisdictions" (Crutchfield et al 1994, 169).

Informed by the power- or racial-threat research of Blalock (1967) and others, Hawkins and Hardy (1989, 84–87) attribute factors such as the racial composition of localities that experienced disruptive Black political movements to "influence the behavior of not only the police themselves but also various other government officials. Hence, prosecutors, judges, correctional officials, and others should be similarly affected and likely produce similar race-related outcomes." Thus, antecedent racial politics influenced policing in some jurisdictions; but more importantly, researchers found the relative small size of a state's Black population in general, and the concentration of a state's urbanized Black population, had the greatest explanatory power in exposing unexplainable disproportionality in incarceration between African Americans and Whites. And Dehais (1983) argues precisely that Blumstein's early work takes for granted that the likelihood of being imprisoned after arrest is relatively the same between African Americans and American Whites (Hawkins and Hardy 1989).

A common theme in the various studies on racial disproportionality is how the inclusion of nonviolent drug-related offenses depresses rates of unexplainable disproportionality by racial involvement (Tonry and Melewski 2008; Blumstein 1995; Austin and Allen 2000). For example, Patrick Langan's (1985) study built on Blumstein's method and combined it with the NCVS, confirming the differential involvement hypothesis with the critical caveat that the *exclusion of drug offenses,* which, Blumstein conceded, had the lowest explanatory value concerning disproportionate incarceration by race and "led to a somewhat inflated aggregate figure of explained disparity between the expected and observed incarceration of Blacks" (Garland et al., 20) In short, arrests and incarceration for drug-related offenses, unlike violent crimes (which may or may not be drug related), are out of base with the major theoretical and empirical research accounting for the massive overrepresentation of African Americans in the American prisons, jails, noncustodial systems. Despite Dilulio's (1996) claims of precisely the opposite, incarceration rates at all levels exploded on drug offenses, while violent crime went into steady decline (Tonry and Melewski 2008).

If all illegal drug use, possession, and sales were taken as "seriously criminal" *for all,* what explains the disproportionate incarceration of a racial group for offenses that they are *less* inclined than others are to engage in? In most cases, the "outdoors" corner drug dealer explanation for easier arrestability makes sense when compared to the more discreet approaches of White drug dealing (Tonry and Melewski 2008, 27–29); but, in the case of marijuana sales, entire regions in Northern California (producing more than 70 percent of all outdoor growth) and Kentucky are known for marijuana cultivation and sales. Broward County, Florida, is also well known for massive sales of prescription drugs, such as oxycodone, but has avoided intense scrutiny as heroine or crack did previously.

Two-thirds of those in the country's 5,000 jails and prisons, according to Glenn Loury, are in for nonviolent crimes. Where Blumstein insists that incarceration rates reflect "differential involvement" by African Americans in serious crimes, Loury makes the point that most of the growth in jailing and imprisonment was not for the most serious crimes, but for petty drug possession and sales in a social and political milieu where citizens, policymakers, and industry "have made a collective decision to increase the rate of punishment" (Loury 2008, 9). Targeting pedestrian drug use with a zero-tolerance approach occurred as a "decline in drug use across the board had begun a decade before the draconian anti-drug efforts of the 1990s were initiated" (Loury 2008, 16). According to federal-prosecutor-turned-professor Paul Butler, "the War on Drugs is the single most important explanation for mass incarceration. Over 80 percent of the increase in the federal prison population from 1985 to 1995 was due to drug convictions. . . . Over 500,000 people are currently in prison in the United State for drug offenses. One in five federal prisoners is a 'low-level drug law violator,' which means 'non-violent offenders with minimal or *no prior criminal history*'" (Butler, 46. Emphasis added).

In a published 2007 symposium with Loury, Loic Wacquant argues, "The share of African Americans among individuals arrested by the police for the four most serious violent offenses (murder, rape, robbery, and aggravated assault) dropped from 51 percent in 1973 to 43 percent in 1996. The rapid 'Blackening' of the prison population even as crime 'Whitened' is due exclusively to the increase in the incarceration of *lower-class* Blacks" (emphasis in original, Loury 2008, 60–61). Disparities across the entire public-policy sphere show African Americans lagging in comparison to American Whites and other groups (2011; Bonilla-Silva 2006; and Mann and Zatz 2002). Butler concludes: "In no aspect of American life are differences between Blacks and Whites as extreme as they are in incarceration" (Butler, 36–37)[4] because of how lawmakers and law enforcers have chosen to execute the drug war.

Although his initial (1982) study supported the differential involvement hypothesis, Blumstein estimated that unexplained disproportionality may account for only 20 percent of hyper-incarceration patterns. But, he conceded that drug offenses were very different from violent crime offenses and the least explainable forms of arrest by race, leading to incarceration. Of all the crimes studied, arrests for drug offenses represented the highest level of unexplained disproportionality at 48.9 percent (Blumstein 1982). This important detail was decidedly less interesting to some scholars than his more explainable disproportionality by race. His updated study (1993), utilizing 1991 prisoner surveys and UCR data, found that explain-able disproportionality by race had declined only to 76 percent; it increased to 93.8 percent when drug-related offenses were excluded (Garland et al., "Racial Disproportionality," 19). Other research using Blumstein's model shows unex-plained disproportionality at the local level to be up to three times as high as the national level (Garland et al., Tonry and Melewski 2008, Hawkins and Hardy 1989, Crutchfield et al. 1994).[5] For instance, in summarizing the various levels and rates of disproportionality, Austin and Allen conclude in their study of Pennsylvania, "drug offending (arrest) provides a rather weak explanation of racial disparity in court commitment for this offense (Austin and Allen 2000, 208). As noted in the introduction, Blumstein (1993) has been a reliable scholarly chronicler of African American violent crime and punishment, which some conservative scholarship (McWhorter 2000, Thernstrom and Thernstrom 1997, Wilson 1989) has justifi-ably touted, but he is certain that War on Drug policies, especially beginning in 1985, took on a Black-in-lieu-of-White character that is *unexplained* by "the race ratio of 'offending.'" For Blumstein (1993), the racial character of the War on Drugs leads to the conclusion that it effectively ameliorated drug-related arrests for some Whites, while shifting attention to African American drug use, sales, and possession. For instance, American juveniles' illicit drug use between 1965 and 1980 led to similar arrest rates. In fact, in the immediate period before the second term of the Nixon War on Drugs (1971–1972) and the Reagan administration's declaration (1982), "the arrest rates for Whites were higher than those of non-Whites." So that by 1974, as arrest rates increased thirty-fold for both groups, with Whites at 329 per 100,000 and non-Whites, mostly African Americans, at 257 per 100,000, a decline in White arrests occurred, according to Blumstein, as "a conse-quence of *the general trend toward decriminalization of marijuana in the United States.* A major factor contributing to that decriminalization was probably a realization that the arrestees were much too often the children of individuals, usually White, in positions of power and influence" (Blumstein 1993, 758).

Blumstein's subsequent (1995, 2003) research is concerned more with the impact of the War on Drugs on African Americans in terms of its attendant violence among the young, and the (previous) 100:1 crack cocaine to powder cocaine disparity. No single feature of punishment in America was as devastat-ing to ordinary African Americans and communities. No aspect of punishment, following Ronald Reagan's 1986 Anti-Drug Abuse Act and the Democratic Par-ty's political ambition to compete on "tough on crime" grounds, exposed the unexplainable African American arrest rates, when compared to American Whites using the identical pharmacological drug, cocaine. Crack has had a nuclear impact on African American life. Like his early work, Blumstein essentially focuses on violent crimes, rather than nonviolent drug offenses. Murder with the use of guns increased in the middle 1980s during the War on Drugs, with both victims and perpetrators being progressively younger. While Blumstein does not issue any support for legalization, he concedes that "any such policy involves a complex weighing of the costs of criminalization, of which homicide is but one, against the probable consequences of greater use of illegal drugs if they were legalized." During testimony before the U.S. Sentencing Commission in 2002, he urged further for a reduction in the cocaine disparities since the market demands and severe violence of the previous two decades had subsided. He also called for grandfathering mandatory minimums and other tough-on-crime political instruments of the national and state legislatures for fear that policymakers would not reevaluate the societal harm done to communities because of the laws.

Given the often mean-spirited polemics and public-policy debates on race and crime in the United States directed toward African American scholars, intellectuals, and also "underclass" Black criminality (DiIulio 1994; Thernstrom and Thernstrom 1997), conservative scholars and think-tank operatives should qualify that the omitted drug offenses are the great exception to the explainable disproportionality in incarceration, widely discussed in scholarly literature. A common sleight occurs in which researchers, who oppose legalization, highlight the dangers, costs, and harms of more serious illegal drugs (with the obligatory mention of "crack babies"), as does James Q. Wilson (1990), only to see marijuana all but ignored. In a footnote, Wilson simply offers, "I do not take up the question of marijuana. For a variety of reasons—its widespread use and its lesser tendency to addict—it presents a different problem from cocaine or heroin. . . . ." (Wilson 1995, 131). With a sleight of emphasis, attention is drawn instead to explainable disproportionality, which exonerates American White criminality in the major area leading to incarceration over the past two decades. No study, whether quantitative or not, has convincingly accounted for the unexplainable discrimination over drug arrests and incarceration. And no recent study has sought to prove the "burden of Whiteness" before the criminal justice system more than that of neoconservative public intellectuals Stephan and Abigail Thernstrom (1997). Claiming that "statistical disparities between groups in matters like arrests or incarcerations are not conclusive evidence of discrimination" (as they invoke Langan 1985), the authors proceed to suggest that the death penalty, rates of prosecutions that end in dismissal of charges or acquittals (for 1992 only), and "race on race" victimization actually work against American Whites. Using both the National Crime Victimization Survey (NCVS) and the Justice Department's UCR data (which are widely accepted but equally contested by law enforcement officials and academic researchers due to serious shortcomings), they point to arrest patterns from the former and a 1993 study of the latter, which "tracked the experience of over 10,000 adult felony defendants arrested in 1990 in the nation's seventy-five largest counties (which include 59 percent of the Black population of the United States). It found that after charges were filed, 66 percent of the accused Blacks were actually prosecuted, versus 69 percent of those who were White. Among those who were prosecuted, 75 percent of Blacks and 78 percent of the Whites were convicted. Again the only hint of racial disparity was to the advantage, not to the disadvantage, of Blacks accused of crimes" (1997, 273).

It is worth noting that with a study that marshals in more than 700 pages of what one student of Black politics has usefully called the "Black Cultural Pathology Paradigm" research (Floyd 2007), the work gives a mere two pages of attention to the question of disparities for drug-related offenses. After asking, "Is the War on Drugs Racist?" the extent of their analysis resorts to diminishing the "not trivial," racial disparities that undermine their argumentation. But these nontrivial statistical exceptions represent thousands of people who are parents, children, guardians, workers, and neighbors caught up in an unforgiving punishment apparatus.

Since the 1980s, the number of people under correctional supervision, either in prison, on probation, or parole, has increased significantly, from 1.8 million in 1980 to 7.3 million, based on statistics reported by the Bureau of Justice Statistics of the U.S. Department of Justice. Blacks make nearly half of the state and federal prison populations, even though they represent about 12 percent of the U.S. population (Bell 2006; Mauer 1999). And the rising rate of incarceration reached unprecedented levels in the 1990s, in part because of drug prosecutions. Since the 1970s, a parallel trend of increasing arrests for drug offenses occurred based on government data. The process starts with the young. The Sentencing Project found that one in four Black males 20 to 29 were under criminal justice supervision in 1989 (Mauer 1999). In 1997, 9 percent of the Black population was in jail or had been jailed compared to 2 percent of the White population, based on government statistics. Young offenders are taken from their families and sent to prison, and these minority young adults are released with criminal records, unable to find a job. For Black women, there was also an increase in their rates of incarceration between 1985 and 1995. Drug convictions can carry felony charges, and thus, some ex-offenders are barred for life from ever voting.

Getting High versus Getting Free: Legalization as a Step toward Carceral System Reform

Legalization, or at least decriminalization, of personal-use marijuana is a vital alternative to draconian laws drawn up in the War on Drugs regime of the past three decades. It is well established that concern and paranoia over petty "crack" cocaine arrests for sales, possession, and use drove the mass warehousing of the state of California's prisons and jails populations to become the largest in the United States (Lusane 1991; Weatherspoon 1998; Reinarman and Levine 1997; Provine 2007). What is less appreciated in light of the fierce reaction to the emergence of crack cocaine in the *middle* 1980s is that marijuana use and related arrests foregrounded the official war on drugs announced by the Reagan administration in October of 1982 (Alexander 2010, 49). The Nixon administration ran on a platform of law and order social control of African Americans in 1968; he implemented his war on drugs. Policing petty drugs would be the means to that end. White House Chief of Staff H. R. Halderman once noted, "[President Nixon] emphasized that you have to face the fact that *the whole problem is really the Blacks.* The key is to *devise a system* that recognizes this while not appearing to" (Baum 1996, 13). The War on Drugs system's primary target was what political operatives and bureaucratic appointees collapsed into the procrustean category, "theyoungthepoortheblack" (Baum 1996, 21). Between the Nixon and Reagan administrations' focus on street-level drug trafficking, sales, possession, and use, marijuana remained at the center.

For instance, the pro-legalization policy group, National Organization for the Reform of Marijuana Laws (NORML), reports that marijuana arrests per hour began a steady increase between 1965 and 1968. Marijuana-related arrests per hour during this period went from a low of two arrests per hour, resulting in roughly 90,000 annual arrests in the country, to more than doubling at 200,000 per year by 1971. By 1973, annual arrests reached 400,000 per year and remained roughly at this level until the early to middle 1980s, when the Reagan administration declared a "war on drugs." Where marijuana arrests (at about 300,000 per year) took a sharp, temporary decline as the "crack epidemic" became the center of attention, beginning in 1992, marijuana arrests, at 33 per hour, increased every year over the next decade, peaking at 700,000 per year in 2000. By 2007, the number of arrests per year rose to more than 850,000 per year, or 99.6 per hour. Noting that marijuana possession constituted nearly 8 of 10 drug-related *arrests* in the 1990s, Michelle Alexander insists that this period of "unprecedented punitiveness" resulted "in prison sentences (rather than dismissal, community service, or probation)" to the degree "in two short decades, between 1980 and 2000, the number of people incarcerated in our nation's prisons and jails soared from roughly 300,000 to more than 2 million. By the end of 2007, more than 7 million Americans—or one in every 31 adults—were behind bars, on probation, or parole" (2010, 59). Thus, marijuana anteceded crack—not in terms of its pharmacological potency or even in fostering the violent, nihilistic crisis associated with crack—but more in how state, local, and national law enforcement has targeted Black and Latino communities for scapegoating and punishment.

There is widespread consensus in reported government statistics, advocacy studies, and policy think tanks that African Americans bear the brunt of law-and-order management of marijuana laws in the United States. How national and local media chose to present the use and abuse of both drugs in *racial terms* that were woefully different from the facts of use, sales, and possession is confirmed in academic and critical legal studies literature. One study focusing on marijuana initiants found that "among Blacks, the annual incidence rate (per 1,000 potential new users) increased from 8.0 in 1966 to 16.7 in 1968, reached a peak at about the same time as Whites (19.4 in 1976), then remained high throughout the late 1970s. Following the low rates in the 1980s, rates among Blacks rose again in the early 1990s, reached a peak in 1997 and 1998 (19.2 and 19.1, respectively), then dropped to 14.0 in 1999. Similar to the general pattern for Whites and Blacks, Hispanics' annual incidence rate rose during late 1970s and 1990s, with a peak in 1998 (17.8)" ("Initiation of Marijuana Use" 2008). During the late 1990s, habitual street-level marijuana use was buttressed in pop culture by West Coast hip-hop rap, especially as associated with rapper Calvin "Snoop Dogg" Broadus. Broadus became so associated with illegal marijuana use and culture that during the 2010 midterm elections, media reports claimed that pre-election polling, which showed the pro-legalization Proposition 19 losing in a tight campaign, may have been suffering from the "Broadus effect," equating it to the "[Tom] Bradley effect" in California politics and might nevertheless pass when likely voters, who otherwise supported legalization, actually showed up at voting booths.

Surveys confirm that White Californians (and Americans) participate in the sales and consumption of marijuana at rates exceeding those of African Americans, Latinos, and Asians in the state. The true face of marijuana in California is not mainly African American or Latino; it is widely understood to be White. In none of the top California counties with the highest marijuana arrest rates per 100,000 citizens (Alpine, Calaveras, Mono, Humboldt, or Inyo) do African Americans comprise more than 1.3 percent of the respective county populations.[6] Arrests in these counties and those that have traditionally ranked high, such as Plumas, Trinity, and Sierra, largely reflect the "supply-side" approach to marijuana inter-diction, targeting industrial production.[7] For instance, as *felony* juvenile and adult drug arrests declined throughout the 1990s, only among White males and females did these arrests increase; marijuana was the main source of both felony and misdemeanor arrest rate increases in the state (Lockyear 2000). On the "demand side," however, a starkly different picture emerges, most devastatingly for African Americans arrested for petty possession.[8] Macallair and Males (2009) suggest that the variation in marijuana arrests at the county level in California makes very little sense. In their study, they include simple marijuana arrests in five of the least and most harsh major counties. Where San Francisco County, Mendocino County, and Alameda County (Berkeley, Oakland) align predictably with the least-harsh arresting counties for petty marijuana possession, given their liberal and progressive political orientations, the alignment of Mendocino County, Santa Cruz County, and Humboldt County with the five harshest is surprising. What is most perplexing, but largely attributed to race in their study, is that a virtual "bait and switch" occurred over the period, where some more liberal counties like San Francisco, moderate Marin County, and Contra Costa County went soft on adult marijuana arrests rates, but focused more severely on young African Americans.

While arrests for all major California demographic groups increased significantly between 1990 and 2008, the arrests for no group out of adult Whites, Asians, Latinos, or women *ends* in 2008 as high as Africa Americans *began* in 1990; where African American rates were 225.6 in 1990, the highest arrest rates per 100,000 in 2008 were among Latinos/Hispanics at 212.2. By then, for African Americans, the rate had exploded to 604 per 100,000, representing a rate increase of 168 percent (Macallair and Males 2009, 4). Based on this data, Macallair and Males conclude: "Dramatic changes have occurred in the demography of marijuana arrestees. . . . In 1990, half of all marijuana possession arrests were European American (White), 60% were 21 or older, and 90% were male; in 2008, 56% were African American or Hispanic, just half were 21 or older, and 88% were male" (2009, 3). While other groups, such as Latinos/Hispanics, females, males of all races, middle-aged to older individuals (for all groups except Asians), and juveniles show dramatic increases, young adult African Americans (20–29 years) *and those 40 years and older* respectively represent the highest arrest rates over three decades (1,316.7) and the highest rate-change increase of 345 percent. Comparing arrest patterns of African Americans in the 20–29 age category (4,761) to those of Whites between 40–69 years of age (2,757), the authors quip, "Do 360,000 African Americans age 20–29 really smoke more pot than *7.2 million* European Americans age 40–69?" (Macallair and Males, 2009, 8. Emphasis in original text).

Nearly half of California's African American population resides in its largest, most *policed* counties and represent the bulk of the resulting disproportionately between their population and marijuana possession arrests. African Americans heavily populate California cities that constitute nearly 30 percent of the state's population. The pro-legalization advocacy group NORML found that, in 2002, "African Americans as compared to Whites in California were arrested at a 5:1 (per capita) ratio on marijuana sales charges."[9] A 2010 Drug Policy Alliance study, "Targeting Blacks: Possession Arrests of African Americans in California, 2004–2008," found disproportionate arrest patterns in each of the state's 25 largest *counties* (Levine, Gettman, and Siegel 2010, 6–8, 12). In each county, the percentage of African American possession arrests was higher than the Black percentage of the total county population. Most surprising was San Francisco. During this period, this liberal Democratic Party bastion, which had an African American woman district attorney, Kamala Harris, who rejected "Tough on Crime" ideology in preference for what she identifies as "Smart on Crime," nonetheless was near the very bottom. Of the 25 counties, only Sacramento and Solano Counties, which both had higher percentages of Black population, arrested a higher percentage of its Black population.[10] Moreover, in none of the counties does the African American marijuana arrest rate outpace that of their White counterparts; in most, the gaps in possession arrest rates were extreme. Disproportionate minority contact is the rule; there are few exceptions. A related 2010 study, commissioned by the California NAACP, "Arresting Blacks for Marijuana in California: Possession Arrests in 25 Cities, 2006–2008," found that in 25 select California *cities*, African Americans were arrested up to 12 times the rate of Whites (Levine, Gettman, and Siegel 2010). The study also found that Los Angeles arrested African Americans for low-level marijuana possession at seven times the rate of Whites. Similar disparities were found in other cities where arrest patterns were wildly disproportionate for African Americans; in Pasadena (African Americans are 11 percent of the population and 49 percent of those arrested), African Americans were arrested at 12 times the rate of Whites; San Diego arrested African Americans for marijuana possession at six times the rate of Whites; and in Sacramento (African Americans 14 percent of the population), African Americans were 51 percent of those arrested for possession. In each of the 25 major cities, the rate of African American to White marijuana possession arrests per 100,00 was, at a minimum, two times more (Compton) where the Black population was 31 per-cent, to a high of 14 times higher in Torrance, which has a Black population of 2 percent, roughly 2,500 African American residents. Torrance also holds the highest Black rate of marijuana arrests per 100,000 at an extreme, 3,227. But it does not stand alone. Burbank, which has an African American population of less than 3 percent, has a 2,077 rate of marijuana arrests per 100,000. Similarly, Glendale, with a Black population of 2.9 percent, has a rate of 1,843 arrests per 100,000. Merced has a Black rate of marijuana arrests of 1,448 per 100,000 citizens. Even the more moderate cases of arrests per 100,000 and Black percentage of marijuana posses-sion arrests are grossly disproportionate. Of the 1,515 persons in California prisons actually incarcerated on marijuana charges in 2010, nearly half—750—were Black Americans.

These out-of-balance arrest patterns persist despite there being roughly a 3.4 percent adult African American population in the state from which to draw.[11] In fact, it might be more useful to describe the racial double standard in the experi-ences of average non-Whites and Whites in California and other states as consti-tuting a face of "bi-raciality." Researchers studying inequality within and among industrialized countries have found that within every state in the United States, the risk of being incarcerated differs by race, with African American youth and adults for nonviolent or violent crimes having the greatest risk (Wilkinson and Pickett 2009). Rejecting the premise that imprisonment reflects incidence of criminal offenses between races, the study affirms, ". . . . African American youth commit fewer drug crimes. But African American youth are overwhelmingly more likely to be arrested, to be detained, to be charged, to be charged as if an adult, and to be imprisoned. The same pattern is true for African American and Hispanic adults, who are treated more harshly than Whites at every stage of judicial proceedings. Facing the same charges, White defendants are far more likely to have the charges against them reduced, or to be offered 'diversion'—a deferment or suspension of prosecution if the offender agrees to certain conditions, such as completing a drug rehabilitation programme" (150). Consistent with most aspects of punishment in the United States, from arrest to sentencing, there remain unofficial "Black codes" that effectively apply to African Americans and those that apply to others.

Beyond research, one need look no further than the NBC cable news networks, MSNBC and CNBC, and their respective crime-and-punishment and drug series. A key feature of the former is a host of "reality" prison series shows produced by 44 Blue Productions, such as *Pitbulls and Parolees, Lockup: Extended Stay, and Behind Bars,* which tend routinely to provide viewers with a foreboding look behind the scenes of U.S. and international prison cultures. Individual inmates, corrections officers, family members, wardens, and health workers are typically cast around notorious Part 1 Index offenses such as homicide, arson, armed robbery, larceny-theft, forcible rape, burglary, and vehicle theft. African Americans, Latinos, and Whites of lower socioeconomic status and education levels are preponderant in this casting. CNBC's primetime shows *Marijuana, Inc., and Marijuana, USA,*[12] present sympathetic market-focused segments such as "The Confused State of Pot Law Enforcement," "How Big is the Marijuana Market?" "State by State Guide to Laws, Consumption, and Costs," and "Marijuana in America: History and Culture." The focus is often places like Mendocino County, California, where estimates suggest that as much as 60 percent of its 86,000 residents cultivate, distribute, or consume high-grade marijuana; its White population is 88 percent, compared to Latinos at roughly 20 percent, Native Americans at 5.8 percent, and African Americans at 0.9 percent. Nevertheless, arrest patterns and conviction rates do not reflect who cultivates, uses, or sells marijuana most in the state or country.

A 2007 National Survey on Drug Use and Health report for the U.S. Department of Health and Human Services found that among racial groups, drug use tends to be lowest in nonmetropolitan counties, (except for individuals claiming two or more racial identities and Native Americans and Alaska Natives) and highest in metropolitan counties.[13] The same pattern among these groups holds specifically for marijuana use, including African American respondents at 7.3 percent reporting past-month use, Whites at 6.2 percent, Latinos at 5.0 percent, and Asians at 1.8 percent. But, this provides only a snapshot of reported use among groups in the country, further highlights the disparity in arrests among African Americans when compared to the reported use of other groups, and is not generalizable as an explanation of marijuana use. For instance, a 2001 iteration of the same survey of reported *lifetime* use (as opposed to past month) showed that Whites reported significantly higher use than African Americans (41.5 to 35.5 percent, respectively) in 2000 and (44.5 to 38.6 percent, respectively) in 2001. The same holds true for reported *past-year* usage respectively, with Whites at 11.2 percent in 2000 to African Americans at 10.9 percent, and again in 2001 respectively, with Whites at 12.9 and African Americans at 12.2 percent. Nevertheless, African Americans are arrested more than the several groups who report higher usage and at rates that far exceed their reported use relative to Whites.

For Blacks throughout the United States, marijuana is more a "gateway drug" for granting local, state, and national law enforcement the capacity to greater mass incarceration of African Americans and other groups than it is for exposure to more serious drug use. Comparing arrest rates for select offenses[14] in 1990 and 2008, research shows marijuana possession to be an extreme outlier (Macallair and Males 2009, 3). As arrests declined for every available category, arrest rates for possession of small quantities of marijuana moved in a positive direction at 127 percent. Small-scale, personal-use marijuana possession arrests far exceeded property crimes, violent crimes, and all other drug possession and sales. As pop culture (e.g., the *TV Guide Network* series *Weeds*), voters, and public opinion show signs of greater tolerance for some form of regulation, decriminalization, and normalization, law enforcement has been unrelenting. Harry G. Levine and his colleagues (2010) insist: "In the last 20 years, California made 850,000 arrests for possession of small amounts of marijuana, and half a million arrests in the last ten years. The people arrested were disproportionately African

Americans and Latinos, overwhelmingly young people, especially young men" (Levine, Gettman, and Siegel 2010). The patterns of disparity, especially between African Americans and Whites, in California's counties and cities are consistent with patterns in cities and states across the United States. For instance, in Syracuse, in Onondaga County, New York, the arrest rate for minor marijuana possession is 1,795 per 100,000, compared to 169 per 100,000 for Whites; the Black population in Syracuse is 10.61, according to NORML. In Cincinnati, Ohio, in Hamilton County, the marijuana arrest gap between African Americans and Whites is 1,292 per 100,000 to 341. Kansas City, Missouri, in Jackson County similarly arrests African Americans for possession at 1,093 per 100,000 to 292 per 100,000 for Whites. Hartford, Connecticut, in Hartford County, yields similar disparities, with African Americans being arrested at a rate 938 per 100,000 and Whites at 206 arrests. Communities like Cleveland, Ohio; Sioux Falls, South Dakota; Duluth, Minnesota; Saginaw, Michigan; Omaha, Nebraska; and Albany, New York, African American per-capita arrests for possession of small quantities of marijuana, when compared to Whites and others, is similarly reflective of the reality that African Americans are treated with a double standard under marijuana laws in the United States. New York City aggressively arrests African American offenders at a ratio of 9:1 when compared to White offenders. According to the author of the Marijuana Policy Project, ". . . 1998 and 2007 the New York police arrested 374,900 people whose most serious crime was the lowest-level misdemeanor marijuana offense. That number is eight times higher than the number of arrests (45,300) from 1988 to 1997. Nearly 90 percent arrested between 1998 and 2007 were male, despite the fact that national studies show marijuana use roughly equal between men and women. And while national surveys show Whites are more likely to use marijuana than Blacks and Latinos, the New York study reported that 83 percent of those arrested were Black or Latino. Blacks accounted for 52 percent of the arrests, Latinos and other people of color accounted for 33 percent, while Whites accounted for only 15 percent" (Mirken 2007). According to NORML, for four years in a row during the previous decade, U.S. marijuana arrests set an all-time record. Marijuana arrests of all groups are currently approaching 850,000 arrests per year.

The plight of African Americans and the extreme disparities they experience in California and other states have become routine. No group of adults in the state or country would benefit more from a reasoned policy of decriminalization. They have become the canary in the mine of the unrelenting War on Drugs that has engulfed members of nearly every major population in the state. Alarmist reaction to "crack" in the 1980s and 1990s at least signaled the emergence of a crisis in rural and urban African American communities to which they could organize and respond. Yet seeping under the radar, marijuana has facilitated the mass criminalization of ordinary African Americans for at least the past three decades. Religious organizations and leaders who decry the human waste and community dissolution associated with mass incarceration and criminalization are mostly hostile to the idea of decriminalization. Marijuana, like homosexuality, has seemingly always been taboo in the African American church, even as members' and parishioners' families and lives are deeply affected. This may be largely due to the social stigma attached to marijuana and the reality that this population has been targeted for all sorts of adverse policies from the undoing of affirmative action, social welfare, education, housing, and public health, including widespread gun violence among their young. Marijuana is more taboo than crisis.

Conclusion

For many, the right to consume marijuana is a matter of freedom to choose and to hold sovereignty in one's person. For African Americans, advocacy for legalization (and to a lesser extent decriminalization) of adult personal use of marijuana must be viewed as a strategic means to eradicating the totalitarian hold which the U.S. criminal justice system holds on more than a million of their lives, with criminological projections that forms of official repression will deepen and intensify if left unabated for the remainder of the twenty-first century. Early in the twentieth century, marijuana, like opiates, was criminalized, racialized, and identified with one or more racial minority groups' ostensible dangerousness in American society. Today, marijuana law enforcement exposes the gross double standards applied to African American and other racial minority groups, in relation to American Whites. Conservative criminology and think-tank intellectuals have offered statistical and analytical support for the differential treatment of African Americans, all but absolving society of responsibility demanded in the individual. It is not a society that has an unmitigated and tortured racial legacy that is responsible for the grossly disproportionate patterns of African American imprisonment, but the irredeemable and behavioral choices of individuals. Meanwhile, the disproportionate and differential involvement for marijuana and other illegal drugs on the part of American Whites is largely ignored by the same research claiming criminal Black deviance. This line continues, even in the face of a full generation of scholarly research that has debunked it. Increasingly, scholars have shown that it is not merely deviant African American individuals' behavior that leads to the many social problems that engulf their communities today; instead, the experience with the entire process, from arrest to incarceration and parole, is believed to have a contagious effect, hardening those who were originally jailed for petty conduct. Against conventional understanding, Van den Brink (2008) views prohibitionist policies as having a "gateway effect" on more serious drug use, not on marijuana itself. He notes, "in some prohibitionist countries the probability of cocaine use in subjects who have never used cannabis is higher (USA 33%) than in some countries with a liberal cannabis policy (the Netherlands, 22%)." For African Americans impacted by the War on Drug ideology of the past four decades, marijuana has been a gateway drug to ever-harsher punishment of African Americans, increasing the risk for many that upon arrest, their lives will not return to any normalcy. This, while their American White peers can anticipate that petty drug consumption or possession will not lead to routine peremptory stops or no-knock warrants (Alexander 2011), or their lives being irrevocably destroyed. The growth in incarceration of poor, urban-dwelling young people between 1980 and 1996 did not reflect increasing crime, leading Glenn Loury to conclude that policymakers made the conscious decision to become increasingly harsh in punishing crimes, especially those committed by racial minorities (Loury 2010, 10).

Like slavery, sharecrop exploitation, the lynch pogroms, and Jim Crow hyper incarceration of mostly ghettoized, poorer, and young African Americans—even for conduct that all segments of the U.S. population engage in more so—represents the greatest obstacle to accessing the broad opportunity structure that makes for the common good. Marijuana and other drug laws are effectively the "Black codes" of the twenty-first century. They must be eradicated for the sake of the "beloved community" that guided the hopes of the civil rights movement, before the present carceral obsession captured the U.S. punishment system.

Notes

1. This phrase is preferred by Loic Wacquant, who insists that the phrase "mass incarceration" unfortunately implies that the targets of ever-harsher laws are evenly distributed among groups in society. For him, the phrase "hyper incarceration" betrays the targeting of specific groups such as young, less educated, poor, racial minority group members. See his comments in the forum of Glenn C. Loury (2008).
2. These observations are all based on the authors' summary of the important criminological work by M. H. Barlow, "Race and the problem of crime in *Time* and *Newsweek* cover stories, 1946–1995," *Social Justice* 25, no. 2 (1998): 149–182. The Building Blocks for Youth conducted its first report, "The Color of Justice" in January 2000; later in 2000, in collaboration with the National Council on Crime and Delinquency (NCCD) Building Blocks for Youth, published "And Justice for Some: Differential Treatment of Minority Youth in the Justice System." A third report, "Youth Crime, Adult Time," was published in October 2000, and "Off Balance: Youth, Race, and Crime in the News," was published in April 2001.
3. Petersilia was a senior researcher in the criminal justice program of the Rand Corporation. See http://articles.chicagotribune.com/1987-07-06/news/8702190186_1_prison-population-crimes-racial-bias (Emphasis is mine.) Moreover, this claim offers that racism in the criminal justice system was disproven by the overrepresentation of other groups in society (males and youth). It implies that race is a *biological equivalent* to age (being young) and gender (male) that scholars widely reject. It is actually the case that combining race and male gender shows salient disproportionality with 8.1 percent of all African American young men age 25 to 29 being incarcerated in 2005, as were 2.6 of Latino young men and 1.1 percent of White males. See also Garland, et al. 2008. And it is true that even *within* gender groups, African American women suffer increasingly higher rates of incarceration than women of other groups. Since the late stages of the War on Drugs, "the fastest growing segment of the imprisoned population is Black women, who are incarcerated for nonviolent offenses," (Brown et al. 2003, 135). Moreover, African Americans' percentage of the population when compared to these groups was significantly small and highly concentrated in urban areas. For instance, at the time, males constituted 48 percent of the U.S. population, while African Americans constituted just 11 percent. It is also pertinent that African Americans are regionally and locally concentrated rather than a "national population" (Hawkins and Hardy 1989,

86), as are the young or males. At no point does Blumstein suggest that the "statistics are not evidence of racism," and the crimes that were sending people to prison and jail were committed by Whites, more than others.

4. Glenn Loury concurs, making acquisition and possession of wealth as the only major exception, Loury, *Race, Incarceration,* p. 37.

5. Hawkins (1986) replicated Blumstein's method in North Carolina with a special focus on examining racial disparity among crime types. He compared Whites with non-Whites (although 97 percent of non-Whites were classified as Black). Using UCR arrest data and prison admissions data and incorporating a one-year lag period (e.g., 1978 arrests compared with 1979 admissions), Hawkins found greater unexplained disparity in North Carolina than what Blumstein observed at the national level (i.e., 20 percent). During 1978–1979, 30 percent of the disproportionality was left unexplained, 41 percent was unexplained in 1980–1981 and 42 percent in 1981–1982. These differences in unexplained disproportionality highlight the importance of examining imprisonment disparity over multiple time periods" (p. 21).

6. Alpine (0.58), Sierra (0.3), Plumas (n/a), Trinity (0.5), and Humboldt (1.2) are significantly smaller than in the state or in the counties where arrests are highest. The others were Sierra (94.9), Trinity (n/a), Humboldt (85.7), and Plumas (89.9). Only in the state's smallest county, Alpine, is the White population (73.6), below the state average (76.4). The others were Inyo, Humboldt (85.7), Alpine, Mono, and Calaveras.

7. California NORML reports these rates in 2002: Alpine (2,955.27), Sierra (759.84), Humboldt (444.19), Plumas (440.04), and Trinity (437.04).

8. Petty possession is considered quantities below one ounce.

9. http://www.canorml.org/background/CAarreststatsNORML. Accessed April 15, 2011.

10. Levine et al., ibid., Appendix: County and State Data.

11. Census reports register the total Black population in California at 6.6 percent, or 2,556,653. Bureau of Justice Statistics Drug Arrests by age show that between 1970 and 2007, arrests among adults have outpaced juvenile arrests, especially between 1980 and 1990. After a brief decline among adults in the early 1990s, the gap in arrests among adults and juveniles showed a pattern of adult arrests dramatically increasing in the middle 1990s through 2007, while arrests among juveniles stabilized over the entire period. See http://bjs.ojp.usdoj.gov/content/glance/drug.cfm. Accessed 3/16/2011.

12. See David Hinckley, *NY DailyNews.com,* 1/22/2009. A 2009 *National Geographic* report conducted by journalist Lisa Ling called "Marijuana Nation," preceded the CNBC reports of reporter Trish Regan and focused on the liberalization of Canadian marijuana laws and mass production and availability in Vancouver, British Columbia. Like CNBC, its reportage was overwhelmingly sympathetic and mostly reflective of White dealers and growers portrayed as entrepreneurs despite their illegal activity. The Marijuana, USA segment did include African American proprietors and cultivators Chef Scott Durrah and his wife Wanda James of Denver, Colorado.

13. Conducted between 2004 and 2005, data in the survey were based on a sample of 136,068 respondents (12 years old or older) to face-to-face interviews at their place of residence. Department of Health and Human Services, SMASHA, Office of Applied Studies.

14. These are listed in order with the rates of change between the two years. Rape (−67%), murder (−63%), property crimes (−49%), robbery (−46%), all misdemeanors (−43%), all offenses (−40%), violent crimes (−34%), all felonies (−33%), all drug sales (−32%), all other drug possession (−29%), assault (−28%), weapons (−26%) and marijuana possession (+127).

8

THE LATINO POLITICS OF PROPOSITION 19

Criminal Justice and Immigration

Melissa R. Michelson and Joe Tafoya

In 2010, as Californians debated the pros and cons of legalizing marijuana, policymakers and analysts debated the possible impacts on the state's large Latino population. What would be the likely impact on the rates of arrest and incarceration of Latino youth, who are disproportionately charged with drug-related crimes (as are African American youth) compared to their White counterparts? Were such likely changes a good reason to vote for the proposal? Others debated the possible impact on immigration policy. Debates about border control and what to do about undocumented immigration are often linked to the problem of smugglers bringing marijuana across the U.S.-Mexican border. Thus, decriminalization had the potential to soften views regarding the negative impact of undocumented immigrants and possibly move immigration politics forward. In this chapter, we open with the history of marijuana laws, illustrating the long-standing link to immigration and Latino politics. We then review contemporary policy debates regarding Latinos, Proposition 19, and immigration and criminal justice policies.

The Anti-Mexican History of Marijuana Laws

Marijuana has long been linked in the public mind to Latinos, especially Mexicans (Musto 1987). From the Mexican Cockroach Song (*La Cucaracha*), which has been around for a century, to Cheech and Chong's *Up In Smoke* (1978), the idea that Mexicans are heavy marijuana users is firm in the public imagination, despite data regarding relatively equal rates of use across racial and ethnic groups. While initial anti-narcotics efforts in California, inspired by anti-Chinese sentiment, focused on the use of opium, attention turned in the early twentieth century to the new "menace" of marijuana. Cannabis had previously been a common ingredient in patent medicines; the new name, marijuana, was meant to sound foreign and associate the drug with immigrants (Holland 2010). A travelogue from 1897 warned:

> In Southern Arizona the jail and prison officials have their hands full in trying to prevent the smuggling into their institution of the seductive mariguana. This is a kind of loco weed more powerful than opium.[1]

The reputation of Mexican marijuana as being a cause of madness was widespread. In 1911, the *Washington Post* printed an article titled, "War on Crazing Drug: California Fears the Dread Loco Weed That Has Menaced Mexico" (November 6, 1911). The article claimed that Mexican laborers were bringing the "loco weed" into California.

In 1913, California lawmakers took action to ban marijuana. Initial crackdowns were centered in Mexican neighborhoods (such as the Sonoratown neighborhood of Los Angeles in 1914).[2] Gieringer (2006) notes the link to Mexicans, and particularly to criminal behavior by Mexicans, as prompting other states to soon follow suit:

> The first true marijuana scare in the country occurred in El Paso, Texas, on New Year's day 1913, when a Mexican bandido, allegedly crazed by habitual marijuana use, shot up the town and killed a policeman, prompting the city to ban marijuana two years later.

Helmer (1975) claims anti-marijuana laws were inspired by anti-Mexican attitudes. Bearman (2010) specifically links the decision in 1937 to make marijuana possession a federal crime to anti-Mexican hysteria.

Mexican-Americans were used as a whipping boy to generate anti-marijuana hysteria. In the 1930s, Harry Anslinger, head of the Federal Bureau of Narcotics, led the propaganda campaign to make marijuana possession a federal crime. He was an avowed racist, as evidenced by this quote about marijuana:

> "I wish I could show you what a small marijuana cigarette can do to one of our degenerate Spanish-speaking residents. That's why our problem is so great; the greatest percentage of our population is composed of Spanish-speaking persons, most of who are low mentality, because of social and racial conditions."

While marijuana use in California, and elsewhere in the Southwest United States, was blamed on the influence of Mexican immigrants who were bringing with them their native addiction to the "loco weed," evidence suggests that use of the drug in Mexico was never particularly widespread (Reuter and Ronfeldt 1992, 93–94). Still, respected sources continue to pin domestic marijuana use to Mexican immigrants. Online supplementary materials for a recent *Frontline* episode, "Busted: America's

War on Marijuana," include an item titled "Mexican immigrants introduce recreational use of marijuana leaf" for the 1900–1920s. The entry notes:

> After the Mexican Revolution of 1910, Mexican immigrants flooded into the U.S., introducing to American culture the recreational use of marijuana. The drug became associated with the immigrants, and the fear and prejudice about the Spanish-speaking newcomers became associated with marijuana. Anti-drug campaigners warned against the encroaching "Marijuana Menace," and terrible crimes were attributed to marijuana and the Mexicans who used it.[3]

In the 1930s, massive unemployment triggered increased fears and resentments of Mexican immigrants. "This instigated a flurry of research which linked the use of marijuana with violence, crime and other socially deviant behaviors, primarily committed by 'racially inferior' or underclass communities."[4]

Current criminal justice and immigration politics continue to reflect this historical linkage between Mexican immigrants and marijuana. Despite evidence that use rates are higher among Whites than among young people of color, Latino and Black youth are more likely to be arrested and charged for violating laws against marijuana possession (Levine, Gettman, and Siegel 2010). Despite evidence that a significant portion of marijuana consumed in the United States is produced domestically, the link to Mexican drug smugglers continues, influencing immigration politics.[5] This includes stories in the U.S. media about the violence of Mexican drug cartels, the cost of fighting drug trafficking along the U.S.-Mexican border, and the issue of undocumented immigrants bringing illegal drugs (including marijuana) into the United States.[6]

Criminal Justice Politics

Numerous studies have documented the racism that corrupts the U.S. criminal justice system. Regarding marijuana laws, a study released during the 2010 campaign by the Drug Policy Alliance noted that although rates of use were higher among White youth, Black and Latino youth were much more likely to be prosecuted for marijuana possession and use (Levine, et al. 2010). At the individual level, this sends Latino youth to jail instead of to college (this includes the increased difficulty that those found guilty of drug crimes will have in obtaining student financial aid), making it more difficult for them to become productive adults; at the societal level, this impacts Latino communities and families, removing and criminalizing the young men who would otherwise serve roles as husbands and fathers. In short, "Marijuana arrests have serious consequences" (Levine et al. 2010, 3, 15):

> For young, low-income Latinos—who use marijuana less than young whites, and who already face numerous barriers and hurdles—a criminal

record for the "drug crime" of marijuana possession can seriously harm their life chances. . . .These marijuana possession arrests, which target young, low-income Californians, serve as a "head start" program for a lifetime of unemployment and poverty.

In part, this disproportional impact on communities of color is due to the perception by many that marijuana is not a serious drug, or one for which possession is normally prosecuted. In a documentary called "Prop 19:The end of the war on marijuana?" produced for the National Radio Project's *Making Contact,* journalist Andrew Stezler drew attention to the criminal justice impact of current marijuana laws.

In 2009, more than 850,000 Americans were arrested for marijuana violations, according to the FBI.That number is the second highest ever, and it means that more than half of the nation's drug arrests were for pot. It's a staggering statistic, but one that runs counter to popular wisdom. More important, as noted in the documentary, is the discretion thus given to law enforcement officers.While some communities experience de facto decriminalization, police patrolling communities of color often disproportionately enforce existing anti-marijuana laws, in part because those communities are more likely to be subject to regular law-enforcement patrols. Thus, although people in *any* neighborhood are likely to be in possession of small amounts of marijuana, low-income Latinos in "high crime" neighborhoods are more likely to be subject to searches of their person and vehicles, resulting in ethnically biased arrests (Levine et al. 2010).

The disparity in arrest rates exists across the state. Levine et al. (2010) used statistics from the California Department of Justice to calculate rates of arrest for Whites and Latinos in 33 California cities from 2006 to 2008.The cities represent a total population of 10 million, a quarter of the state population, and a third of the state's Latinos. As Table 8.1 shows, the bias is consistent across these cities.

These data show that the bias against Latinos exists statewide; despite lower levels of use than Whites, Latinos are more likely to be arrested and charged. Pasadena and Santa Monica are the cities with the highest ratios in the state at 2.9 and 2.7, respectively, meaning that for every one White person the police arrest for possession, nearly three Latinos were arrested. In the state's largest city, Los Angeles, the arrest rate for Latinos is twice that of Whites.

Such disparities are not unique to California. A recent *New York Times* article noted that nearly 90 percent of those arrested for personal possession in New York City are Black or Latino, despite "rampant" use by young affluent Whites (Dwyer 2011). Michelle Alexander notes in *The New Jim Crow: Mass Incarceration in the Age of Colorblindness* (2010, 96–97) that the War on Drugs has resulted in the mass incarceration of Black and Latino men:

The number of 2000 drug admissions for Latinos was twenty-two times the number of 1983 admissions.Whites have been admitted to prison for drug offenses at increased rates as well—the number of whites admitted for

TABLE 8.1 White and Latino Marijuana Possession Arrest Rates in 33 California Cities, 2006–2008

City, County	White Rate of MJ Poss Arrests per 100,000 Whites	Latino Rate of MJ Poss Arrests per 100,000 Latinos	Times the Latino Arrest Rate is Greater than the White Arrest Rate	City Pop	Latino % of Pop	Latino % of MJ Arrests
Alhambra, LA	168	455	2.7	85,949	35.5	74.6
Burbank, LA	586	900	1.5	104,191	25.7	34.9
Covina, LA	397	525	1.3	54,114	47.9	56.3
Downey, LA	110	191	1.7	115,800	70.4	75.4
Glendale, LA	462	981	2.1	195,505	17.4	29.9
Long Beach, LA	246	409	1.7	462,556	40.2	36.2
Los Angeles, LA	73	146	2.0	3,749,058	48.4	48.3
Lynwood, LA	75	155	2.1	71,138	83.1	73.7
Monrovia, LA	303	535	1.8	37,155	34.3	46.9
Pasadena, LA	137	395	2.9	137,885	33.5	33.1
Santa Monica, LA	166	452	2.7	87,935	11.8	22.5
Whittier, LA	171	349	2.0	88,207	64.9	78.3
Fullerton, Orange	146	225	1.5	133,484	33.0	45.8
Irvine, Orange	336	661	2.0	193,872	8.7	19.5
Mission Viejo, Orange	193	250	1.3	95,378	15.9	19.0
Orange, Orange	508	692	1.4	137,855	37.5	45.1
Santa Ana, Orange	88	123	1.4	327,681	79.0	87.9
Tustin, Orange	216	388	1.8	72,232	36.8	51.0
Bakersfield, Kern	82	104	1.3	318,436	42.2	36.3
Chino	392	616	1.6	78,446	51.4	63.6
Corona, Riverside	123	158	1.3	156,525	40.9	48.6
El Centro, Imperial	273	361	1.3	39,979	75.0	78.5
Escondido, San Diego	133	205	1.5	137,991	45.1	55.4
Fremont, Alameda	165	221	1.3	206,241	14.6	26.7
Fresno, Fresno	98	174	1.8	472,179	44.6	49.7
Modesto, Stanislaus	76	110	1.4	204,070	34.4	40.1
Oxnard, Ventura	107	188	1.8	175,906	70.1	82.3
Salinas, Monterey	85	131	1.5	143,853	72.0	78.0
San Diego, San Diego	145	181	1.2	1,251,184	27.3	27.0
San Jose, Santa Clara	121	263	2.2	905,180	31.5	54.7
Santa Barbara, Santa Barbara	353	451	1.3	86,087	32.1	37.0
Upland, San Bernardino	200	336	1.7	76,446	35.8	41.3
Visalia, Tulare	67	152	2.3	116,306	40.6	60.7

Source: Levine et al. (2010), p. 12.

drug offenses in 2000 was eight times the number admitted in 1983—but their relative numbers are small compared to blacks' and Latinos'. Although the majority of illegal drug users and dealers nationwide are white, three-fourths of all people imprisoned for drug offenses have been black or Latino.

These differences are not due to differences in rates of illegal drug use. Alexander cites the U.S. Department of Health and Human Services' *Summary of Findings from the 2000 National Household Survey on Drug Abuse,* which reports that 6.4 percent of Whites, 6.4 percent of Blacks, and 5.3 percent of Hispanics were current illegal drug users in 2000. These drug convictions, of course, have consequences; convicted felons are often excluded from jury service and from voting, and are often legally discriminated against in housing, unemployment, education, financial aid, and public benefits (Alexander 2010).

Evidence from current anti-drug laws suggests that the impact of such a law would have been reduced criminalization of Latinos, particularly of young Latino men. Decriminalization would have decreased the discretion available to police departments and enforcement officers, reducing their ability to prosecute and criminalize young Latinos engaging in behaviors that are no different (and, in fact, less common) from those affluent Whites engage in. Decriminalization in California, if successful, might even have led to decriminalization efforts in other states, with potential widespread consequences for the mass incarceration of young men of color. These considerations were noted by Latino organizations that endorsed Proposition 19. The California chapter of the League of United Latin American Citizens (LULAC) urged passage of the measure, noting the disproportionate rates with which Latino youth are charged with possession and cultivation of marijuana. The endorsement of Prop 19 by leading Latino organizations such as LULAC of California and the Latino Voters League, however, was insufficient to overcome public concern that the measure would have negative consequences, and Latinos generally did not support the measure.

Immigration Politics

As noted above, marijuana has long been linked to Mexican immigrants, often to illegal smugglers. The degree to which the marijuana used in California originates in Mexico is unknown. A recent report from California's Bureau of Narcotics Enforcement estimated three times as much marijuana was grown in state as was seized along the entire U.S.-Mexico border (Isackson 2010). Rios (2010) claims that 50 percent of the cannabis used in the United States is grown domestically. The United Nations (UNODC 2006) estimates that this number is closer to one-third. Due to the unreliability of various sources of information used to produce these estimates, including consumption rates and plant-yield estimates, Kilmer et al. (2010) instead give a range for imports from Mexico as comprising 40–67 percent of the marijuana used in the United States.

Nonetheless, debates about immigration and securing the border thus often refer to the danger of illegal drugs. If Proposition 19 had been approved, it would have reduced any incentive Mexican drug cartels and other producers might have had to attempt to sneak supplies across the U.S.-Mexican border, thus theoretically reducing border violence and undocumented immigration. Because this is not truly the source of most marijuana in the state, the actual effects in these areas would likely have been minimal. Yet, the impact on immigration debates might have been noticeable. Marijuana possession arrests bring immigrants under the federal radar and thus the public eye. If the public links border control and undocumented immigration to the trafficking of marijuana, then the legalization of marijuana might have also reduced fears about border security and undocumented immigrants. There is some possibility that this would have allowed domestic debates about immigration policy to make a leap forward. As Bearman (2010) notes:

> Legalization could also aid the war on terror by freeing immigration and other border control resources to target terrorists and WMDs rather than the illegal drug trade. Under prohibition, moreover, terrorists piggyback on the smuggling networks established by drug lords and more easily hide in a sea of underground, cross-border trafficking.

According to Holland, "Mexican drug cartels make 70 percent of their profits from marijuana sales . . . the warfare that is waged on both sides of our borders is primarily marijuana-driven" (2010: 3). At a press conference at Latino Voters League (LVL) headquarters on August 13, 2010, LVL coordinator Antonio Gonzalez argued that "approving Proposition 19 will strike a blow to violent gangs and Mexican cartels that prey on our communities by removing their profit incentive."[7]

This interpretation of the possible impact of Prop 19, however, was rejected by many analysts, who noted that other drugs would remain illegal and that marijuana would have remained illegal in other states. Mexican drug cartels, to be sure, smuggle many other drugs (Isackson 2010). According to Joe Garcia, a special agent with Immigration and Customs Enforcement:

> They diversified, there's a larger increase in manufacturing of meth in Mexico. Eighty percent of what U.S. authorities seize comes from Mexico," says Garcia. Besides, he says Proposition 19 wouldn't touch cartels' profits from their other illegal activities, "Heroin, cocaine, extortion, gun running, bulk cash smuggling, whatever. They're going to find a way to do it." And the violence that comes with smuggling those drugs, cash and guns will continue. (Isackson 2010)

Across the border, Mexican officials denounced Proposition 19. President Felipe Calderón criticized the idea as inconsistent with federal efforts against drug trafficking and said it was unreasonable for the United States to ask for supply to decrease while encouraging consumption. This was in marked contrast to the support for legalization often voiced by former Mexican President Vicente Fox, who served from 2000–2006, and to statements in favor of a new debate about decriminalization voiced by the subsequent president of Mexico, Enrique Peña Nieto, who was elected in July 2012. Peña Nieto's endorsement of a debate on legalization aligned him with an increasingly large list of leaders of Latin American countries. As of July 2012, the presidents of Colombia, Uruguay, Belize, and Guatemala were calling for a debate on decriminalization, hoping to limit escalating drug violence.[8] "I'm not saying we should legalize," Peña Nieto said in an interview on the PBS *NewsHour* July 3, 2012. "But we should debate in Congress, in the hemisphere, and especially the U.S. should participate in this broad debate. . . . It is quite clear that after several years of this fight against drug trafficking, we have more drug consumption, drug use and drug trafficking. That means we are not moving in the right direction. Things are not working." This increasing regional support for decriminalization hints that future efforts similar to Proposition 19 might be forthcoming, perhaps in a different political arena. At the time, however, President Calderón's opposition was consistent with that of most Mexican leaders.

Other Mexican officials feared that the passage of Proposition 19 would mean even more smuggling through border towns such as Tijuana, or a shift to more domestic sales. A study released in October 2010 by the nonpartisan RAND Drug Policy Research Center in Santa Monica, CA, claimed that passage of Proposition 19 would have had minimal impacts on Mexican drug-trafficking organizations (DTOs):

> California accounts for about one-seventh of U.S. marijuana consumption, and domestic production is already stronger in California than elsewhere in the United States. Hence, if Prop 19 *only* affects revenues from supplying marijuana to California, DTO drug export revenue losses would be very small, on the order of 2–4 percent (Kilmer et al. 2010, 3).

The study also rejected claims that passage of Proposition 19 would reduce violence in Mexico, noting: "There are fundamental issues related to the justice system that need to be addressed before anyone can expect significant improvements in the security situation in Mexico" (Kilmer et al. 2010, 4).

Closer to home, passage of Proposition 19 would have removed one of the pathways to deportation that face many young Latinos convicted of marijuana possession. Levine et al. (2010) note that one conviction for marijuana possession can mean that immigrants who leave the country can be denied reentry, while those with two convictions can be deported. According to Human Rights Watch, from 1997 to 2007, the United States deported 1,063 individuals whose sole or highest charge against them was possession of marijuana, nearly 80 percent of whom were from Mexico (Human Rights Watch, 2009). Just before the vote on

Proposition 19, California Governor Arnold Schwarzenegger signed Senate Bill 1449, which changed possession of less than an ounce of marijuana to an infraction rather than a misdemeanor. Yet, such infractions still appear in criminal justice databases, thus producing the same negative consequences for those found to have a "drug offense" on their record.

Other U.S. cities and states are decriminalizing marijuana. In June 2012, the Chicago City Council, with the encouragement of Mayor Rahm Emanuel, approved decriminalization of possession of 15 grams or less of marijuana. Before the vote, several aldermen noted the disproportionate effect of drug laws on Black and Latino communities.

> "If you had been white and privileged, marijuana has already been decriminalized," said Ald. Howard Brookins, 21st, who voted for the measure. "The only people arrested for these crimes have been black and brown individuals. . . . This is a way to potentially level the playing field."[9]

By June 2012, 15 states had decriminalized possession of small amounts of marijuana, and several others were considering legalization, including Oregon, Colorado, and Washington.[10] In his attempt to add New York to the list, Governor Andrew Cuomo noted the disproportionate effect of marijuana laws on Black and Latino youth. Data released by the governor's office noted that in 2011, more than 50,000 arrests for possession of marijuana were made in New York. Fifty percent of those arrested were under 25 years old, and 82 percent were Black or Latino.[11] The effort was blocked by State Senate Republicans, and New York lawmakers promised to revisit the issue in the future.[12]

At the national level, legalization in the near future is unlikely, and even the limited legalization of medical marijuana allowed by different states has been subject to attack. President Barack Obama has admitted that he smoked marijuana as a young man. Yet, he opposes decriminalization, and his Department of Justice has moved to crack down on medical marijuana dispensaries in California and Colorado. In February 2012, *Rolling Stone* magazine published a story detailing what it called "Obama's War on Pot: In a shocking about-face, the administration has launched a government-wide crackdown on medical marijuana."[13] Despite promising during the 2008 campaign that he would end the Bush administration's high-profile raids on providers of medical marijuana, the Obama administration instead unleashed "a multi-agency crackdown on medical cannabis that goes far beyond anything undertaken by George W. Bush."

> The feds are busting growers who operate in full compliance with state laws, vowing to seize the property of anyone who dares to even rent to legal pot dispensaries, and threatening to imprison state employees responsible for regulating medical marijuana. With more than 100 raids on pot dispensaries during his first three years, Obama is now on pace to exceed Bush's record

for medical-marijuana busts. "There's no question that Obama's the worst president on medical marijuana," says Rob Kampia, executive director of the Marijuana Policy Project.[14]

Representative Barney Frank, a member of the U.S. House from Massachusetts, has since 1997 repeatedly introduced a bill (The Medical Marijuana Patient Protection Act) that would leave enforcement of medical marijuana to the states, but the bill dies in committee every session.[15] In sum, while legalization at the city and state level continues apace, movement at the national level seems unlikely.

Conclusion

Accurately or not, the origin of recreational marijuana use in the United States has long been linked to Mexican immigrants. Anti-Mexican sentiment in the early twentieth century thus led to the demonization of the "loco weed" and its criminalization. Today, cannabis production and distribution is associated with Mexican drug-trafficking organizations (DTOs), and thus, with the issues of border control, border security, and drug violence. Domestically, this perpetuates anti-Latino and anti-immigrant stereotypes of criminality, and works against resolution of ongoing political debates about how to reform current immigration laws. Discretion given to law-enforcement officers under current antidrug laws results in disproportional numbers of Latino youth, particularly young men, being arrested and prosecuted for marijuana possession. With these facts in mind, many Latino political leaders, including Antonio González, have advocated for legalization and supported Proposition 19. While legalization would likely not have impacted the Mexican DTOs or significantly reduced violence in Mexico, it would have decriminalized a significant portion of the Latino community and perhaps allowed for a reduction in resources used to patrol the border. Thus, the politics of Proposition 19 ranged far beyond the specific language of the proposal, with massive possible impacts on Latino politics in California and across the country. Californians rejected the measure, but in other cities and states throughout the country, decriminalization is spreading, often with the specific aim of reducing the disproportionate impact of drug laws on young Black and Latino men. At the same time, opposition to legalization by the Obama administration indicates that movement at the national level is unlikely in the foreseeable future.

Notes

1. "It Brings Ravishing Dreams of Bliss," *San Francisco Call,* October 24, 1897, p. 17.
2. "Wagonload of Dreams Seized," *Los Angeles Times,* September 10, 1914, p. 2, cited in Gieringer 2006.
3. http://www.pbs.org/wgbh/pages/frontline/shows/dope/etc/cron.html, accessed 06/13/11
4. http://www.pbs.org/wgbh/pages/frontline/shows/dope/etc/cron.html, accessed 06/13/11

5. http://www.medicalmarijuanaadvisor.net/2010/02/27/where-does-your-weed-come-from/, accessed 06/10/11, on the percentage of domestic marijuana grown in Mexico. http://www.economist.com/node/10000884, accessed 06/10/11 on the size of the California marijuana agricultural market

6. http://topics.nytimes.com/top/news/international/countriesandterritories/mexico/drug_trafficking/index.html, accessed 06/10/11 on Mexican drug trafficking

7. http://yeson19.com/node/105, accessed 05/16/11.

8. http://www.businessweek.com/news/2012–07–17/legal-marijuana-debated-as-belize-joins-regional-push-on-drugs, accessed July 31, 2012.

9. http://articles.chicagotribune.com/2012–06–28/news/ct-met-chicago-city-council-0628–20120628_1_pot-possession-possession-of-small-amounts-pot-tickets, accessed July 31, 2012.

10. http://www.foxnews.com/us/2012/06/10/efforts-to-relax-pot-rules-gaining-momentum-in-us/, accessed July 31, 2012.

11. http://articles.cnn.com/2012–06–04/justice/justice_new-york-marijuana_1_marijuana-laws-decriminalize-possession-small-amounts?_s = PM:JUSTICE, accessed July 31, 2012.

12. http://www.nytimes.com/2012/06/20/nyregion/cuomo-bill-on-marijuana-doomed-by-republican-opposition.html, accessed July 31, 2012.

13. http://www.rollingstone.com/politics/news/obamas-war-on-pot-20120216 #ixzz22Ebz6uHW, accessed July 31, 2012.

14. ibid.

15. http://www.rollingstone.com/politics/blogs/national-affairs/pot-legalization-is-coming-20120726, accessed July 31, 2012.

9

NO HALF-MEASURES

Mexico's Quixotic Policy on California's Proposition 19

Nathan Jones

President Felipe Calderón of Mexico has led an ambitious militarized assault on organized crime throughout his *sexenio*. The results of that strategy have been mixed, especially in terms of increased drug-related homicides, which now total more than 60,000 since his term began in 2006 ("Mexico's presidential election" 2012). With the introduction of California's Proposition 19, which would have legalized marijuana for recreational consumption in California, domestic and foreign policy in Mexico collided in a strange and unpredictable way. Mexico staunchly opposed the legislation, yet had earlier taken steps toward the decriminalization of small amounts of drugs domestically. Later, Calderón would even discuss "market alternatives" to the "drug war" as a viable area for discussion. How can these seemingly contradictory policies be reconciled? What has been missing in the explanations of President Calderón's foreign policy on Proposition 19? What was the impact of Proposition 19 on the legalization debate in Mexico?

While the other contributors to this volume have focused on the domestic political and societal implications of Proposition 19 in the United States, I will emphasize the Mexican foreign policy response. I argue that the Calderón administration's drug policy, while seemingly quixotic, actually forms a rational and coherent drug policy operating under quite difficult circumstances. Proposition 19 may have even helped to push Calderón personally and politically toward openness, or to what I call an "international legalization" policy. Others, such as Patrick Corcoran, argue that the Calderón administration's policy was a poorly thought out "knee-jerk reaction" to the proposition (Corcoran 2012).

I argue instead that the thinking of the administration was that while drug legalization may address the market forces underlying the drug trade (Andreas 2003, 2011; Friman and Andreas 1999; Naím 2005), incomplete legalization proposals would exacerbate the security problems of Mexico as a drug transit nation by increasing U.S. consumption. The statements of Calderón administration officials make this plain, as does their willingness to discuss "international legalization."

California's Proposition 19 represented a partial legalization of marijuana consumption in the United States but did not purport to satisfy total U.S. demand ("Legalizing Marijuana in California Will Not Dramatically Reduce Mexican Drug Trafficking Revenues | RAND" 2010). Thus, for Calderón, Proposition 19 would simply have exacerbated U.S. consumption by signaling to the U.S. consumer that legalization was imminent, while not legalizing the production of the drug throughout the country. This situation would have worsened Mexico's position as a drug-transit nation. However, a *global* legalization policy would have addressed the underlying supply-and-demand factors that cause Mexico to suffer from drug-related violence. Understood in this context, Calderón's policy is coherent and predictable, though counterintuitive.

This chapter will proceed as follows: (1) provide a background of the security situation related to Mexican drug-trafficking organizations (MDTOs); (2) describe the drug-policy debates in Mexico; (3) flesh out the debate on the efficacy of Proposition 19 in combating MDTOs; (4) trace Calderón's statements on Proposition 19; (5) elucidate the existing Latin-American movement for legalization; (6) present the responses of Mexico security and policy experts on Calderón's seemingly quixotic policies; and (7) describe how Calderón's apparently contradictory policies are predictable given Mexico's precarious position and why, for Calderón, there could be "no middle ground."

Mexico's Battle against Organized Crime

Felipe Calderón Hinojosa of the Partido Acción Nacional (PAN) came to office in 2006 amid a contested election and rising organized crime violence. As Calderón would later argue, his predecessor President Vicente Fox, also of the PAN, did not sufficiently address the rising power of organized crime in the country (Archibold 2010; Booth and Miroff n.d.; Spagat 2010). The Calderón strategy initially deployed 30,000 federal troops to confront organized crime in "hotspots" around the country. Later, the number of troops deployed grew to more than 60,000 in more than 18 Mexican states. Given the investment of blood and treasure in a supply-side counternarcotics strategy, it is noteworthy that the center-right Calderón administration would entertain any form of legalization discussion (Bittel 2009; Marosi 2010).

U.S. Cooperation in the Drug War

The United States has assisted and pushed Mexico in its battle against MDTOs extensively during the Calderón administration's tenure (2006–2012). In public statements and private conversations, U.S. officials have referred to unprecedented support from the Calderón administration on the fight against MDTOs. President Calderón broached the subject of a partnership agreement in a meeting with President George W. Bush on the Yucatan Peninsula in the city of Merida (Johnson, 2008).

The Merida Initiative is a partnership agreement between the two nations first discussed in 2007. In broad strokes, it provided $1.4 billion over three years in equipment and training to the Mexican government to fight organized crime. The equipment was military-intensive, providing, among other items, two CASA planes for surveillance and eight B12 helicopters. In addition, the United States agreed to do more about the southbound flow of weapons and chemical precursors (Cook, Rush, & Seelke n.d.; Johnson 2008).

The equipment was slow to be delivered and was heavily criticized in Mexico. According to state department cables released by Wikileaks, Mexican officials have since acknowledged that the initiative was too equipment intensive and should have focused more on training and capacity building (Barclay 2009; Carroll 2010; Martinez-Amador 2011).

Mexico as a Consumer Nation

We should also note that drug use in Mexico has increased dramatically in the last decade. The consumption of methamphetamine or *cristal* has had a powerful social impact upon Mexico, a nation accustomed to being a transportation hub for illicit narcotics, not a production and consumption market. Secretary of Public Security Genaro Garcia Luna described a quadrupling of methamphetamine use in the last decade and a tripling of cocaine use from 2006 to 2008 ("Growing Drug Abuse in Mexico adds to Crime and Violence—Frontera Norte Sur," 2010).

A 2009 United Nations report estimated 1.7 million Mexicans, or about 2.4 percent of the population, use cocaine. In comparison with the U.S., where an estimated 88 tons of cocaine are consumed annually, Mexico, with about one-third of the population as its northern neighbor, consumes an estimated 27.65 tons of the drug every year. If the UN's numbers are fairly accurate, Mexico is rapidly catching up to the U.S. as a leading consumer of cocaine ("Growing Drug Abuse in Mexico adds to Crime and Violence— Frontera Norte Sur," 2010).

We can attribute this uptick in domestic drug consumption to multiple factors including, but not limited to, poverty, unemployment, lack of education, lack of economic opportunity, economic dislocations following NAFTA/ destruction of the *ejido* system, organized crime groups' diversifying their markets, increased U.S. enforcement of the border in the post-9/11 environment, a *narco-cultura* that glorifies drug traffickers, widespread impunity, and the globalization of a drug-using culture abetted by increased access to film, television, and telecommunications (Astorga 1997; Danelo n.d.-a, n.d.-b; Friedman 2010; Grayson 1995, 2008; Johnson 2011; Luhnow and De Cordoba 2009; Marosi, 2010; Wilkinson and Ellingwood n.d.). Whatever the causes, Mexico is no longer simply a drug-transport nation, but is a consuming and producer nation as well.

With the rising popularity of cheap methamphetamines in Mexico, we have seen an increase in drug use. According to Mexican Attorney General Eduardo Medina Mora, "It is clear to everyone that our nation has stopped being a transit country for drugs going to the United States and become an important market as well. We are experiencing a phenomenon of greater drug supplies in the streets, at relatively accessible prices ("Mexico grapples with drug addiction")."

Previous Mexican Drug Decriminalization

Interestingly, the Calderón administration supported drug decriminalization domestically in Mexico in 2009. The rationale for this legislation was that the legalization of small quantities of drugs would free law enforcement to focus on organized crime. The "decriminalization" of small quantities of drugs went beyond marijuana to include cocaine, LSD, and ecstasy (Miller Llana 2009). *The Economist* pointed out that decriminalization reduced the scope of crimes for which corrupt police could demand bribes ("Mexico and drugs: Thinking the unthinkable | The Economist," 2010). This decriminalization has had almost no impact on drug use, consumption, or the treatment of addicts by police (Wagner 2010).

Mexican Voices for Change in Drug Policy

Calderón is not the first Mexican politician to support discussions on drug legalization. Former Mexican Presidents Ernesto Zedillo (Partido Revolucionario Institucional, or PRI) and Vicente Fox (PAN) have both argued in favor of legalization. According to Fox, "In order to get out of this trap (of drug violence caused by organized crime), I'm specifically proposing the legalization of the drug." Zedillo and other Latin-American leaders signed a report in 2009 from the Latin American Commission on Drugs and Democracy, which concluded:

> Prohibitionist policies based on the eradication of production and on the disruption of drug flows as well as on the criminalization of consumption have not yielded the expected results. We are farther than ever from the announced goal of eradicating drugs (Romo 2011).

The Global Commission on Drug Policy, which "builds upon the success" of the aforementioned report, has also written similar reports. The commission is notable in that it includes former President Mexican Vicente Fox and Mexican intellectuals like Carlos Fuentes ("Global Commission on Drug Policy | The

Commission," n.d.). They have joined a chorus of scholars and intelligentsia in Mexico making similar arguments, including scholars like Jorge Chabat of CIDE, who has long advocated for turning drug use into a public-health issue (Chabat 2002; Jorge Chabat n.d.).

Questionable Potential of Proposition 19

The value of Proposition 19 for Mexico was hotly debated in the months leading up to the November ballot. Some in Mexico and California argued that the legalization of marijuana would deprive MDTOs of profits. The *Washington Post* quoted U.S. estimates that marijuana accounts for 60 percent of all MDTO profits (Fainaru & Booth 2009).

Others argued that Proposition 19 was unlikely to have an impact on MDTOs, given their diversified business models, which include kidnapping, and the sales of other drugs like *crystal,* cocaine, heroin, copyright piracy, etc. According to Alejandro Poiré, the administration's press secretary at the time, "Legalization of drugs will not put an end to violence and legalizing marijuana in a unilateral and isolated way, will not impact the patterns of consumption, nor will it reduce addiction and it could increase it."[1]

In the midst of the debate, a RAND report utilizing complicated statistical methods was released. The report concluded that the passage of Proposition 19 in California would have little impact on marijuana prices in the United States or on MDTOs. It found that Prop 19's passage would result in 2–4 percent reduction of Mexican DTO profits, with the codicil that if California marijuana were to be shipped out of state in quantities large enough to undercut Mexican produce marijuana, it could reduce MDTO revenues by "approximately 20 percent" ("Legalizing Marijuana in California Will Not Dramatically Reduce Mexican Drug Trafficking Revenues | RAND," 2010).

Scholars such as David Shirk, director of the Trans-Border Institute, have argued that while legalizing marijuana would be unlikely to harm MDTO profits, it would free government resources to pursue organized crime. Shirk points out that 98 percent of all illicit narcotic tonnage seized at the border is marijuana and 6 percent of all U.S. arrests are marijuana related. Thus, decriminalization of marijuana would free significant law-enforcement resources for "hard" drugs (Shirk 2011). This position is echoed by Jorge G. Castaneda, Mexico's former foreign minister from 2000–2003, and Hector Aguilar Camín, editor of *Nexos* Magazine, in a joint opinion piece in the *Washington Post* six months before the election (Castañeda & Aguilar Camin 2010).

> Legalizing marijuana would free up both human and financial resources for Mexico to push back against the scourges that are often, if not always correctly, attributed to drug traffickers and that constitute Mexicans' real bane: kidnapping, extortion, vehicle theft, home assaults, highway robbery and

gunfights between gangs that leave far too many innocent bystanders dead and wounded. Before Mexico's current war on drugs started, in late 2006, the country's crime rate was low and dropping. Freed from the demands of the war on drugs, Mexico could return its energies to again reducing violent crime (Castañeda & Aguilar Camin 2010).

Other Mexican scholars, such as Edgardo Buscaglia, pointed out that Mexico was unlikely to benefit from legalization because Mexican state capacity is too weak. According to Buscaglia, "you need to have regulatory capacity in place . . . Mexico does not even have the capacity to regulate its pharmaceutical products" (see also, Johnson 2010).

Tracing Calderón's Statements on Proposition 19

Calderón made major statements against California's Proposition 19 in English-language media, about once a month in the six months prior to voting in California, and increased public statements dramatically in the month before the election. This behavior suggests a conscious counter-Proposition 19 strategy from the administration. Support for Proposition 19 declined in public-opinion polls in California (see also Chapter 4 of this volume). In the month prior to the election, no poll registered more than 50-percent support. In a more sophisticated analysis of all polls, Nate Silver of the *New York Times* identified the same downward trend in the month prior to the election. He also identified the governor's race as a factor making voter turnout likely to be older and more conservative on the issue of legalization (Silver 2010). Thus, Calderón's statements may have been important factors in its defeat of Proposition 19.[2]

The timing of the decline in support coincides with an uptick in English-language criticism of Proposition 19 from the Calderón administration in the month prior to the ballot (see Table 9.1). This criticism, combined with the opposition of U.S. government actors such as the Obama administration, various law-enforcement agencies, and the federal government generally, likely contributed to the electoral defeat. Thus, the importance of the Calderón administration's views on Proposition 19 and their impact upon the failure of the initiative cannot be underestimated (Booth and Miroff n.d.; Spagat 2010; "Latin Leaders Question Move to Legalize Marijuana | CNSnews.com," n.d.).

In August 2010, President Calderón spoke at forums on Mexican insecurity where the issue of legalization arose repeatedly. Calling unilateral legalization "absurd," he said:

> If there is not an international approach, Mexico will pay the costs and will get none of the benefits. . . . The price of drugs is not determined by Mexico. The price of drugs is determined by the consumers in Los Angeles, New York and Chicago (Booth and Miroff n.d.).

TABLE 9.1 Timeline of Calderón's Statements on Proposition 19

Selected Statements from Mexican President Felipe Calderón on California's Proposition 19	Date	Source
"absurd" and "If drugs are not legalized in the world, or if drugs are not legalized at least in the United States, this is simply absurd, because the price of drugs is not determined in Mexico. The price of drugs is determined by consumers in Los Angeles, or in New York, or in Chicago or Texas."	Aug-10	http://www.mcclatchydc.com/2010/09/08/100271/weary-of-drug-war-mexico-debates.html#storylink=misearch
"The growing acceptance by the American public of marijuana as a medicinal drug is absurd . . . I think they have very little moral authority to condemn a Mexican farmer who for hunger is planting marijuana to sustain the insatiable North American market for drugs."	8-Oct-10	http://latimesblogs.latimes.com/lanow/2010/10/mexican-president-felipe-calderón-strongly-criticizes-marijuana-legalization-measure-proposition-19.html
". . . serious consequences for American and Mexican society."	8-Oct-10	http://latimesblogs.latimes.com/lanow/2010/10/mexican-president-felipe-calderón-strongly-criticizes-marijuana-legalization-measure-proposition-19.html
"Drugs kill in production. Drugs kill in distribution, as is the case in the violence in Mexico, and drugs kill in consumption."	8-Oct-10	http://latimesblogs.latimes.com/lanow/2010/10/mexican-president-felipe-calderón-strongly-criticizes-marijuana-legalization-measure-proposition-19.html
"Any revisions to the regulatory framework of the production, transportation and consumption of drugs should be comprehensive and globally [sic]."	2-Nov-10	http://www.eluniversal.com.mx/notas/720642.html
"terrible inconsistency"	October, 2010	http://cnsnews.com/news/article/latin-leaders-question-move-legalize-marijuana
"absurd" and "inconsistent"	25-Oct	http://www.mcclatchydc.com/2010/09/08/100271/weary-of-drug-war-mexico-debates.html#storylink=misearch

Selected Statements from Mexican President Felipe Calderón on California's Proposition 19	Date	Source
"They have exerted pressure and demanded for decades that Mexico and other countries control, reduce, and fight drug trafficking, and there is no discernible effort to reduce the consumption of drugs in the United States . . ."	25–Oct–10	http://cnsnews.com/ news/article/latin-leaders- question-move-legalize- marijuana
First reference to "market alternatives"	26–Aug–11	http://www.mcclatchydc. com/2011/09/20/124679/ mexican-leader-hints- again-at.html
First reference in United States: "We have to do whatever it takes to reduce demand for drugs. But if drug consumption can't be contained, then decision makers must look for solutions, including market alternatives, to reduce the astronomical profits of these criminal organizations."	20–Sep–11	http://www.mcclatchydc. com/2011/09/20/124679/ mexican-leader-hints- again-at.html

Source: Compiled by author.

This marked one of the first times that a sitting Mexican president appeared willing to discuss the issue of international legalization. These forum questions were prompted by California's Proposition 19 and the debate it inspired in Mexico. As for global legalization, particularly if drug consumption cannot be brought down, Calderón has since been surprisingly consistent on the need to find an international solution; for instance, renegotiate the international regime of norms, treaties, and institutions dedicated to drug production, distribution, and use (Marosi 2010; Johnson 2010, 2011). In an interview shortly before the Proposition 19 vote, Calderón said:

> The growing acceptance by the American public of marijuana as a medicinal drug is absurd. . . . I think they have very little moral authority to condemn a Mexican farmer who for hunger is planting marijuana to sustain the insatiable North American market for drugs (Marosi, 2010).

Less than a year later, Calderón appeared to change his position on legalization, averring that "decision makers must look for other solutions, including market alternatives. . . . I'm talking about market alternatives, market solutions" (Johnson, 2011). These two seemingly contradictory statements connote both an evolution and a broader global perspective on the existing "prohibition" regime.

After the debate over Proposition 19 had subsided, Calderón faced one of the most difficult moments of his presidency. In Monterrey, Mexico, on August 25, 2011, MDTO hit men, likely affiliated with the cartel known as *Los Zetas,* entered and set fire to a casino, and prevented the patrons from leaving. The deaths of 52 people in that brazen attack came to embody the violence spawned by Calderón's military assault on Mexican organized crime (Ellingwood 2011). It was in the immediate aftermath of this event that Calderon made those first references to "market alternatives."

Supply-and-demand factors drive the drug trade, and without the elimination of the vast U.S. and European consumer markets, the only market alternative is to legalize and regulate the commodities in question. Calderón has signaled he is willing to consider ending the "prohibition" regime that has characterized the drug war as declared by Richard Nixon in 1970, but only as part of a regional or international policy change (Gray 2001).

Historians will likely debate Calderón's motivations for promoting international legalization, while aggressively lobbying against California's efforts to legalize marijuana. Was Calderón's claim to be open to international legalization discussions a mechanism to sabotage California's legalization efforts? Was it an attempt to delay the issue until he was out of office and could discuss the issue free of the responsibility of maintaining a secure nation, as Fox and Zedillo had? Or was it simply an inconsistent "knee jerk" strategy, as Mexican analysts such as Patrick Corcoran have argued?

These are all likely motivators for Calderón's seemingly quixotic policy. But for Calderón, the leader of a primarily drug-transit nation, there could be no half measures. With partial legalization, Mexico would have paid the highest price in the context of organized crime violence. We know that the administration's official statements were surprisingly consistent among his chief advisors, suggesting that a coherent policy existed. There would be talk of "international legalization," or no talk of legalization at all.

An International Drug Prohibition Regime Change

There has been a surprisingly high degree of willingness to discuss legalization of drugs within the Latin-American region, even among its conservative leadership. This is significant given that many of these governments receive millions—and for some billions—in aid from the U.S. government to combat drug trafficking. Colombia is the staunchest U.S. supporter in the region, due in large part to U.S. assistance in dismantling the Medellin and Cali cartels and later supporting Colombia's fight against FARC. Colombia's success, it should be noted, has not been in slowing or even reducing the flow of drugs, but in the security gains the country has made (Bowden 2001; Ford 2008).

At a conference in Cartagena Colombia on October 27, 2010, Colombian President Juan Manuel Santos said of inconsistent national policies, "It's confusing for our people to see that, while we lose lives and invest resources in the fight against drug trafficking, in consuming countries initiatives like California's referendum are being promoted (Miller Llana, 2010).

Similarly reflecting his new international legalization policy, Calderón, on November 2, 2010 tweeted, "Any revisions to the regulatory framework of the production, transportation and consumption of drugs should be comprehensive and globally [sic]."[3]

This trope is consistent among Latin-American leaders. All recognize the difficulty of addressing drug trafficking unilaterally. Only former leaders, long out of office, have made the push for unilateral changes.

The present regime of international treaties regarding the drug trade is prohibitionist and obliges signatory nations to combat the drug trade rather than consider legalization. This places national leaders in a difficult position in developing national policies that differ from the current prohibitionist regime. Former Latin-American leaders, such as President Vicente Fox of Mexico 2000–2006, have suggested that leaders should push ahead regardless of international treaties stating:

> It is not necessary that there is a global change . . . always, in every human action, there are leaders. There are people that go ahead, that see problems before the rest, that take decisions before the rest. . . . It is a shame that the proposal [Proposition 19] to legalize did not prosper. . . . It would have been a great thing, a benefit to California, the United States and for Mexico. It would have been a first step (Grillo & Del Rincon 2011).

There has been a surprising degree of regional solidarity among leaders calling for discussions on rethinking the global drug regime. Tied by international treaties and bilateral commitments, principally to the United States, these nations have difficulty forging unilateral policies. The global drug prohibition regime appears to have a powerful path-dependence[4] that leaders who may want to change find difficult to overcome (Peters 1999).

Much like U.S. immigration policy—where in lieu of reform, the existing policy is one of increased enforcement—international drug policy in lieu of comprehensive international reform will continue to be focused on the interdiction of drugs ("Lost in Detention | FRONTLINE | PBS," 2011). If individual states reform these policies beyond decriminalizing the possession of drugs, they risk a "pariah" status in the international community (Bowden 2001).

At the Summit of the Americas in April 2012 in Cartagena, President Obama faced significant pressure from violence-wary Latin-American leaders, including President Calderón, who sought to change hemispheric drug policy. Obama reiterated the U.S. position that legalization is "not the answer" ("Obama: Drug legalization not the answer to cartels—CBS News," 2012). But, President Santos of Colombia, President Perez Molina of Guatemala, and other Latin-American leaders attempted to push Obama toward a more liberalized drug policy (Ellsworth 2012; Epatko 2012; Perez Molina 2012).

Most recently, the administration of Jose Mujica, president of Uruguay, is considering legalizing, regulating, and selling marijuana in a bid to reduce cocaine consumption. This "unorthodox" approach is a response to the rising domestic drug consumption of coca paste and increased levels of violence in a country that has boasted the lowest levels of violence in Latin America. The premise is that if marijuana is legalized, regulated, and sold by the government, it will attract users away from drugs such cocaine paste, which is similar to crack (Ramsey 2012).

All these events and public statements paint a picture of a region growing tired of the supply-side approach of the drug war. Regional leaders, prompted by escalating organized-crime violence, are seeking alternatives. Like Calderón, they are reticent to act alone, understanding that this global market will need to be addressed regionally, if not globally, for any change in strategy to have an effect.

Other Expert Analyses

Not all view the Calderón administration's stance toward California's Proposition 19 as part of a coherent whole. For some scholars of Mexico interviewed in the course of research, the administration's policies on legalization can be characterized as either avoiding deeper issues of governance or being "knee-jerk" responses to perceived U.S. hypocrisy on the "drug war" (Cope 2012, Corcoran 2012).

Colonel (Ret.) John Cope, Fellow at the National Defense University's Institute for National Strategic Studies and head of Western Hemispheric Affairs, holds a counter viewpoint. For him, like Calderón administration advisor Joaquin Villalobos, the legalization debate is a means by which to avoid deep problems of governance in Latin America.

> I think the way Joaquin [Villalobos] sees the drug fight as a symptom of a larger set of problems is correct, but only Uribe [president of Colombia early 2000's] has been willing to face the broader challenge. Calderón and his Central American counterparts are not willing to face reality. The whole legalization initiative is an attempt to find an easy out of a problem that has no easy solution (Cope 2012).

For Cope, like Villalobos, the issue for Latin-American countries, Mexico in particular, posed by drug-trafficking organizations is one of state capacity and governance that will require complex reforms, resources, and political will that many of these countries do not currently possess. Thus, legalization has become a convenient avoidance strategy.

Patrick Corcoran, *Insight Crime* and *Este Pais* contributor, views Calderón's vehement rejection of California's Proposition 19 as a "knee-jerk" policy that seemed inconsistent with the administration's efforts fight drug trafficking organizations (Corcoran 2012).

I really don't think his reaction to Prop. 19 was guided by a logical, thorough consideration of the issue by Calderón as policy-maker; it seemed much more knee jerk to me. I think there's a pretty good case to be made that interrupting the flow of money to the marijuana exporters could have a significant impact on the stability of the Mexican drug trade and should be opposed for that reason, but he never made that argument. With regard to his past efforts, the only real difference was that the 2009 decrim[inalization] in Mexico applied only to very small amounts, but philosophically Prop. 19 and Calderón's decriminalization seem to be well aligned.

Later, as he warmed to the issue a bit, he has talked about the need to consider legalization in an international context, so that is probably an element in his frustration. But that was something he started to emphasize a bit later, I believe. Regardless, the criticism applies probably more to Mexico's decriminalization that to California's vote, because the United States is such a large market that it can affect the size and structure of the black market through a legalization much more easily than Mexico can. What I mean is that the Mexican decriminalization essentially disappeared into the ether and had no appreciable impact; I doubt that would be the case if the United States were to decriminalize (Corcoran, 2012).

Conclusions

California's Proposition 19 inspired a debate in Mexico on the issue of legalization. The violence resulting from the government's assault on MDTOs and support from former leaders and Mexican intelligentsia contributed to the mainstreaming of the legalization debate. Mexico *had* suffered 28,000 confirmed drug-related homicides (the number as of June 2012 was closer to 60,000) from December 2006 when Calderón began his militarized assault on the country's cartels until the summer of 2010 when the debate on Proposition 19 began in earnest. Yet Calderón had previously supported the decriminalization of small amounts of drugs, a policy ostensibly justified by the need to free resources to fight organized crime. In the context of increased violence, California's Proposition 19 was viewed as potentially increasing demand for marijuana and thus increasing violence in Mexico. His willingness to support *international* legalization discussions stemmed from his free-market economic views and his representation of a drug-transit nation positioned below the largest drug consumption market in the world, the United States of America (Johnson, 2011). While seemingly quixotic, they represented the coherent policies of the leader of a primarily drug-transit nation, bounded by the international drug prohibition regime and a powerful drug-consuming market neighbor controlling significant military aid and an important economic relationship.

As Calderón steps down as president of Mexico at the end of 2012, it will be interesting to see if his views on the legalization of drugs deepen. Will he move toward the views of Fox, joining the chorus of former Mexican and Latin-American leaders on drug legalization? We can only speculate answers to these questions given Calderón's public statements up to now. They appear to suggest that he could prove an important, but controversial, voice among the former Latin-American leaders promoting a fundamental change in drug policy, because he will likely promote nothing short of "international legalization."

The next president of Mexico is likely to continue similar drug policies, given the foreign-policy constraints of U.S. military and economic aid. The "path dependence" of the current international drug-prohibitionist regime is strong and continues to have U.S. support (Peters 1999). Even if a pan–Latin American agreement to alter the international drug-prohibition regime could be achieved, it would likely not have much impact without some matching reforms in the United States.

Proposition 19 forced Calderón to consider legalization. The evolution in his policy that resulted was his willingness to discuss only "international legalization." For the leader of a drug-transit nation, hard-hit by organized crime violence, no half measures could do. This debate has inspired a broader hemispheric debate on a new drug policy that now includes leaders in nations like Mexico, Colombia, and Guatemala, nations that have historically supported U.S. drug policy.

Notes

1. Author's translation provided. (Gonzalez, 2010; "México seguirá lucha contra narcotráfico: Poiré—El Universal—México," 2010)
2. Based upon the author's Lexis-Nexis search of key terms including "Proposition 19" and "Calderón."
3. Translation provided by Google Translate (Ramos Perez, 2010).
4. Path-dependence is a concept borrowed from economics which suggests that present decisions may be constrained by past decisions, especially formative events. Thus, the global drug prohibition may be presently suboptimal for Mexico, but is very costly to leave once entered (Peters 1999).

10

THE "CHRONIC"[1] AND COERCION

Exploring How Legalizing Marijuana Might Get the U.S. Government off the Backs and Throats of African Americans (or, Not)

Christian Davenport

Many African Americans have been there: hanging out at the park, on a stoop in front of a friend's building, or on some corner. Doing nothing in particular, just kind of chilling and hanging out—talking about the latest game, scandal, political development, or scientific discovery. Now, there may or may not be some marijuana/weed/chronic in circulation and/or some alcohol at the time, but that is beside the point—actually. The point is that Blacks well know what would transpire if the police[2] rolled by at that moment. If that happened, everyone at the park, on the stoop, or on the corner would tense up for a few seconds that seem to last a lifetime, wondering what the police were going to do next. Essentially, there are two ways this can go: if the police continue to move on, then the pause button is released and everyone's life goes back to what they were doing. If the police do not move on, however, they bust a U-turn, flash the lights, hit the siren *(whup, whup),* pull up, get out, and slowly walk up with a remark or two; that is when the all-too-familiar scene emerges.

Here, a game of ghetto 21 ensues:[3] "What's in the bag," "do you know what time it is," "what are your names," "do you have a job," "would you mind emptying your pockets," "could I look through your jacket," "is there anything in the coat that I should know about"? It continues (that was only seven questions after all). This game is not like 21 "questions." Rather, it is more like 21 "opportunities": 21 opportunities for the police to feel slighted; 21 opportunities for them to point out exactly who has weapons readily at their disposal, as well as the right to ask anything they please whenever the mood strikes them; 21 opportunities for the police to escalate to a level of antagonism that they deem appropriate; and 21 opportunities for Blacks to demonstrate exactly how compliant they can be.

As an African American from Manhattan (first the upper west and then the lower-east side), the scenario above is one of the major reasons why I became a political scientist and later a sociologist. Upon reading Machiavelli and Hobbes, I knew the police, their ideas, and their behavior all too well as it related to this work. It was all about power, and keeping it. Upon reading Antonio Gramsci, Frantz Fanon, James Scott, and Robin Kelley, it was also familiar and all too clear: it was all about resisting power and trying to obtain it. In the park, on the stoop, and on the corner, the police had most of the power, at least one form of it (the coercive kind), and at the moments at the park, stoop, or corner, Blacks were trying to survive the power attempt and get some power over their lives, and the places associated with it as well.

When approached by the editors of this book about California Proposition 19 (the Regulate, Control, and Tax Cannabis Act of 2010) regarding the effort to legalize marijuana for personal use and gauge its relevance for African Americans, I immediately thought of the scenario above. Specifically, I wondered how would the passage of Prop 19 change things for Blacks, like when they were on the block or any of the other locales noted above, if at all? Would it make things better, worse, or have no impact whatsoever? How would the scenario change after passage (or not), and why? These questions all occurred to me.

My take on these issues is fairly straightforward. I think enough evidence exists that the relationship between the political authorities of the U.S. government and African Americans has been a complex one, as well as one filled with the former's coercive activity being used extensively against the latter—indeed, whole institutions and sections of the U.S. budget have been allocated for such tasks. This situation is not new. From the first moment Blacks were brought to the country, they were subject to significant degrees of identification, monitoring, regulation, constraint, subjugation, and violence. Over time, the methods have changed, but a case can be made that they have literally and figuratively been the "whipping" boys (and girls) for the nation—to observe, to enjoy, and to learn from. Breaking Black bodies and spirits might not be discussed as frequently as other American pastimes or legacies, but looking at the horrors of slavery, Reconstruction, Jim Crow, the Red Summer, antiriot behavior, police brutality, hostile protest policing and counter-movement activity, extremely aggressive policing, and high rates of arrest, detention, conviction, sentencing, death penalty, parole rejections, and hate crimes,[4] it appears that the agents of coercion have had their hands, feet, weapons, and institutions at the backs, as well as throats, of African Americans for quite some time. This all says nothing about the activities of vigilantes and ordinary citizens, who have added yet another layer of discrimination into the scenario.

While this behavior is logical in certain respects (applied in an effort to extract labor and protect the social, economic, and political inequality at the founding of the nation and for much of its history), the historical treatment of American Blacks is somewhat puzzling for it moves against general patterns discussed by important theorists like Michel Foucault (1977), who argue that over the last 50 years, we should not see such displays of state coercion. Indeed, he argued that because of increased political accountability, as well as normative concerns with what was deemed legitimate for political institutions to do against citizens, during the period in question, authorities around the globe should have reduced overt manifestations of violence and removed such activities from (public) sight—leaving the mystery of the unseen prison to establish and maintain socio-political control. This misses an important innovation, however, countries like the United States have created. Rather than hide their efforts at socio-political control and leave something to the imagination of Americans, these political authorities have decided to openly subjugate the Black community and display it like the flag to be covered/popularized/communicated on TV, film, newspapers, and in textbooks. Oprah, Obama, Tiger, Colin, and Michael notwithstanding, the message has been clear: watching the "colored coercion show" that is the excessive coercion of African Americans, U.S. citizens end up knowing what coercive power the government holds and potentially employs through its treatment of the Blacks in its territorial jurisdiction. Acknowledging this, it is not just myself, friends, and depoliticized associates who were targeted, but seemingly most African American males who were hit by armed government officials over the last 20–30 years, as well as those directly interested in social movements, those interested in raising controversial claims against political authorities, and anyone who looked potentially threatening (whatever categorized as such by relevant government agents).

This coercive behavior is largely justified in different ways, but one of the most prevalent recently has been the war against drugs. Here, in an effort to protect the rest of the country from the rampaging Black drug lord and/or user—both of whom are capable of wreaking havoc on regular citizens—the coercive arm of the state has been unleashed, including police, courts, and correctional facilities, and an industry that has distributed images/stories of the problem as well as battlefront via diverse media.

Set within this context, the "legalization" of marijuana (i.e., the systematic allowance of production and sales for the relevant drug under specific regulatory guidelines and taxation) looks as if it could serve as a major force for reducing the use of state coercion against Blacks. With the most legitimate of reasons removed, it is possible that the parks, stoops, and corners would be safe(r) and that African Americans would be less likely to encounter the coercive arm of the U.S. state. Although that is one argument, I will actually maintain that while legalization of marijuana would probably decrease certain elements of state-sponsored coercion against the Black community, without "decriminalization" (the systematic reduction of penalties and the stigma levied upon those who use and/or are associated with the relevant drug) or "depenalization" (where "sale and possession are proscribed, but the prohibition on possession is backed only by such sanctions as fines or mandatory substance abuse treatment, not incarceration"), it would likely not have much of an impact on overall levels of coercive government behavior directed against African Americans. Moreover, it would also likely bring newer agencies of the state into contact with Blacks, which, as with many such interactions, would not be healthy for Blacks—physically, psychologically, politically, economically, or socially. Evidence from the Netherlands regarding marijuana, various European countries concerning diverse drugs, Thailand regarding prostitution, and gambling in the United States tend to support this idea. Legalization moves in the right direction, but it does not go far enough for African Americans.

Below, I discuss the basic parameters of the American drug war and think about how it has influenced African Americans. I then address the issue of how the drug war has intersected with a broader and historically more consistent project of Black subjugation. Within the following section, I consider how legalization might offset these dynamics, but then I address what legalization will not be able to accomplish as it relates to improving the African American condition. Finally, I conclude with how far we probably need to go before we would see some substantive change.

The War against the Chronic (or, the Chronic War)

The objectives of the latest U.S. war on drugs might seem pretty obvious: destroy the creation and distribution of drugs, and reduce the use of relevant substances in the country as well as the violence associated with it.[5] There are, however, numerous means that one could use to these ends, and the path selected in the United States is important for our topic of discussion of decreased Black victimization from state-sponsored coercive behavior. With some minor variation, the U.S. model has followed a simple formula: approaches advocating law enforcement (i.e., transit and source-country interdiction/seizures, crop eradication, and enforcement—mandatory sentencing and increased prisons) generally trump treatment, education, and prevention (quite frequently combined).[6]

While there are different arguments put forward for this approach, one of the more logical ones is articulated in a RAND report concerning a different drug (cocaine) by Peter Rydell and Susan Everingham (1994) in a report entitled "Controlling Cocaine." As they state, drawing on economic theory:

> The direct result of supply reduction programs (like interdiction, etc.) is to increase the price of cocaine. The indirect result and ultimate purpose is to reduce cocaine consumption through current users reducing their consumption in response to the price increase and the number of future users decreasing as inflows of new users decrease and outflows of existing users increase in response to the price increase (Rydell and Everingham 1994, 61).

How is this achieved?

Supply reduction causes the price of cocaine to increase in three different ways. When production expands to replace seizure losses, the sales price goes up to cover the replacement cost of the seizures. Additional price increases occur to cover the costs of financial sanctions imposed on producers (seized assets and arrests and imprisonment of drug dealers or their agents). Finally, cocaine producers do not passively accept product seizures and financial sanctions. They actively take precautions to avoid the supply-control penalties to the extent possible. These precautions increase the processing costs at each production stage (Rydell and Everingham 1994, 61–62).

The logic here suggests that the approach would only be successful if the United States could somehow impose enough damage on the drug trade to impact the cost. By interfering with the drug business, the price of doing business would be adjusted and the increased price would be passed on to the customer. With the increased cost, users would eventually stop seeking the production. This is how it is supposed to work.

According to some research (Lusane 1991, 36), the specific war on marijuana largely began after World War I with prohibitions being established in Washington D.C. (1906), Wyoming (1915), Texas (1919), and several other states. Following these earlier efforts, the Federal Bureau of Narcotics was created in 1930 under the directorship of Harry Anslinger—who, like Hoover at the FBI, stayed in power for several decades. In 1937, the United States adopted the Marijuana Tax Act, making possession, transfer, or sale outside of a medical context illegal throughout the country. In medical contexts, severe taxes were applied.[7] After this time, a few notable highlights represent significant changes. For example, in 1952 and 1956, the Boggs and Narcotics Control Acts were passed (respectively), which made first-time marijuana possession automatically punishable with 2–10 years. In the waxing and waning of the law, this was repealed in 1970 (in The Comprehensive Drug Abuse Prevention and Control Act), but the creation of "three strikes" laws through the Sentencing Reform Act of 1984 and the Anti-Drug Abuse Act of 1986 once again made things worse. It should be noted that while decriminalization (punishment of those holding/using) has experienced some variation, legalization efforts (i.e., allowance of production and sale) have been relatively untried, except with regard to medical exemptions and a few isolated efforts.

As for what has been done in the name of the war on drugs, the picture is fairly clear. Billions of dollars have been spent and are being spent on trying to destroy crops at the source and intercept drug traffickers en route to the United States. The amounts destroyed and intercepted are sizeable, but they appear to pale in comparison to the amount being produced and eventually finding its way into the United States. The linkage between the two is very important. As David Passage, U.S. ambassador to Colombia, stated in 2000:

> The test of the effectiveness of our effort to stamp out the production and trans-shipment of illegal narcotics to the United States is not how many hectares on the back side of the Andes have been burned, how many acres of coca or opium poppies have been sprayed, how many labs have been smashed, 55-gallon barrels of precursor chemicals poured into the headwaters of the Orincoco and Amazon, drug kingpins arrested, cartels broken up,

small drug-carrying aircraft forced or shot down, or "mules" arrested at U.S. ports of entry (Peavie 2001, 38).

At one point, such information was provided to Americans almost daily. Rather, he continued:

The only valid test of the effectiveness of our effort is its impact on street-corner availability of drugs within a 5-block radius of the average American middle school (Peavie 2001, 38).

By this measure, efforts have proven ineffective and, indeed, suggest that the problem may never be resolved.

While the activity concerning other countries is quite newsworthy and worth mentioning, the more frequently discussed activity and one most of interest to the current study concerns arrests in the United States—especially those concerning African Americans. By almost any indicator, the situation is horrible. According to Pamela Oliver (2008, 2–3), who undertook an extensive evaluation of patterns from 1925 to 2000:

(t)he Black/White racial disparity on top of the already-high rate for the majority population in the United States gives African Americans an incarceration rate that is without parallel anywhere in the world. The Bureau of Justice Statistics estimates that 12% of Black men in their twenties are incarcerated (9% in prison and 3% in jail) and that 40% of all Black men are under the supervision of the correctional system: in prison, in jail, or being supervised while on probation or parole. Petit and Western (2004) estimate that 60% of Black men, age 30–34 who are not high school graduates, have been incarcerated.

Criminologists documented and monitored this rise in arrest and incarceration of Black people as it happened, showing that it was largely due to an increased level of punitiveness in responding to crime, not to rising crime rates. Crime rates in the late 1960s and early 1970s were high, but incarceration continued to climb, even when crime went down in the early 1980s and the 1990s. One study in 1999 showed that only 12 percent of the rise in incarceration between 1980 and 1996 was due to changes in crime rates, while changes in sentencing policies accounted for 88 percent (Blumstein and Beck 1999). That is, for a given crime, people were much more likely to be sentenced to prison, and to be sentenced for a longer time. The rising Black/White disparity in incarceration was due primarily to the drug war and especially the intense policing of Black communities after 1986 around the "crack epidemic." The racial disparity in incarceration for ordinary crime remained relatively constant—that is, rate of increase was similar for both races—while the racial disparity for drug offenses rose steeply (Mauer and Huling 1995), reaching 20 to 1 by the mid-1990s.

She continues:

> Black people are subject to extraordinarily high rates of surveillance and
> arrest. For (her) state of Wisconsin, using data supplied by the state's Office
> of Justice Assistance, (Oliver) calculated an average annual arrest rate for
> Blacks for 1997–1999 of 41.7 per 100, while the comparable rate for Whites
> (including Hispanics) in Wisconsin was 6.0 per 100. A majority of these
> arrests are for low-level (drug) offenses, as is true in other jurisdictions
> (Miller 1996). Virtually all young Black men in segregated poor Black urban
> neighborhoods have been stopped and questioned by the police, and most
> have been arrested. In short, the United States is one of the most repressive
> countries on earth. Our Black population is living under a level of surveil-
> lance that can only be characterized as a police state (Oliver 2008, 2–3).

Other such evaluations exist.[8] For example, a legal article by Richard Banks
(2003, 595–596) states that:

> A recent study by the Bureau of Justice Statistics found that in 2001 nearly
> seventeen percent of black men were currently or previously imprisoned.
> Black men are more than five times as likely as white men to enter prison.
> Black women are six times as likely as white women to enter prison, and
> nearly as likely as white men to do so. These disparities have grown dramati-
> cally in recent years. While a variety of factors account for these develop-
> ments, the importance of the drug war is beyond dispute. From 1990 to
> 2000, drug offenders accounted for a greater proportion of prison popula-
> tion growth among black inmates than among any other racial group.

The outcome of all this effort has been the creation of a terrorized, as well as
depleted, community in terms of lost rights that have been overrun, lost people
who have (again) been extracted from their families and friends, lost opportunity
from coming in contact with or being incarcerated, as well as the often legal
stigma of those who have served time and lost hope from having had to deal with
such a problem for so long with seemingly no improvement.

Now, I do not mean to suggest that there has not been some push back to
these efforts from diverse levels. Within communities affected by these various
state policies, there has long been discussion/criticism and some efforts to get the
government to take a less heavy-handed approach. This said, communities have
frequently been divided on this issue, and thus the resistance to relevant efforts
(coming from the most important political actors in the country) has not been
effectively countered. There have been some legal and political efforts as well.
For example, a few states have attempted to reduce the high level of punitiveness
directed against drug offenses in opposition to federal law (e.g., Hawaii, California,
and Oregon), but these efforts have either been defeated (as in the case of Prop 19)
or they have resulted in lawsuits as the federal government has attempted to (re)

assert its right to override state initiatives (e.g., *Gonzales v. Raich* 2005). For the most part, life in the Black communities of America has been not only "nasty, brutish and short" but dissected, degraded, deprived, and decimated.

What I am suggesting here is a different type of evaluation than is usually considered when individuals speak of alternative drug regimes (i.e., legalization, decriminalization, and depenalization), which normally concerns issues like the amount of drug use that would likely follow from the adoption of one over the other. Rather than consider drug use or the price of drugs, I wish to consider what impact legalization like Prop 19 would have on African Americans and their persecution at the hands of U.S. coercive agents (briefly described above). In short, I wish to explore how changing drug regimes could remove the boot, nightstick, gun and prison cell from the face, neck back and lives of American Blacks.

To understand the impact of the drug war on the Black community, one would first have to reconstruct Black life and consider the diverse points of possible intersection. As with other Americans, Blacks work, go to school, search for work, socialize, eat, play sports, catch a show/game, and so forth. On the way to or from any of these activities, African Americans could be observed, stopped, questioned, harassed, arrested, or shot as authorities attempt to identify, monitor, constrain, or remove individuals they believe to be taking part in the drug trade. Even those staying at home are not immune from such activities. Consequently, Blacks provide authorities with a lifetime of opportunity to intersect with the war on drugs—an opportunity that authorities appear to employ broadly across the African American community as one considers the practices known as "driving while Black," "walking while Black," "sentencing while Black," "protesting while Black," and so on. Indeed, it is interesting that what people used to just call racism has been broken into various subcomponents that individuals examine separately under the stricter rules of evidence put forward by a society that collectively believes it has done away with such evil. Nevertheless, the practices persist, and it is in this context that one needs to evaluate legalization. For the African American community is subject to the extensive engagement with political authorities because they are believed to be the most at risk to use, the most likely to engage in violence in support of such activity, and the most logical target of any antidrug effort. The evidence for these beliefs is highly contested, but most analyses identify that the focus on African Americans lies disproportionate to their actual participation. This makes change highly unlikely since the practices are not based on reality, but rather on racist beliefs, practices, and institutions.

Legalization

Since the drug war is failing, as it's commonly asserted (i.e., drug use and violence is not diminished but increased), numerous attempts have been made to resolve the situation. The legalization of drugs, with initiatives like Prop 19, is one of the most frequently advocated alternatives. On the surface, the idea of legalization has much appeal. If drugs were legalized, then the whole noxious network of drug traffickers, smugglers, and money launderers stretching from the jungles of South America to the streets of American cities would suddenly disappear. This is the idea at least. If this were to happen, prices would go down, competition would be diminished, and with it, the corresponding violence would diminish, too. Drug agents would no longer barge unannounced into apartments, teenagers would no longer be busted for smoking pot, and motorists would no longer be stopped on the New Jersey Turnpike (a frequent stopping point). These reductions would be relevant for the population generally but especially for African Americans. These are just the immediate effects. Over time, shows like *Cops* would be diminished in their characterization of current expectations/presentations of Black drug dealers, and representations of the troubled Black dealers would be diminished on news programs, as well as in films. Never again would Denzel Washington (the premier African American actor) have to play and receive accolades for dealing to Blacks.

Yet, as with all things, legalization entails some real risks. If hard drugs like heroin or crack were suddenly sold in state stores or made available through prescriptions, use—and abuse—could increase. The end of alcohol prohibition, for instance, resulted in a sharp rise in alcohol consumption, along with many unfortunate side effects. And, while no one wants to revive that disastrous experiment, it does suggest that the sudden legalization of an intoxicant can lead to an increase in consumption. This prospect makes many Americans recoil from the idea of legalizing drugs—or at least hard ones. I believe a far more convincing case can be made for legalizing, or at least decriminalizing, marijuana, a much less toxic substance; but as long as legalization is seen as the main alternative to the drug war, the movement toward reform will stall.[9]

How would legalization influence the dynamics identified above? Well, the identification of creators, distributors, and users of the drugs, as well as the violence associated with these activities, would shift. Creation and/or distribution would be state run, and users would be less of interest except for identifying minors. Turf wars would be diminished because turf, as such, would cease to exist—holdovers would be dealt with violently but the safety and civility of a CVS-like delivery system would make the street dealer disappear. You can't get a soda, toothpaste, some chocolate, and some weed with your local street dealer. Given the reduced violence that would accompany a regulated industry, organizational priorities and training of the U.S. government would give way from military and undercover operations to something more akin to a regulatory agency. The result of this would be reduced monitoring and disruption of Black life by at least the most coercive elements of the U.S. government. Now, given the pressure of other crimes in the Black community, I do not expect all coercive agents to disappear, but many operations and agencies might be reduced in number if not priority, and the state of siege currently existing within African American communities might be reduced. At least, this should be the case over time.

I would expect new organizations to come into existence to handle the creation and enforcement of news rules, which will pay disproportionate attention to African Americans involved with, or potentially involved with, marijuana. For example, I expect licensing boards to be less likely to certify and be more likely to close facilities in Black communities, as well as more likely to let poorer quality drugs to be found there. One would expect greater numbers of banks and insurance investigators to raise hurdles/questions with Black proprietors and those serving this community. American racism does not go away—it evolves.

This brief thought experiment could be extended to reflect on how a Netherlands-like marijuana drug regime would be applied in the U.S. context. As stated in a recent review:

> (b)etween 1976 and 1986, a set of guidelines emerged stipulating that coffee shop owners (in the Netherlands) could avoid prosecution by complying with five rules: a) no advertising; b) no hard drug sales on the premises; c) no sales to minors; d) no sales transactions exceeding the quantity threshold; and e) no public disturbances (MacCoun and Reuter 2001, 123).

If the United States were to follow a similar policy, one would expect diverse institutions to emerge addressing each element, or some combination of elements. Consequently, one or several organizations would monitor, investigate, and prosecute violators of advertising, hard-drug sales, sales to minors, threshold limitations, and disturbances. The last would be the most obvious problem for African Americans with regard to state coercion since this community likely would be associated with the most disturbances or the most violent ones, continuing a perception of Black criminality and violence. This could lead to greater investigation and/or preparation for such activities in this community. The other areas of concern could involve coercive action in the form of raids and undercover operations where force could be used; but, given the legal nature of the enterprise, I believe the overall levels of coercion would be frowned upon—if not initially, then over time.

A related problem could emerge with the anticipated increased use of marijuana within the Black community and the likely psychological as well as institutional aftereffects of such use. For example, extensive marijuana use is associated with a distorted sense of time and short-term memory loss, which could result in increased monitoring of/punishment for truancy issues. These problems could exacerbate already existing problems with achievement in school, leading to tracking and/or remedial efforts in educational facilities. Also among common aftereffects are anxiety, paranoia, and depression. Given the issue of Blacks being more likely evaluated negatively in psychological evaluations and the already discussed hostile interactions with authorities who frequently judge African American behavior/demeanor as antisocial or hostile, these will only exacerbate existing tensions. This could potentially shift criminal policing from drugs to an increase in summary offenses such as drunkenness or disorderliness. These would be especially problematic because they involve high levels of discretionary power from officers on the street. Pernicious effects are likely to exist with regard to advertising as well, which although not coercive could negatively influence African Americans. For example, it would be expected that legalization would increased efforts to commercialize the sales. Historically, this involves targeting Blacks, with them receiving the most potent as well as questionable-quality products.

Drug "Wars" and Breaking Blacks: On Disciplining and Punishing

Acknowledging what he believed to be a widely emerging trend at the time, Foucault (1977) argued that modern nation-states in general and democratic states in particular would reduce the amount of coercion used against citizens and they would move such activities away from public view. There were two reasons for this: (1) to decrease public outrage that had begun to emerge as state-sponsored violence around the world was beginning to be viewed as unjust and immoral; and, (2) political authorities preferred to wield their coercive behavior against the minds and imaginations of their subjects as opposed to directly targeting their bodies. Beyond Foucault, various theorists have also argued that modern governments in general and democracies in particular would diminish the use of coercion against those within their territorial jurisdiction, but for different reasons. Under the label of democratic or liberal peace theory (Davenport 2007), there was a widespread turn against overt manifestations of coercion because they tended to delegitimize the political authorities involved. It was also noted that democracies decreased coercion because they had alternative mechanisms of control (i.e., normative and material power), they established mechanisms for "channeling" political opposition into institutions that could be regulated/controlled, and they feared the electoral backlash that could be levied against them if coercive behavior was not deemed acceptable.

Governments could adopt a different path, however, and the United States appears ready to embrace it wholeheartedly. Specifically, political authorities could identify a part of the population that was the least connected, the most politically vulnerable, numerically small but not negligible, and subject these people to the full repertoire of state coercive behavior. This would be communicated to the rest of the population in a wide variety of ways—employing all of the tools of modern communication (e.g., radio, TV, newspapers, advertising, and the Internet). Through these government "performances," the rest of the population would learn what the state was capable of, but without directly feeling that such activity was directed against them—at least not in a straightforward manner. Here, the imagination is invoked, as Foucault suggested, because every citizen would come to view the targeted subject as somehow representative of them, but with enough critical distance and otherness that widespread sympathy would not be aroused. The behavior itself, however, would be far more public than Foucault suggested. Little would be left of the imagination.

Authorities engaged in such activity would have to maintain an important balancing act. The behavior enacted against the targeted population could not appear to be disproportionate or vicious. This would not be viewed positively and could lead to backlash. Somehow, the target would need to be viewed as transgressing some boundary of the acceptable, and in this light, state coercion would be seen as legitimate as well as perhaps required. If the government uses coercion where it seems it is necessary to do so, it would be providing a service.

I argue that African Americans have served as the target of state-repressive violence and that, in certain respects, the coercion of Black people has facilitated the socio-political order—the polity and order itself being created as well as sustained with every whip of the lash, every attempted lynching, every arrest, every defeated protest, every assassination of a Black leader. These events would not be hidden from popular consumption and, in fact, they have not been. Instead, they would be served up in newspaper articles, trading cards, TV reports, popular films, and even government investigations. Indeed, think for a second of all the representations you have seen regarding some aspect of state power being used against African Americans: the execution of the Black prisoner in the film *The Green Mile,* the removal of Kunta Kinte's foot in the *Roots* miniseries, the often-viewed beating of Rodney King, the legal investigations of Michael Jackson and Michael Jordan, the arrest of Wesley Snipes, the random Black male on *Cops,* or the search for some African American on a local TV news program.

Clearly, there is some variation here. Southern attacks on Blacks during the civil rights movement provoked northern Whites to feel some sympathy and even on occasion attempt to intervene. This point is known and widely discussed, but what is not discussed is that the response to the Black claims-makers was largely accepted as normal within the society where it took place: White Southerners tolerated the abuse of Black Southerners for decades. The problem with such behavior was seemingly less an issue of how Blacks should be treated but rather that northern intrusion into southern lives was likely to become a reality again if things didn't calm down. Going back into the Jim Crow period, anti-Black activity was widely accepted. In large part, this is because the behavior was believed to be a legitimate response to perceived illegitimate challenges from Blacks to improve their situation.

Post-civil rights, with increased aggressiveness on behalf of Blacks, with the Black power movement as well as newly perceived illegitimacy, increased coercive behavior against African Americans was once again viewed as legitimate. Indeed, a concerted effort was put into making sure that young Black males in particular were not able to wreak the havoc that they had during the period of the riots. To avoid appearing unprovoked and illegitimate, the drug war was declared. This brought African Americans into contact with not just police officers, court officials, and prison guards but also welfare agents, social workers, and a large cadre of other government officials who assisted in the identification, monitoring, regulation, and even elimination of Blacks. All of this took place under the watchful gaze of a transfixed nation that appeared to not be able to get enough; indeed, in the words of the film *Gladiator*—America was very much amused with the treatment of African Americans.

How does one get to such a level of investigation, monitoring, harassment, punitiveness, incarceration, and violence? I would say that this is done through a twofold process. First, the African American community has been so thoroughly segregated (Massey and Denton 1987) but at the same time penetrated (Giddens 1987) that it approaches descriptions of the Panapticon.[10] At every turn in the Black community, there is a camera, an informant, a patrolman, a police station, or some agent of the government. In addition to the structure of Black segregation, a network of institutions assures that problematic individuals are consistently identified, as well as dealt with in some manner (e.g., being sent to tracked classrooms, detention centers and/or prison). As Foucault argues (Garland 1990, 151):

> (t)here exists a kind of carceral continuum which covers the whole social body, linked by the pervasive concern to identify deviance, anomalies, and departures from the relevant norms. This framework of surveillance and correction stretches from the least irregularity to the greatest crime and brings the same principles to bear upon each. The idea of the 'continuum' is important here, not just to describe the relations of one institution to another, but also to suggest the similarities that exist between societies.

Unlike Foucault, however, I do not maintain that such treatment is equal across the population within the territorial jurisdiction of the relevant government. Instead, the least connected and most vulnerable are selected.

Second, the nature of the interaction is professionalized but distant as in any developed bureaucratic practice, and the overall level of coerciveness is high across all encounters. At every engagement, African Americans appear to be at the severe end of the continuum. They are normally the ones initially suspected, investigated, accused, stopped, questioned, arrested, sentenced, beaten, and/or shot. They are likely given harsher sentences and harsher treatment when in custody, as well as less likely to be released or incorporated back into society after release.

Notice that unlike discussions of racial profiling, I do not highlight any ethnic animosity at the root of this treatment. In fact, I have not really identified any root at all except that distinct institutions and logics of behavior have emerged which act in the service of the very behavior identified above. This identifies that Blacks are more likely stopped by police without having to establish that every police officer is racist, without intent having embodied in agents, and left only with behavior, vague/professionalized ideology, and institutions. This makes the situation that much harder to identify, as well as that much harder to change. At the same time, this does not make the reality in American parks, stoops, corners, cars, prisons, detention centers, barbershops, and schools any less real.

Chronic Conclusions

I undertook this research in an attempt to understand whether the legalization of marijuana would be better or worse for African Americans with specific interest in how governments used diverse coercive activities against this population. Considering the discussion above, I am skeptical about what legalization would do other than adding a few more institutions into the colored coercion show (i.e., the excessively well-covered monitoring, arrest, incarceration, and abuse of Blacks). While legalization would begin to weaken the highly stigmatized Black community by associating it with a then legal substance, if such an effort were not associated with decriminalization, however (removing the stigma associated with the use of marijuana), then I fear that the change would not be significant enough. From this vantage point, the key to Black freedom and equality is to have Blacks interact less with political authorities, change how the culture views African Americans in general, and understand exactly what has been done against them—individually and collectively. Legislation takes us part of the way but not far enough. It's like offering up a mule but holding back the 40 acres.

This issue is not simply one of justice for African Americans, but it is one of political legitimacy itself. As Ralph Bunche argued years ago:

> If democracy is survive the severe trials and buffetings to which it is being subjected in the modern world, it will do so only because it can demonstrate that it is a practical, living philosophy under which all people can live the good life most abundantly. It must prove itself in practice, or be discredited as a theory. Democratic nations such as our own have an obligation to all mankind to prove that democracy, as a form of government, as a practical means of human relationships, is a working and workable concept. This America can do only by abandoning the shallow, vulgar pretense of limited democracy—under which some are free and privileged and others are permanently fettered. The Negro, and especially the Negro in the South, already has had too vivid an experience with embryonic fascism in the very shadow of democracy. Within our own gates are found intense racial hatreds, racial ghettoes, and racial differentials that saturate the political, economic and social life of the nation (Bunche 1973, 106).

He continues that Blacks have a right to be skeptical but should not give up completely. As he states:

> Negroes are all too familiar with the many and serious shortcomings of American Democracy; but they know, through they do not always recall,

that democracy as a concept, as a way of life, had afforded them the sole basis for whatever progress they have made as a group since slavery, for the heroic struggle they have incessantly waged, for their aspirations in the future. Democracy, even imperfect democracy, has been the ideological foundation upon which Negro life has been based; it has been the spiritual lifeblood for Negroes. As an ideal, it has not progressed very rapidly in the world we know. But what else has the world to offer the Negro? (Bunche 1973, 110).

In this context, U.S. political democracy is to be judged by its treatment of African Americans. Here, until the lash is put away, the prison doors open, and the bodies and minds healed through discussion, investment, truth telling, and (where deemed necessary) compensation, there is no American democracy. Proposition 19 is not just about marijuana, therefore; it's about who the United States would like to be; either the country has its foundations and continuation in the areas of democracy and human rights, or it has its foundations and continuation in the areas of racism and its legacy.

Notes

1. This is a slang term for high-grade marijuana popularized by Dr. Dre in his first solo album by the same name after he left NWA (Niggaz Wit Attitude).
2. See: http://en.wikipedia.org/wiki/List_of_slang_terms_for_police_officers.
3. This is not blackjack, mind you, although one might be involved.
4. Research finds that these are essentially antiblack activities, with African American targets being the majority of relevant events.
5. It is fairly well known that there have been numerous "cycles" of drug wars: e.g., Lawrence Friedman, David Musto, and Michael Tomry [drug wars in black and white].
6. Eva Bertram et al. (1996) makes this argument in Drug War Politics.
7. See: http://www.druglibrary.org/schaffer/hemp/taxact/mjtaxact.htm.
8. For an interesting study of marijuana-relevant arrests in New York City, see Geller and Fagen (2010).
9. See: http://www.salon.com/health/feature/2000/02/22/massing.
10. See: http://en.wikipedia.org/wiki/Panopticon.

REFERENCES

An act to amend Section 11357 of the Health and Safety Code, and to amend Section 23222 of the Vehicle Code, relating to controlled substances, SB 1449. 2010. California State Legislature.

Alexander, Michelle. 2010. *The New Jim Crow: Mass Incarceration in the Age of Colorblindness.* New York: The New Press.

Alonso, M. B. 2011. *Cannabis Social Clubs in Spain: A Normalizing Alternative Underway.* Series on Legislative Reform of Drug Policies, No. 9. Transnational Institute, Amsterdam.

Alvarez, R.M. 1997. *Information and Elections.* Ann Arbor: University of Michigan Press.

Alvarez, R.M. and John Brehm. 2002. *Hard Choices, Easy Answers: Values, Information, and Public Opinion.* Princeton, NJ: Princeton University Press.

Amsterdam Tourist Information. 2007. Why Is Amsterdam So Tolerant? http://www.dutchamsterdam.nl, May 4.

Andreas, Peter. 2011. "Illicit Globalization: Myths, Misconceptions, and Historical Lessons." *Political Science Quarterly,* Vol. 126, No. 3, pp. 403–425.

Archibold, R. C. 2010. "Prop. 19 California vote watched closely in Mexico." *SFGate,* October 20. Retrieved December 19, 2011, from http://articles.sfgate.com/2010–10–20/news/24143327_1_legalization-drug-consumption-drug-war

Astorga, L. 1997. "Los corridos de traficantes de drogas en México y Colombia. *Revista Mexicana de Sociología,"* Vol. 59, No. 4, pp. 245–261.

Austin, Roy and Mark Allen. 2000. "Racial Disparity in Commitment to Pennsylvania Prisons." *Journal of Research and Crime Delinquency,* Vol. 37, pp. 200–220.

Australian Institute of Health and Welfare 2008. 2007 National Drug Strategy Household Survey: State and territory supplement (Drug Statistics Series, Number 21), August. Canberra. www.aihw.gov.au/publications/phe/ndshs07-sats/ndshs07-sats.pdf

Banks, Richard. 2003. "Beyond Profiling: Race, Policing and the Drug War." *Stanford Law Review* 56: 571–603.

Barclay, C. V. 2009. Wikileaks—Cable Viewer—Viewing cable 09Mexico193, The Battle Joined: NARCO Violence Trends in 2008, January 23. Retrieved December 13, 2010, from http://213.251.145.96/cable/2009/01/09MEXICO193.html

Baum, Dan. 1996. *Smoke and Mirrors: The War on Drugs and the Politics of Failure.* New York: Back Bay Books.

Bearman, David. 2010. "Yes on Prop 19: a 'Yes'Vote is Clear, Particularly for Groups Being Marginalized by Current Policy." *Latino Politics Blog,* October 20. (http://latinopolitic-sblog.com/2010/10/20/yes-on-prop-19-a-yes-vote-is-clear-particularly-for-groups-being-marginalized-by-current-policy/, accessed 05/07/11).

Beatty, P., Petteruti, A. and Ziedenberg, J. 2007. "The Vortex: The Concentrated Racial Impact of Drug Imprisonment and the Characteristics of Punitive Counties." *Justice Policy Institute.*

Bell, Derrick. 2004. Silent Covenants: *Brown v. Board of Education* and the Unfulfilled Hopes for Racial Reform. New York: Oxford University Press.

Bell, James. 2006. "Correcting the System of Unequal Justice." In *The Covenant,* Tavis Smiley, Ed. Chicago: Third World Press.

Bertram, Eva, Morris Blachman, Kenneth Sharpe, and Peter Andreas. 1996. *Drug War Politics: The Price of Denial.* Berkeley: University of California Press.

Biderman, Albert D. and Albert J. Reiss. 1967. "On Exploring the 'Dark Figure' of Crime," *The Annals of the American Academy of Political and Social Science,* Vol. 374, No. 1 (November), pp. 1–15.

Bieleman, B., A. Beelen, R. Nijkamp, and E. de Bie 2009. *Coffeeshops in Nederland 2007.* Groningen: Intraval.

Bittel, J. S. 2009. "Mexico's Drug-Related Violence." Services, Congressional Research.

Blumstein, Alfred. 1982. "On the Racial Disproportionality of United States' Prison Populations." *Journal of Criminal Law and Criminology,* Vol. 73, No.3 (Fall), pp. 1259–1281.

Blumstein, Alfred. 1993. "Racial Disproportionality of U. S. Prison Populations Revisited." *University of Colorado Law Review,* Vol. 64, pp. 743–760.

Blumstein, Alfred and Allen J. Beck. 1999. "Population Growth in U. S. Prisons, 1980–1996." *In Crime and Justice: A Review of the Research,* M. Tonry and J. Petersilia, Eds., Vol. 26 (Prisons), pp. 17–61. Chicago, IL: University of Chicago Press.

Bonilla-Silva, Eduardo. 2006. *Racism without Racists: Color-blind Racism and the Persistence of Racial Inequality in the United States.* Lanham, MD: Rowman & Littlefield Publishers.

Booth, W., & Miroff, N. (n.d.). Racked by Drug Violence, Mexico Wary of Calif. Vote on Legalizing Marijuana." Retrieved September 12, 2010, from http://www.washingtonpost.com/wp-dyn/content/article/2010/09/09/AR2010090906988_pf.html

Booth, William and Nick Miroff. 2010. "Racked by Drug Violence, Mexico Wary of California Vote on Legalizing Marijuana." *Washington Post,* October 19.

Bowden, Mark. 2001. *Killing Pablo: The Hunt for the World's Greatest Outlaw.* New York: Atlantic Monthly Press.

Bowler, Shaun and Donovan, Todd. 1998. *Demanding Choices: Opinion, Voting, and Direct Democracy.* Ann Arbor: University of Michigan Press.

Brewer, Paul R. 2003. "The Shifting Foundations of Public Opinion about Gay Rights." *Journal of Politics,* Vol. 65, No. 4, pp. 1208–1220.

Brook, J. S., Brook, D. W., Arencibia-Mireles O., Richter, L., Whiteman, M. 2001. "Risk Factors for Adolescent Marijuana Use Across Cultures and Across Time." *The Journal of Genetic Psychology: Research and Theory on Human Development,* Vol. 162, No. 3, pp. 357–374.

Brown, Michael K., Martin Carnroy, Elliott Currie, Troy Duster, David Oppenheimer, Marjorie Shultz, and David Wellman. 2003. *Whitewashing Race: The Myth of a Color-Blind Society.* Berkley, CA: The University of California Press.

Buckley, William F. 2004. "Free Weeds: The Marijuana Debate." *National Review* June 29.

Bunche, Ralph. 1973. *The Political Status of the Negro in the Age of FDR.* Chicago: University of Chicago Press.

Bureau of Justice Statistics. 2007. Sourcebook of Criminal Justice Statistics Online. Table 4.38.2007. Retrieved December 24, 2011, from http://www.albany.edu/sourcebook/pdf/t4382007.pdf

Bureau of Justice Statistics. 2010. State Court Processing Statistics (SCPS). Washington, D.C.: U.S. Department of Justice, Office of Justice Programs, Bureau of Justice Statistics.

Bureau of Justice Statistics. 2011. Jail Inmates at Midyear 2010—Statistical Tables. Washington, D.C.: U.S. Department of Justice, Office of Justice Programs, Bureau of Justice Statistics.

Bureau of Labor Statistics. 2010. CPI inflation Calculator Retrieved December 23, 2011, from http://www.bls.gov/data/inflation_calculator.htm

Butler, Paul. 2009. *Let's Get Free: A Hip Hop Theory of Justice.* New York: The New Press.

California Attorney General. 2010. California Criminal Justice Profile, 2009. Retrieved December 23, 2011, from http://stats.doj.ca.gov/cjsc_stats/prof09/

California Department of Corrections and Rehabilitation. 2007. Report to the California State Legislature: A roadmap for effective offender programming in California. Sacramento, CA: California Department of Corrections and Rehabilitation, Expert Panel on Adult Offender Reentry and Recidivism Reduction Programs.

California Department of Corrections and Rehabilitation. 2009. Daily jail rate manual for reimbursements under Section 4016.5 of the Penal Code and Section 1776 of the Welfare and Institutions Code. Sacramento, CA: California Department of Corrections and Rehabilitation, Division of Adult Parole Operations.

California Department of Corrections and Rehabilitation. 2010. "California Prisoners & Parolees, 2009." Sacramento, CA: California Department of Corrections and Rehabilitation, Offender Information Services Branch, Estimates and Statistical Analysis Section, Data Analysis Unit.

California Department of Corrections and Rehabilitation. 2011a. "Prison Census Data as of December 31, 2010." Sacramento, CA: California Department of Corrections and Rehabilitation, Offender Information Service Branch, Estimates and Statistical Analysis Section, Data Analysis Unit.

California Department of Corrections and Rehabilitation. 2011b. "Second and Third Striker Felons in the Adult Institution Population." Sacramento, CA: California Department of Corrections and Rehabilitation, Offender Information Service Branch, Estimates and Statistical Analysis Section, Data Analysis Unit.

California Department of Justice. 2005. Asset forfeiture: Annual report 2004. Sacramento, CA: California Department of Justice, Division of Law Enforcement, Bureau of Narcotic Enforcement.

California Legislative Analyst's Office. 2009a. Achieving better outcomes for adult probation. Sacramento, CA: California State Legislature, Legislative Analyst's Office.

California Legislative Analyst's Office. 2009b. Fiscal impact of legalizing marijuana. Sacramento, CA: California State Legislature, Legislative Analyst's Office.

California Legislative Analyst's Office. 2010. Proposition 19: Changes California law to legalize marijuana and allow it to be regulated and taxed. Initiative statute. Sacramento, CA: California State Legislature, Legislative Analyst's Office.

Calvert, Kyla. 2010. "Would Legalizing Marijuana Cut Law Enforcement Costs?" *KPBS San Diego Public Broadcasting,* October 8. Retrieved December 23, 2011, from http://www.kpbs.org/news/2010/oct/08/will-prop-19-cut-law-enforcement-costs/

Carey, S. M., Crumpton, D., Finigan, M. W., & Waller, M. 2005. "California Drug Courts: A Methodology for Determining Costs and Benefits. Phase II: Testing the Methodology Final Report." Portland, OR: NPC Research.

Carey, S. M., and M. Waller. 2008. "California Drug Courts: Costs and Benefits. Phase III: DC-CSET statewide launch, Superior Court of Sacramento County, Sacramento Drug Court site-specific report." Portland, OR: NPC Research.

Carroll, R. 2010. "US Has Lost Faith in Mexico's Ability to Win Drug War." *The Guardian,* December 2. Retrieved December 3, 2010, from http://www.guardian.co.uk/world/2010/dec/02/us-mexico-drugs-war-wikileaks

Carsey, Thomas M. and Geoffrey C. Layman. 2010. "Party Identification, Party Polarization, and 'Conflict Extension' in the American Electorate." In *Understanding Public Opinion,* 3d, Barbara Norrander and Clyde Wilcox, Eds. Washington, D.C.: CQ Press.

Castañeda, J. G. and H. Aguilar Camin. 2010. "California's Prop 19, on Legalizing Marijuana, Could End Mexico's Drug War." *Washington Post,* May 9. Washington, D.C. Retrieved January 24, 2012, from http://jorgecastaneda.org/index.php?newsId = 575777C2–0486–1A62–903B-E23A4AD8B9A6

Caulkins, J. P., Kilmer, B., MacCoun, R. J., Pacula, R. L. & Reuter, P. 2012. "Design Considerations for Legalizing Cannabis." *Addiction,* Vol. 107, No. 1, pp. 61–78.

CBS News. 2012. "Obama: Drug legalization not the answer to cartels," April 14. Retrieved June 25, 2012, from http://www.cbsnews.com/8301–250_162–57414151/obama-drug-legalization-not-the-answer-to-cartels/

Chabat, Jorge. 2002. "Mexico's War on Drugs: No Margin for Maneuver." *The Annals of the American Academy of Political and Social Science,* Vol. 582, No. 1.

Chabat, Jorge. n.d. "Mexico's Drug War—Stories, Photos, Videos—Mexico Under Siege—World News." *Los Angeles Times.* Retrieved January 26, 2012, from http://projects.latimes.com/mexico-drug-war/#/question-and-answers

Chavez, Lydia. 1998. *The Color Bind, California's Battle to End Affirmative Action.* Berkley, CA: University of California Press.

Clayton and Mosher, 2007 [[Chapter 2]].

Christie, P. and R. Ali. 2000. "Offences under the Cannabis Expiation Notice Scheme in South Australia." *Drug and Alcohol Review* Vol. 19, pp. 251–256.

Clear, T. R., D. R. Rose, and J. A. Ryder. 2001. "Incarceration and the Community: The Problem of Removing and Returning Offenders." *Crime and Delinquency,* Vol. 47, pp. 335–351.

Clements, K. W. 2010. *Three Facts about Marijuana Prices.* Unpublished manuscript, University of Western Australia Business School.

CNS News. n.d. "Latin Leaders Question Move to Legalize Marijuana." *CNSnews.com.* Retrieved January 26, 2012, from http://cnsnews.com/news/article/latin-leaders-question-move-legalize-marijuana

Cohen, Cathy J. 2010. *Democracy Remixed: Black Youth and the Future of American Politics.* New York: Oxford University Press.

Coleman, Clive and Jenny Moynihan. 1996. *Understanding Crime Data: Haunted by the Dark Figure.* Maidenhead, Berkshire, UK: Open University Press.

Cook, C., Rush, R. G., & Seelke, C. R. (n.d.). Merida Initiative: Proposed U.S. Anti-crime and Counterdrug Assistance for Mexico and Central America 06.03.08 CRS Report.pdf (application/pdf Object). Retrieved November 29, 2008, from http://www.wilsoncenter.org/news/docs/06.03.08%20CRS%20Report.pdf

Cope, J. 2012. Proposition 19 Email Response to questions, January 17.

Crutchfield, Robert D., George S. Bridges, and Susan R. Pitchford. 1994. "Analytical and Aggregation Biases in Analyses of Imprisonment: Reconciling Discrepancies in Studies of Racial Disparity." *Journal of Research in Crime and Delinquency,* Vol. 31, pp. 166–182.

Danelo, D. 2010. "A New Approach is needed in Anti-crime Fight in Mexico." Retrieved December 21 from http://www.mexidata.info/id2896.html

Danelo, D. 2010. "E-Notes: The Geopolitics of Northern Mexico—FPRI." Retrieved November 15, from http://www.fpri.org/enotes/201011.danelo.mexico.html

Davenport, Christian. 2007. *State Repression and the Domestic Democratic Peace.* New York: Cambridge University Press.

Davidson, Julia O'Connell. 2002. "The Rights and Wrongs of Prostitution." *Hypatia, Inc.,* Vol. 17, No.2, Feminist Philosophies of Love and Work, pp. 84–98.

Davis, Darren W. 1995. "Exploring Black Political Intolerance." *Political Behavior,* Vol. 17, No. 1, pp. 1–22.

Dawson, Michael C. 1994. *Behind the Mule: Race and Class in African American Politics.* Princeton, N.J.: Princeton University Press.

Dehais, Richard J. "Racial Disproportionality in Prisons and Racial Discrimination in the Criminal Justice Process: Assessing the Empirical Evidence." Paper presented at 1983 American Society of Criminologists.

Department of Health and Human Services. 2008. "Initiation of Marijuana Use: Trends, Patterns, and Implications." SAMSHA, Office of Applied Studies, National Survey on Drug Abuse, 1999 and 2000, June 16. http://www.oas.samhsa.gov/MJinitiation/chapter3.htm.

DiChiara, Albert, and John F. Galliher. 1994. "Dissonance and Contradictions in the Origins of Marihuana Decriminalization." *Law and Society Review,* Vol. 28, No. 1, pp. 41–78.

Di Forti, M., et al. 2009. "High Potency Cannabis and the Risk of Psychosis." *The British Journal of Psychiatry,* Vol. 195, pp. 488–491.

Dilulio, John. 1995. "The Coming Superpredators," *The Weekly Standard,* Vol. 1, No. 11 (November 27), p. 23.

Dilulio, John. 1996. "Lock 'em Up or Else Huge Wave of Criminally Inclined Coming in Next 10 Years." *The Ledger,* March 23, p. A11.

Donnelly, Neil, Wayne Hall, and P. Christie. 1998. *Effects of the Cannabis Expiation Notice scheme on levels and patterns of cannabis use in South Australia: Evidence from the National Drug Strategy Household Surveys 1985–1995.* Canberra: Commonwealth Department of Health and Aged Care, Commonwealth of Australia.

Downs, Anthony. 1957. *An Economic Theory of Democracy.* New York: Harper.

Dwyer, Jim. 2010. "A Smell of Pot and Privilege in the City." *New York Times,* July 21, 2010. http:/www.nytimes.com.

Dwyer, Jim. 2011. "Side Effects of Arrests for Marijuana." *New York Times,* June 17, 2011, p. A26.

Earleywine, Mitch. 2002. *Understanding Marijuana: A New Look at the Scientific Evidence.* New York: Oxford University Press.

Ebenstein, Lanny. 2009. *Milton Friedman: A Biography.* New York: Macmillan.

Economist, The. 2010. "Mexico and Drugs: Thinking the Unthinkable," August 12. Retrieved December 16, 2011, from http://www.economist.com/node/16791730

Economist, The. 2012. "Mexico's Presidential Election: Back to the Future," June 23. Retrieved from http://www.economist.com/node/21557332

Eddy, Mark. 2010. *Medical Marijuana: Review and Analysis of Federal and State Policies.* Washington, D.C.: Congressional Research Service.

El Universal. 2010. "México seguirá lucha contra narcotráfico: Poiré," November 2. Retrieved January 24, 2012, from http://www.eluniversal.com.mx/notas/720620.html

Ellingwood, Ken and Tracy Wilkinson. 2011. "Searchers Comb Ruins of Monterrey Casino Where 52 died in Fire: The day after a Monterrey casino is set afire by three carloads of gunmen, President Felipe Calderon decries the attack by 'true terrorists' in the once-tranquil city in northern Mexico." *Los Angeles Times,* August 27. http://articles.latimes.com/2011/aug/27/world/la-fg-mexico-fire-20110827.

Ellsworth, B. 2012. "Despite Obama Charm, America's Summit Boosts U.S. isolation." *Reuters,* April 16. Retrieved June 25, from http://www.reuters.com/article/2012/04/16/us-americas-summit-obama-idUSBRE83F0UD20120416

EMCDDA 2010. *Statistical Bulletin 2010.* European Monitoring Centre for Drugs and Drug Addiction. http://www.emcdda.europa.eu/stats10

Epatko, L. 2012. "Legalizing Drugs: Why Some Latin American Leaders Are OK with It." *PBS Newshour,* April 16. Retrieved June 25, 2012, from http://www.pbs.org/newshour/rundown/2012/04/legalizing-drugs.html

ESPAD. 2009. *The 2007 ESPAD Report.* European School Survey Project on Alcohol and Other Drugs. http://www.espad.org/documents/Espad/ESPAD_reports/2007/The_2007_ESPAD_Report-FULL_091006.pdf

Everhardt, V. and D. Reinking. 2011. "Cannabis Clubs in the Netherlands, Closed Circuits as a Means to Reduce Health Hazards and to Demarginalize Recreational Use (for Adults, 18+)." Paper presented at the International Society for the Study of Drug Policy, Utrecht, The Netherlands, May 23.

Fainaru, S. and W. Booth. 2009. "Cartels Face an Economic Battle." *Washington Post,* October 7. Retrieved April 26, 2010, from http://www.washingtonpost.com/wp-dyn/content/article/2009/10/06/AR2009100603847.html

Farabee, D., J. Yang, D. Sikangwan, D. Bennett, and U. Warda. 2008. "Final report on the Mental Health Services Continuum Program of the California Department of Corrections and Rehabilitation—Parole Division: UCLA Integrated Substance Abuse Programs," Semel Institute for Neuroscience and Human Behavior, David Geffen School of Medicine at UCLA. Prepared for the California Department of Corrections and Rehabilitation, Division of Parole.

Federal Bureau of Investigation. 2011. National Gang Threat Assessment. Retrieved from http://www.fbi.gov/stats-services/publications/2011-national-gang-threat-assessment/).

Fishman, Laura T. 2002. "The Black Bogeyman and White Self-Righteousness." In Cora-mae Richey Mann and Marjorie S. Zatz (Eds.), *Images of Color, Images of Crime: Readings,* 2nd ed. Los Angeles, CA: Roxbury Publishing Company, pp. 177–191.

Ford, J. 2008. "Plan Colombia: Drug Reduction Goals Were Not Fully Met, but Security Has Improved; U.S. Agencies Need More Detailed Plans for Reducing Assistance." Office, Government Accountability: GAO. Retrieved from http://www.gao.gov/products/GAO-09–71

Foucault, Michel. 1977. *Discipline and Punishment: The Birth of the Prison.* London, Vintage Press.

Friedman, T. L. 2010. "Narcos, No's and Nafta." *New York Times,* May 2. Retrieved from http://www.nytimes.com/2010/05/02/opinion/02friedman.html

Frontera Norte Sur. 2010. "Growing Drug Abuse in Mexico adds to Crime and Violence." February 1. Mexidata.info. Retrieved December 17, 2011, from http://mexidata.info/id2541.html

Frontline PBS. 2011. "Lost in Detention," October 18. Retrieved from http://www.pbs.org/wgbh/pages/frontline/lost-in-detention/

Gandhi, Allison, Erin Gruner, Anthony Murphy-Graham, Sara Petrosino, Chrismer Schwartz, and Carol H. Weiss. 2007. "The Devil Is in the Details: Examining the Evidence for 'Proven' School-Based Drug Abuse Prevention Programs." *Evaluation Review*, Vol. 31, No. 1, pp. 43–74.

Garland, David. 1990. *Punishment and Modern Society: A Study in Social Theory.* Chicago: The University of Chicago Press.

Garland, Brett E., Cassia Spohn, and Eric J. Wodahl. 2008. "Racial Disproportionality in the American Prison Population: Using the Blumstein Method to Address the Critical Race and Justice Issue of the 21st Century." *Justice Policy Journal*, Vol. 5, No. 2 (Fall), pp. 1–42.

Geller, Amanda, and Jeffrey Pagan. 2010. "Pot as Pretext: Marijuana, Race, and the New Disorder in New York City Street Policing." *Journal of Empirical Legal Studies*, Vol. 7, No. 4, pp. 591–633.

Geller A, I. Garfinkel, and B. Western. 2011. "Paternal Incarceration and Support for Children in Fragile Families." *Demography*, Vol. 48, pp. 25–47.

Geller, Amanda, Irwin Garfinkel, and Bruce Western. 2006. "The Effects of Incarceration on Employment and Wages: An Analysis of the Fragile Families Survey." Unpublished Paper. Center for Research on Child Wellbeing.

Gibson, James L. 1988. "Political Intolerance and Political Repression during the McCarthy Red Scare." *American Political Science Review*, Vol. 82, pp. 511–529.

Gibson, James L. 1992. "Alternative Measures of Political Tolerance: Must Tolerance Be Least-Liked?" *American Journal of Political Science*, Vol. 36, pp. 560–577.

Giddens, Anthony. 1987. *The Nation-State and Violence.* Berkeley: University of California Press.

Gieringer, Dale H. 2009. "Benefits of Marijuana Legalization in California." California NORML Report. Retrieved December 23, 2011, from http://www.canorml.org/background/CA_legalization2.html

Gieringer, Dale H. 2011 "The Origins of Cannabis Prohibition in California." 2006. Originally published as "The Forgotten Origins of Cannabis Prohibition in California," *Contemporary Drug Problems*, Vol. 26, No. 2, (http://www.canorml.org/background/caloriginsmjproh.pdf, accessed 06/08/11).

Global Commission on Drug Policy. 2006. "The Commission." Retrieved December 17, 2011, from http://www.globalcommissionondrugs.org/Commission

Global Commission on Drug Policy. 2012. "The War on Drugs and HIV/AIDS: How the Criminalization of Drug Use Fuels the Global Pandemic," June.

Goldstein P. The Drugs/Violence Nexus: a Tripartite Conceptual Framework. *Journal of Social Issues* (Fall 1985), pp. 493–506.

Gonzalez, L. 2010. "Legalización no acabará con violencia: Poiré—El Universal—México." *El Universal*, November 2. Retrieved January 24, 2012, from http://www.eluniversal.com.mx/notas/720630.html

Gray, J. 2001. *Why Our Drug Laws Have Failed and What We Can Do About It: A Judicial Indictment of the War on Drugs.* Philadelphia, PA: Temple University Press.

Grayson, G. W. 1995. *The North American Free Trade Agreement?: Regional Community and the New World Order.* Lanham, MD: University Press of America.

Grayson, G. W. 2008. "Mexico and the Drug Cartels." December 19. Retrieved from http://www.fpri.org/enotes/200708.grayson.mexicodrugcartels.html

Grillo, Ioan and San Francisco Del Rincon. 2011. "Mexico's Ex-Leader Vicente Fox: Legalize Drugs to End War." *Time*, January 19. Retrieved December 16, 2011, from http://www.time.com/time/world/article/0,8599,2040882,00.html

Gurin, Patricia, Shirley Hatchett, and James S. Jackson. 1989. *Hope and Independence: Blacks' Response to Electoral and Party Politics.* New York: Russell Sage Foundation.

Hall, W. and L. Degenhardt. 2009. "Adverse Health Effects of Non-Medical Cannabis Use." *The Lancet,* Vol. 374, pp. 1383–1391.

Harris, Kamala. 2011. "Crime in California, 2010." Sacramento, CA: California Department of Justice, Office of the Attorney General.

Harris-Lacewell, Melissa. 2004. *Barbershops, Bibles, and Bet: Everyday Talk and Black Political Thought.* Princeton, NJ: Princeton University Press.

Hawkins, Darnell F. and Kenneth A. Hardy. 1989. "Black-White Imprisonment Rates: A State- by-State Analysis." *Social Justice,* Vol. 16, No. 4, pp. 75–94.

Hazekamp, A. 2006. "An Evaluation of the Quality of Medicinal Grade Cannabis in the Netherlands." *Cannabinoids,* Vol. 1, pp. 1–9.

Helmer, John. 1975. *Drugs and Minority Oppression* New York: Seabury Press.

Holland, Julie, ed. 2010. *The Pot Book: A Complete Guide to Cannabis: Its Role in Medicine, Politics, Science, and Culture.* Rochester, NY: Park Street Press.

Human Rights Watch. 2008. *Targeting Blacks: Drug Law Enforcement and Race in the United States.* NY: New York.

Human Rights Watch. 2009. *Forced Apart (By the Numbers): Non-Citizens Deported Mostly for Nonviolent Offenses.* http://www.hrw.org/node/82173, accessed 6/28/11.

Humphreys, K. 2011. "Mis-Imagining Marijuana Inc." *Washington Monthly,* July 26.

Iguchi, M. Y, J. A. London, N. G. Forge, L. Hickman, T. Fain, and K. Riehman. 2002. "Elements of Well-Being affected by Criminalizing the Drug User." *Public Health Reports,* Vol. 117, No. S1, pp. S146–S150.

Illinois Department of Corrections. 2004. "Governor Blagojevich Launches New State-wide Community Safety and Reentry Working Group."

International Centre for Prison Studies. 2010. World Prison Brief. Accessed 05/03/2011 at http://www.kcl.ac.uk/depsta/law/research/icps/worldbrief/

Isackson, Amy. 2010. "US, Mexican Authorities Say Prop. 19 Won't Squelch Drug Cartel Violence." KPBS Envision San Diego, 10/11/10. (http://www.kpbs.org/news/2010/oct/11/many-us-and-mexican-authorities-say-prop-19-will-n/, accessed 06/13/11).

Jeffreys, Sheila. 1997. *The Idea of Prostitution.* North Melbourne, Australia: Spinifex.

Johnson, D. T. 2008. "The Merida Initiative: Examining U.S. Efforts to Combat Transnational Criminal Organizations," June 5. Retrieved November 30, 2008, from Johnson R. 2009. "Ever-increasing Levels of Parental Incarceration and the Consequences for Children." In S. Raphael and M. Stoll, Eds., *Do Prisons Make Us Safer? The Benefits and Costs of the Prison Boom.* New York, NY: Russell Sage Foundation.

Johnson, Tim. 2010. "Weary of Drug War, Mexico Debates Legalization." *McClatchy,* September 8. Retrieved January 24, 2012, from http://www.mcclatchydc.com/2010/09/08/100271/weary-of-drug-war-mexico-debates.html#storylink = misearch

Johnson, Tim. 2011. "Free Trade: As U.S. Corn Flows South, Mexicans Stop Farming." *McClatchy,* February 3. Retrieved February 3, 2011, from http://www.mcclatchydc.com/2011/02/01/107871/free-trade-us-corn-flows-south.html

Johnson, Tim. 2011. "Mexican Leader Hints Again at U.S. Drug Legalization." *McClatchy,* September 20. Retrieved December 16, 2011, from http://www.mcclatchydc.com/2011/09/20/124679/mexican-leader-hints-again-at.html

Katel, Peter. 2009. "Legalizing Marijuana." *CQ Researcher,* Vol. 19, June 12, pp. 525–548. Retrieved August 18, 2010, from CQ Researcher Online, http://library.cqpress.com/cqresearcher/cqresrre2009061200.

Khan, A. J., E. P. Simard, W. A. Bower, H. L. Wurtzel, M. Khristova, K. D. Wagner, K. E. Arnold, O. V. Nainan, M. LaMarre, and B. P. Bell. 2005. "Ongoing Transmission of

Hepatitis B Virus Infection among Inmates at a State Correctional Facility." *American Journal of Public Health,* Vol. 95, pp. 1793–1799.

Kilmer, Beau, Jonathan P. Caulkins, Brittany M. Bond and Peter H. Reuter. 2010. "Reducing Drug Trafficking Revenues and Violence in Mexico: Would Legalizing Marijuana in California Help?" RAND International Programs and Drug Research Center, Occasional Paper 325, http://www.rand.org/content/dam/rand/pubs/occasional_papers/2010/RAND_OP325.pdf, accessed 06/13/11).

Kilmer, B., J. P. Caulkins, R. L. Pacula, R. J. MacCoun, and P. Reuter. 2010. *Altered State? Assessing How Marijuana Legalization in California Could Influence Marijuana Consumption and Public Budgets.* Santa Monica, CA: RAND.

Kinder, Donald R. and Cindy D. Kam. 2009. *Us against Them: Ethnocentric Foundations of American Opinion.* Chicago: University of Chicago Press.

Kinder, Donald R. and Lynn M. Sanders. 1996. *Divided by Color: Racial Politics and Democratic Ideals.* Chicago: University of Chicago Press.

King, R. S. and M. Mauer. 2005. *The War on Marijuana: The Transformation of the War on Drugs in the 1990s.* The Sentencing Project, May.

Kingdon, John. 1984. *Agendas, Alternatives, and Public Policies.* Boston: Little Brown and Company.

Kjellstrand, J. M. and J. M. Eddy. 2011. "Parental Incarceration during Childhood, Family Context, and Youth Problem Behavior across Adolescence." *Journal of Offender Rehabilitation,* Vol. 50, No. 1, pp. 18–36.

Kleiman, Mark A. R. 1992. *Against Excess: Drug Policy for Results.* New York: Basic Books.

Kleiman, Mark A. R. 2010. "California Can't Legalize Marijuana." *Los Angeles Times,* July 16. www.latimes.com

Langan, Patrick. 1985. "Racism on Trial: New Evidence to Explain the Racial Composition of Prisons in the United States." *Journal of Criminal Law and Criminology,* Vol. 76, pp. 666–683.

LaVigne, Nancy G. Cynthia A. Mammalian, Jeremy Travis, and Christy Visher. 2003. "A Portrait of Prisoner Reentry in Illinois. Urban Institute, Justice Policy Center, Research Report. April.

Lempert, Richard. 1974. "Toward a Theory of Decriminalization." University of Michigan. Public Law and Legal Theory Working Paper Series. No. 209 (August 2010 reprint, original 1974).

Lenton, S. 2011. "Understanding the Recriminalization of Cannabis Use in Western Australia—Implementation Issues, Political Machinations, and Framing of Evidence." Paper presented at the International Society for the Study of Drug Policy, Utrecht, The Netherlands, May 23.

Lenton, S. and S. Allsop. 2010. "A tale of CIN—the Cannabis Infringement Notice scheme in Western Australia." *Addiction,* Vol. 105, pp. 808–818.

Levine, Harry G., Jon B. Gettman and Loren Siegel." 2010. "Arresting Latinos for Marijuana in California: Possession Arrests in 33 Cities, 2006–2008." Drug Policy Alliance, L.A., October 2010.

Liccardo Pacula, Rosalie. 2009. "Legalizing Marijuana: *Issues to Consider Before Reforming California State Law,"* Testimony presented before the California State Assembly Public Safety Committee on October 28, 2009. Santa Monica, CA: RAND Corporation.

Lichtenstein B. 2009. "Drugs, Incarceration, and HIV/AIDS among African American Men: A Critical Literature Review and Call to Action." *American Journal of Men's Health,* Vol. 3, pp. 252–264.

Lockyear, Bill. 2000. Office of the Attorney General, Bureau of Criminal Information and Analysis Criminal Justice Report Series, "Report on Drug Arrests in California, from 1990 to 1999."Vol. 2, No. 2.

Los Angeles Times. 2008. "Mexico Grapples with Drug Addiction," October 15. Retrieved from http://www.latimes.com/news/nationworld/world/la-fg-mexaddict15–2008oct15,0,4364637.story

Los Angeles Times. 2012. "Fallout from Deadly Mexico Casino Fire Sparks Political Brawl." Retrieved January 26, 2012, from http://articles.latimes.com/2011/sep/22/world/la-fg-mexico-casino-fallout-20110922

Loury, Glenn C. 2008. *Race, Incarceration, and American Values.* Cambridge, MA: MIT Press.

Luhnow, D. and J. De Cordoba. 2009. "The Drug Lord Who Got Away." *Wall Street Journal,* June 13. Retrieved October 26, 2010, from http://online.wsj.com/article_email/SB124484177023110993-lMyQjAxMTIwNDE0ODgxNDgxWj.htmlLa

Lupia, Arthur. 1994. "Shortcuts versus Encyclopedias: Information and Voting Behavior in California Insurance Reform Elections." *American Political Science Review,* Vol. 88, pp. 63–76.

Lurigio A, T. Lyons, L. Brookes, and T. Whitney. 2010. *Illinois Disproportionate Justice Impact Study Commission: Final Report.* Chicago, IL: The Illinois Disproportionate Impact Study Commission.

Lusane, Clarene. 1991. *Pipe Dream Blues: Racism and the War on Drugs.* Boston, MA: South End Press.

Lynch, T. 2010. "Pot Shots at Prop 19 Fall Flat." *Huffington Post,* October 20. Retrieved from http://www.huffingtonpost.com/tim-lynch/pot-shots-at-prop-19-fall_b_769946.html

Lyons, Thomas and A. Lurigio. 2010. "The Role of Recovery Capital in the Community Reentry of Prisoners with Substance Use Disorders." *Journal of Offender Rehabilitation,* Vol. 49, No. 7, pp. 445–455.

Macallair, Daniel and Mike Males. 2009. "Marijuana Arrests and California's Drug War: A Report to the California Legislature," Center on Juvenile and Criminal Justice, Legislative Policy Study, October.

MacCoun, Robert J. 2010. "HYPERLINK "http://conium.org/%7Emaccoun/MacCoun2010_Addiction%20_add_2936.pdf" The Implicit Rules of Evidence-Based Drug Policy, Updated." *Addiction, Vol. 105* (July), No. 8, pp. 1335–1336.

MacCoun, Robert. J. 1993. "Drugs and the Law: A Psychological Analysis of Drug Prohibition." *Psychological Bulletin,* Vol. 113, pp. 497–512.

MacCoun, Robert. J. 2011. "What Can We Learn from the Dutch Cannabis Coffeeshop System?" *Addiction,* Vol. 106, pp. 1899–1910.

MacCoun, Robert J., R. L. Pacula, P. Reuter, J. Chriqui, and K. Harris. 2009. "Do Citizens Know Whether They Live in a Decriminalization State? State Marijuana Laws and Perceptions." *Review of Law & Economics,* Vol. 5, pp. 347–371.

MacCoun, Robert J., and P. Reuter. 1997. "Interpreting Dutch Cannabis Policy: Reasoning by Analogy in the Legalization Debate." *Science,* Vol. 278, pp. 47–52.

MacCoun, Robert J. and P. Reuter. 2001. *Drug War Heresies: Learning from Other Vices, Times, and Places.* New York: Cambridge University Press.

MacCoun, Robert J., and P. Reuter. 2011. "Drug Prohibition and Its Alternatives: A Guide for Agnostics." *Annual Review of Law & Social Science,* Vol. 7, pp. 61–78.

MacCoun, Robert J., Reuter, P., & Schelling, T. 1996. "Assessing Alternative Drug Control Regimes." *Journal of Policy Analysis and Management,* Vol. 15, pp. 1–23.

Maguire, Kathleen, ed. 2004. *Sourcebook of Criminal Justice Statistics.* University at Albany, Hindelang Criminal Justice Research Center, Table *5.46.* Available: http://www.albany.edu/sourcebook/pdf/t5462004.pdf. [Accessed 6/09/2013].

Maclachlan, M. 2009. "What would Marijuana Legalization Look Like?" *Capitol Weekly*, November 19. Retrieved from http://www.capitolweekly.net/article.php?xid = yf9mqcx5j7t2f5

Mann, Coramae Richey and Marjorie S. Zatz (Eds.) 2002. *Images of Color, Images of Crime: Readings*, 2nd ed. Los Angeles, CA: Roxbury Publishing Company.

Markus, Hazel and R. B. Zajonc. 1985. "The Cognitive Perspective in Social Psychology." In *The Handbook of Social Psychology, 3d*, Gardner Lindzey and Elliot Aronson, Eds. New York: Newbery Award Records, Inc.

Marosi, Richard. 2010a. "Official: Tijuana Massacre may be Related to Pot Bust," *Los Angeles Times*, October 25. Retrieved July 26, 2011, from http://latimesblogs.latimes.com/laplaza/richard-marosi/

Marosi, Richard. 2010b. Mexico's Calderon Strongly Criticizes Pot Measure Prop. 19 in interview with The Times." *Los Angeles Times*, October 8. Retrieved December 16, 2011, from http://latimesblogs.latimes.com/lanow/2010/10/mexican-president-felipe-calderon-strongly-criticizes-marijuana-legalization-measure-proposition-19.html

Martinez-Amador, D.C. 2011. "A War of Information: US Intervention in Mexico's Drug War," August 19. Insightcrime.org. Washington, D.C. Retrieved from http://insightcrime.org/insight-latest-news/item/1437-a-war-of-information-us-intervention-in-mexicos-drug-war

Massey, Douglas and Nancy Denton. 1993. *American Apartheid: Segregation and the Making of the Underclass*. Cambridge: Harvard University Press.

Massing, Michael. 1998. *The Fix*. New York, NY: Simon & Schuster.

Mauer, Marc. 1990. "Young Black Men and the Criminal Justice System: A Growing National Problem." Washington, D.C.: The Sentencing Project.

Mauer, Marc. 1999. *Race to Incarcerate*. New York: The New Press.

Mauer, Marc and Ryan S. King. 2007. *Uneven Justice: State Rates of Incarceration by Race and Ethnicity*. Washington, D.C.: The Sentencing Project.

Mauer, Marc and Tracy Huling. 1995 (October). "Young Black Americans and the Criminal Justice System: Five Years Later." Washington, D.C.: The Sentencing Project.

McClosky, Herbert and Brill, Alida. 1983. *Dimensions of Tolerance: What Americans Believe about Civil Liberties*. New York: Russell Sage Foundation.

McWhorter, John W. 2000. *Losing the Race: Self-Sabotage in Black America*. New York: Simon and Schuster.

Miller, Lisa L. 2008. *The Perils of Federalism: Race, Poverty, and the Politics of Crime Control*. New York: Oxford University Press.

Miller Llana, S. 2009. "Mexico Quietly Decriminalizes Drug use." *CSMonitor.com*, August 24. Retrieved December 17, 2011, from http://www.csmonitor.com/World/Global-News/2009/0824/mexico-quietly-decriminalizes-drug-use

Miller Llana, S. 2010. "Latin America's Leaders Condemn California's Prop. 19 to Legalize Marijuana." *CSMonitor.com*, October 27. Retrieved January 23, 2012, from http://www.csmonitor.com/World/Americas/2010/1027/Latin-America-s-leaders-condemn-California-s-Prop.-19-to-legalize-marijuana

Ministry of Security and Justice. 2011. *Coffeeshop to be a Private Club for the Local Market*. Press release, May 27.

Mirken, Bruce. 2007. "Marijuana Arrests Set New Record for Fourth Year in a Row," Marijuana Policy Project, September 27.

Miron, J. A. 2005. *Budgetary Implications of Marijuana Prohibition*. Cambridge, MA: Harvard University.

Miron, Jeffrey. 2010. *The Budgetary Implications of Drug Prohibition.* Report funded by the Criminal Justice Policy Foundation. Boston: Harvard University.

Monshouwer, K., M. van Laar, and W. A. Vollebergh. 2011. "Buying Cannabis in 'Coffee Shops.'" *Drug and Alcohol Review,* Vol. 30, pp. 148–156.

Mosher, Clayton J. and Scott Akins. 2007. *Drugs and Drug Policy: The Control of Consciousness Alteration.* Thousand Oaks, CA: Sage Publications.

Muhammad, Khalil Gibran. 2010. *The Condemnation of Blackness: Race, Crime, and the Making of Modern Urban America.* Cambridge, MA: Harvard University Press.

Mumola C. J. 2006. "Parents under Correctional Supervision: National Statistics." Presented at the conference, "Children of parents in the criminal justice system: Children at risk," Bethesda, MD, November 6.

Murakawa, Naomi. 2008. "The Origins of the Carceral Crisis: Racial Order as 'Law and Order' in Postwar American Politics." In *Race and American Political Development,* Joseph Lowndes, Julie Novkov, and Dorian T. Warren, Eds. New York: Routledge.

Murphy, P. 1994. *Keeping Score: The Fragilities of the Federal Drug Budget.* Santa Monica, CA: RAND Corporation.

Murray, J. and D. P. Farrington, I. 2005. "Parental Imprisonment: Effects on Boys' Antisocial Behavior and Delinquency through the Life-Course." *Journal of Child Psychology and Psychiatry & Allied Disciplines,* Vol. 46, Issue 12, pp. 1269–1278.

Murray J., D. P. Farrington, I. Sekol, and R. F. Olsen. 2009. "Effects of Parental Imprisonment on Child Antisocial Behaviour and Mental Health: A Systematic Review." Retrieved from http://campbellcollaboration.org/lib/

Musto, David. 1987. (Originally 1973.) *The American Disease: Origins of Narcotic Control.* New Haven, CT: Yale University Press.

Musto, David S. 1999. *The American Disease: Origins of Narcotic Control, 3rd Ed.* New York: Oxford University Press.

Musto, David, and Pamela Korsmeyer. 2002. *The Quest for Drug Control: Politics and Federal Policy in a Period of Increasing Substance Abuse, 1963–81.* New Haven, CT: Yale University Press.

Myers B. J., T. M. Smarsh, K. Amlund-Hagen and S. Kennon. 1999. "Children of Incarcerated Mothers." *Journal of Child & Family Studies,* Vol. 8, No. 1, pp. 11–25.

Naím, M. 2005. *Illicit?: How Smugglers, Traffickers and Copycats are Hijacking the Global Economy.* Washington, D.C.: Centro Cultural del BID.

National Center for State Courts. 2002. California Judicial Workload Assessment. Final Report. Williamsburg, VA: National Center for State Courts.

Newcomb, M. D. and M. Felix-Ortiz. 1992. "Multiple Protective and Risk Factors for Drug Use and Abuse: Cross-sectional and Prospective Findings." *Journal of Personality and Social Psychology,* Vol. 63, No. 2, pp. 280–296.

O'Connell Davidson, Julia. 1998. *Prostitution, Power and Freedom.* Cambridge, UK: Polity Press.

Oliver, Pamela. 2008. "Repression and Crime Control: Why Social Movement Scholars Should Pay Attention to Mass Incarceration as a form of Repression." *Mobilization,* Vol. 13, No. 1, pp. 1–24.

Openbaar Ministrie 2010. "Frequently Asked Questions about the Dutch Drug Policy." Accessed on 1 June 2010. http://www.om.nl/vast_menu_blok/english/frequently_asked/

Orange County Grand Jury. 2007. "2006–2007 Orange County Grand Jury: The State of Orange County Jails and Programs." Orange County, California.

Orey, Bryon D'Andra. 2004. "Explaining Black Conservatives: Racial Uplift or Racial Resentment?" *The Black Scholar,* Vol. 34, No. 1, pp. 18–34.

Pacula, R. L., MacCoun, R., Reuter, P., Chriqui, J., Kilmer, B., Harris, K., Paoli, L., & Schaefer, C. 2005. "What Does It Mean to Decriminalize Marijuana? A Cross-national Empirical Examination." In B. Lindgren & M. Grossman, Eds., *Substance Use: Individual Behaviour, Social Interactions, Markets and Politics.* Elsevier/North-Holland.

Pager D, B. Western B, and B. Bonikowski. 2009. "Discrimination in a Low-Wage Labor Market: A field Experiment." *American Sociological Review,* Vol. 74, No. 5, pp. 777–799.

Parenti, Christian. 1999. *Lockdown America: Police and Prisons in the Age of Crisis.* New York: Verso Books.

Peavie, Barrett. 2001. *United States War on Drugs: Addicted to a Political Strategy of No End.* Forth Leavenworth: School of Advanced Military Studies.

Perez Molina, O. 2012. "Stop Blindly Following a Failed Policy—Room for Debate." *New York Times,* May 31. Retrieved June 25, 2012, from http://www.nytimes.com/roomfordebate/2012/05/30/should-latin-america-end-the-war-on-drugs/stop-blindly-following-a-failed-policy

Peters, B. G. 1999. *Institutional Theory in Political Science: The New Institutionalism.* London; New York: Pinter.

Petersilia, Joan R. 1987. "Blacks In Prison: It's Not Racism." *The Chicago Tribune,* Opinion Section, July 6. See http://articles.chicagotribune.com/1987-07-06/news/8702190186_1_prison-population-crimes-racial-bias.

Petersilia, J. 2003. *When Prisoners Come Home: Parole and Community Reentry.* New York Oxford University Press.

Phillips I. 2007. "Community Re-entry Challenges Daunt Ex-offenders Quest for a Fresh Start." Illinois Criminal Justice Information Authority Research Briefs, March.

Piehl, A. M., and G. Williams. 2010. *Institutional Requirements for Effective Imposition of Fines.* New Brunswick, NJ: Rutgers University Press.

Pijlman, F. T. A., S. M. Rigter, J. Hoek, H. M. J. Goldschmidt, H. M. J., and R. J. M. Niesink. 2005. "Strong Increase in Total Delta-THC in Cannabis Preparations Sold in Dutch Coffee Shops." *Addiction Biology,* Vol. 10, pp. 171–180.

Pizzi, William T., Irene V. Blair, Charles M. Judd. 2005. "Discrimination in Sentencing on the Basis of Afrocentric Features," *Michigan Journal of Race & Law,* Vol. 10, pp. 327–353.

Popkin, Samuel L. 1991. *The Reasoning Voter: Communication and Persuasion in Presidential Campaigns.* Chicago, IL: The University of Chicago Press.

Premiere Bail Bonds. 2011. "LA County Men's Jail (MCJ)." Retrieved December 23, 2011, from http://www.bailbonds-los-angeles.com/la-central.html

Provine, Doris Maris. 2007. *Unequal under Law: Race in the War on Drugs.* Chicago: University of Chicago Press.

Ramos Perez, J. 2010. "FCH Plantea Revisión Integral Sobre Drogas." *El Universal,* November 2. Retrieved January 24, 2012, from http://www.eluniversal.com.mx/notas/720642.html

Ramsey, G. 2012. "Uruguay: Another Latin American Country Goes Against US Drug Policy." *Christian Science Monitor,* CSM Blog: Latin America Blog, June 22. Retrieved from http://www.csmonitor.com/World/Americas/Latin-America-Monitor/2012/0622/Uruguay-Another-Latin-American-country-goes-against-US-drug-policy.

RAND. 2010. "Legalizing Marijuana in California Will Not Dramatically Reduce Mexican Drug Trafficking Revenues," October 12. Retrieved December 19, 2011, from http://www.rand.org/news/press/2010/10/12.html

Reagan, Ronald. 2004. *Reagan's Path to Victory: The Shaping of Ronald Reagan's Vision.* New York, N.Y.: Simon & Schuster.

Reed, Jr., Adolph. 2000. *Class Notes: Posing as Politics and Other Thoughts on the American Scene.* New York: The New Press.

Reinarman, C., P. D. A. Cohen, and H. L. Kaal, 2004. "The Limited Relevance of Drug Policy: Cannabis in Amsterdam and in San Francisco." *American Journal of Public Health,* Vol. 94, pp. 836–842.

HYPERLINK "http://www.amazon.com/s/ref=ntt_athr_dp_sr_1?_encoding= UTF8&field-author=Craig%20Reinarman&search-alias=books&sort=relevancerank" Reinarman, Craig and HYPERLINK "http://www.amazon.com/s/ref=ntt_athr_dp_sr_2?_encoding=UTF8&field-author=Harry%20G.%20Levine&search-alias=books&sort=relevancerank" Harry G. Levine (Eds.). 1997. *Crack in America: Demon Drugs and Social Justice.* Berkeley, CA: University of California Press.

Reuter, Peter. 2006. "HYPERLINK "http://faculty.publicpolicy.umd.edu/sites/default/files/reuter/files/what_drug_policies_cost.doc" What Drug Policies Cost. Estimating Government Drug Policy Expenditures." *Addiction,* Vol. 101, pp. 312–322.

Reuter, P., and M. A. R. Kleiman. 1986. "Risks and Prices: An Economic Analysis of Drug Enforcement." *Crime and Justice: An Annual Review,* Vol. 7, pp. 289–240.

Reuter, Peter and David Ronfeldt. 1992. "HYPERLINK "http://faculty.publicpolicy.umd.edu/sites/default/files/reuter/files/QUEST_FOR_INTEGRITY%5B1%5D.doc" Quest for Integrity: The Mexican–U.S. Drug Issue in the 1980s." Journal of Interamerican Affairs, Vol. 34, pp. 89–153.

Richman, J. 2010. "Hazy Math: How Much Do We Spend to Incarcerate Pot Users? Not as Much as They Say." *Oakland Tribune,* October 3.

Rios, Viridiana. 2010. "Evaluating the Economic Impact of Drug Traffic in Mexico." Working paper, http://www-old.gov.harvard.edu/student/rios/MexicanDrugMarket_Riosv2.doc, accessed 06/13/11.

Romo, R. 2011. "Former Mexican President Urges Legalizing Drugs." *CNN,* July 26. Retrieved December 16, 2011, from http://articles.cnn.com/2011–07–26/world/mexico.drugs_1_drug-cartels-drug-policy-drug-violence?_s = PM:WORLD

Rydell, C. Peter and Susan Everingham. 1994. *Supply Versus Demand Programs.* Santa Monica: Drug Policy Research Center.

Scherlen, Renee 2012. "The Never-Ending Drug War: Obstacles to Drug War Policy Termination." *PS: Political Science & Politics,* Vol. 45, pp. 67–73.

Schlosser, Eric. 2003. *Reefer Madness: Sex, Drugs, and Cheap Labor in the American Black Market.* New York, NY: Houghton Mifflin.

Schnittker J., M. Massoglia and C. Uggen. 2011. "Incarceration and the Health of the African American Community." *Du Bois Review,* Vol. 8, No. 1, pp. 133–141

Schroeder, Richard C. 1980. *The Politics of Drugs: An American Dilemma.* Washington, D.C.: Congressional Quarterly Press.

Schuman, H., Steeh, C. and Bobo, L. 1985. *Racial Attitudes in America: Trends and Interpretations.* Cambridge, MA: Harvard University Press.

Shirk, D. A., V. Rios and C. Molzahn. 2012. "Drug Violence in Mexico: Data and Analysis through 2011." San Diego, California: Trans-Border Institute, USD. Retrieved from http://justiceinmexico.org/publications/justice-in-mexico-project/

Shirk, David. 2011. "The Drug War in Mexico: Confronting a Shared Threat." Council Special Report No. 60. Council on Foreign Relations. Retrieved from http://www.cfr.org/mexico/drug-war-mexico/p24262

Sigelman, Lee and Welch, Susan. 1991. *Black Americans' Views of Racial Inequality: The Dream Deferred.* New York: Cambridge University Press.

Silver, Nate. 2010. "Is Proposition 19 Going Up in Smoke?" *NYTimes.com,* October 21. Retrieved January 24, 2012, from http://fivethirtyeight.blogs.nytimes.com/2010/10/21/is-proposition-19-going-up-in-smoke/

Sloman, Larry. 1979. *Reefer Madness: The History of Marijuana in America.* New York, N.Y.: St. Martin's Griffin.

Sniderman, Paul M., Richard A. Brody, and Philip E. Tetlock. 1991. *Reasoning and Choice: Explorations in Political Psychology.* New York: Cambridge University Press.

Sorenson, Jon and Don Stemen. 2002. "The Effect of State Sentencing Policies on Incarceration Rates." *Crime and Delinquency,* Vol. 48, pp. 456–475.

Spagat, Elliot. 2010. "Mexico Upset By California Efforts To Legalize Pot." *Huffington Post,* October 8. Retrieved December 16, 2011, from http://www.huffingtonpost.com/2010/10/08/mexico-upset-by-californi_n_755356.html

Spaulding Anne C., Ryan M. Seals, Victoria A. McCallum, Sebastian D. Perez, Amanda K. Brzozowski, and N. Kyle Steenland. 2011. "Prisoner Survival Inside and Outside of the Institution: Implications for Health-Care Planning." *American Journal of Epidemiology,* Vol. 173, No. 5, pp. 479–487.

Spohn, Cassia and Jerry Cederblom. 1991. "Race and Disparities in Sentencing: A Test of the Liberation Hypothesis." *Justice Quarterly,* Vol. 8, No. 3, pp. 305–327.

Stateman, A. 2009. "Can Marijuana Help Rescue California's Economy?" *Time,* March 13.

Stouffer, Samuel. 1955. *Communism, Conformity, and Civil Liberties.* New York: Doubleday.

Sullivan, John L., James E. Piereson, and George E. Marcus (1982). *Political Tolerance and American Democracy.* Chicago: The University of Chicago Press.

Superior Court of California County of Riverside. 2009. "Felony and Misdemeanor Bail Schedule." Riverside, CA: Superior Court of California County of Riverside.

Tate, Katherine. 1994. *From Protest to Politics: The New Black Voters in American Elections, Enlarged Ed.* Cambridge, MA: Harvard University Press and the Russell Sage Foundation.

Tate, Katherine. 2010. *What's Going On? Political Incorporation and the Transformation of Black Public Opinion.* Washington, D.C.: Georgetown University Press.

Terry-McElrath Y. M., P. M. O'Malley and L. D. Johnston. 2009. "Reasons for Drug Use among American Youth by Consumption Level, Gender, and Race/ethnicity: 1976–2005." *Journal of Drug Issues,* Vol. 39, No. 3, pp. 677–714.

Thernstrom, Stephan and Thernstrom, Abigail. 1997. *America in Black and White: One Nation, Indivisible.* New York: Simon & Schuster.

Time. 1975. "Jack Ford: 'My Turn to Sacrifice,'" 20 October.

Tolbert, Carolyn J. and Rodney E. Hero. 1996. "Race/Ethnicity and Direct Democracy: An Analysis of California's Illegal Immigration Initiative." *Journal of Politics,* Vol. 58, No. 3 (August), pp. 806–818.

Tonry, Michael and Matthew Melewski. 2008. "The Malign Effects of Drug and Crime Control Policies on Black Americans." *Crime and Justice,* Vol. 37, No. 1, pp. 1–44.

UNODC. 2010. "World Drug Report 2010." United Nations Publication, Sales No. E.10. XI.13.

Van den Brink, Wim. 2008. "Decriminalization of Cannabis." *Current Opinion in Psychiatry,* Vol. 21, pp. 122–126.

Vigne N. and C. A. Mamalian. 2003. *A Portrait of Prisoner Re-entry in Illinois.* Washington, D.C.: Urban Institute.

Wagner, D. 2010. "Drug Law Changes Little for Life in Mexico." *Azcentral.Com,* January 10. Retrieved January 26, 2012, from http://www.azcentral.com/news/articles/2010/01/10/20100110mex-drugs.html

Wallace J. M. 1998. "Explaining Race Differences in Adolescent and Young Adult Drug Use: The Role of Racialized Social Systems." *Drugs & Society,* 1998, Vol. 14, No. 1–2, pp. 21–36.

Walters, Ronald W. 2008. *The Price of Racial Reconciliation.* Ann Arbor, MI: University of Michigan Press.

Weatherspoon, Floyd B. 1998. *African American Males and the Law: Cases and Materials.* Lanham, MD: University Press of America.

Weaver, Vesla Mae. 2007. "Frontlash: Race and the Development of Punitive Crime Policy." *Studies in American Political Development,* Vol. 21, pp. 230–265.

West, Steven L., and Keri K. O'Neal. 2004. "Project D.A.R.E. Outcome Effectiveness Revisited." *American Journal of Public Health,* Vol. 94, No. 6, pp. 1027–1029.

Whitney T. and M. Heaps. 2005. "Disproportionate Sentencing of Minority Drug Offenders in Illinois." Chicago: Illinois Criminal Justice Information Authority.

Wilkins, David E. 2007. *American Indian Politics and the American Political System, 2nd Ed.* Boulder, CO: Rowman & Littlefield Publishers, Inc.

Wilkinson, T., & Ellingwood, K. n.d. "Mexican Drug Cartels Find Youths to Be Easy Prey." Los Angeles Times, Retrieved February 21, 2011, from http://www.latimes.com/news/nationworld/world/la-fg-mexico-foot-soldiers-20101219,0,642757.story

Wilkinson, Richard and Kate Pickett. 2009. *The Spirit Level: Why Greater Equality Makes Societies Stronger.* London: Bloomsbury Press.

Williams, J. 2004. "The Effects of Price and Policy on Marijuana Use: What Can Be Learned from the Australian Experience?" *Health Economics,* Vol. 13, pp. 123–137.

Wilson, James Q. "Against the Legalization of Drugs." 1990. *Commentary,* February. http://www.commentarymagazine.com/article/against-the-legalization-of-drugs/. Accessed 6/9/2013.

Wise, Tim, 2011. *Colorblind, The Rise of Post-Racial Politics and the Retreat from Racial Equity.* San Francisco, CA: City Lights Books.

Wright, Douglas and Teresa R. Davis, "Youth Substance Use: State Estimates from the 1999 National Household Survey on Drug Abuse," Department of Health and Human Services, Substance Abuse and Mental Health Services Administration http://www.samhsa.gov/data/NHSDA/99YouthState/chapter6.htm#6.3 (accessed 6/8/2013). .

Zuberi, Tuku. *Thicker Than Blood: How Racial Statistics Lie.* 2001. Minneapolis, MN: The University of Minnesota Press.

LIST OF CONTRIBUTORS

R. Michael Alvarez is Professor of Political Science at the California Institute of Technology. He is the codirector of Caltech/MIT Voting Technology Project, a research endeavor aimed at evaluating the reliability of U.S. voting systems. He is the co-editor of *Political Analysis*. His coauthored books include *New Faces, New Votes: The Hispanic Electorate in America* (Princeton University Press 2010) and *Hard Choices, Easy Answers: Values, Information and American Public Opinion* (Princeton University Press 2002). His research focuses on U.S. electoral behavior, election technologies, and U.S. minority politics.

Jonathan P. Caulkins is H. Guyford Stever Professor of Operations Research and Public Policy at Carnegie Mellon University's Heinz College and Qatar campus. Dr. Caulkins specializes in systems analysis of problems pertaining to drugs, crime, terror, violence, and prevention—work that won the David Kershaw Award from the Association of Public Policy Analysis and Management, a Robert Wood Johnson Health Investigator Award, and the INFORMS President's Award. Other interests include reputation and brand management, software quality, optimal control, black markets, airline operations, and personnel performance evaluation. He has taught his quantitative decision-making course on four continents to students from 50 countries at every level from undergraduate through Ph.D. and executive education. Dr. Caulkins has published more than 100 journal articles and 8 books and monographs—most recently, *Drugs & Drug Problems: What Everyone Needs to Know* with Mark Kleiman and Angela Hawken. At RAND, he has been a consultant, visiting scientist, codirector of RAND's Drug Policy Research Center (1994–1996), and founding director of RAND's Pittsburgh office (1999–2001). Dr. Caulkins received a B.S. and M.S. in Systems Science from Washington University, an S.M. in Electrical Engineering and Computer Science and Ph.D. in Operations Research, both from M.I.T.

Christian Davenport is a Professor of Peace Studies, Political Science & Sociology at the Kroc Institute, University of Notre Dame, Director of the Illustrative Information Interface (III), the Radical Information Project (RIP) and Stop Our States (SOS), as well as Associate Editor of the *Journal of Conflict Resolution*. Primary research interests include political conflict (e.g., human rights violations, genocide/politicide, torture, political surveillance, civil war, and social movements), measurement, racism, and popular culture. Dr. Davenport is the author of numerous books. His most recent book, *Media Bias, Perspective and State Repression: The Black Panther Party* (Cambridge University Press 2010), was voted the best book in racial power and social movement theory by the American Political Science Association's Race, Ethnicity and Politics section. In addition to just completing a novel (BE and the Movements in Stasis—the Book of Change, or Not), Dr. Davenport is currently working on numerous projects. For more information, see his webpage: www.christiandavenport.com.

Nathan Jones is a doctoral candidate at UC Irvine in political science and an adjunct instructor at the University of San Diego where he teaches international relations. His dissertation, "The State Reaction: A Theory of Illicit Network Resilience," focuses on the relationship between the business models of Mexican drug-trafficking organizations and their resilience. His case study was the Arellano-Felix Organization, popularly known as the Tijuana Cartel. He was a 2010–2011 Institute for Global Conflict and Cooperation (IGCC) Dissertation Fellow, which allowed him to conduct six months of fieldwork in Tijuana and three in Mexico City. While in both locations, he interviewed relevant scholars, journalists, government officials, and law enforcement in Mexico and San Diego. Jones has published with major think tanks like the Woodrow Wilson Institute, Center for Strategic and International Studies, and InsightCrime, on varied topics like the flow of guns into Mexico from the United States and levels of drug-related violence in Mexico. His primary research interests include security in Latin America, illicit networks, drug policy, and the just war doctrine of the Catholic Church. Jones completed his bachelor's degree with high honors in political science at UC Berkeley in 2003, where he wrote his honors thesis on regime stability in Syria.

Beau Kilmer is a senior policy researcher at the RAND Corporation and codirector of the RAND Drug Policy Research Center. His primary fields of interest are public policy, illicit markets, community corrections, substance use and treatment, and the future of drug testing. He is currently the principal investigator of an NIH-funded evaluation of South Dakota's 24/7 Sobriety Project and co–principal investigator on four RAND projects: evaluating innovative approaches to closing open-air drug markets; measuring community-level effects of drug treatment; assessing illicit drug markets in the European Union; and estimating the cost-effectiveness of a brief voluntary alcohol and drug intervention for middle school youth. Dr. Kilmer also completed projects for the European Commission to develop indicators for assessing the effectiveness of drug enforcement and estimate the size of the global drug market. Dr. Kilmer is an assistant editor for *Addiction,* and his recent work was published in *Proceedings of the National Academy of Sciences, Foreign Policy, Drug and Alcohol Dependence,* and *Journal of Quantitative Criminology.* He was the lead author on two RAND reports that shaped the discussion about Proposition 19: *Altered State? Assessing How Marijuana Legalization in California Could Influence Marijuana Consumption and Public Budgets* and *Reducing Drug Trafficking Revenues and Violence in Mexico: Would Legalizing Marijuana in California Help?* Before earning his Ph.D. at Harvard University, Kilmer received a Judicial Administration Fellowship that supported his work with the San Francisco Drug Court.

Jaclyn R. Kimble is a Ph.D. student at the California Institute of Technology. She received her B.A., with distinction, in Economics from Yale University in 2009. She completed her M.S. in Social Science at Caltech in 2011. Her current research focuses on election law, redistricting, and racially polarized voting.

Thomas Lyons is a medical anthropologist and an assistant professor and director of the HIV/AIDS Research and Policy Institute at Chicago State University on Chicago's South Side. He received his Ph.D. in anthropology from the University of Chicago. He has published on the role of peer support groups in reducing HIV risk among drug using men who have sex with men, as well as on prisoner reentry issues. At Treatment Alternatives for Safe Communities (TASC), he was the chief research analyst for the Disproportionate Justice Impact Study Commission, an Illinois legislative commission investigating racial disparities in incarceration under the drug laws. Dr. Lyon's interests focus on interventions for drug-using men who have sex with men and persons involved in the criminal justice system.

Robert J. MacCoun holds a Ph.D. in Psychology, but he has spent his career at the boundaries where psychology meets public policy and the law. He spent seven years as a Behavioral Scientist at the RAND Corporation, and then joined the UC Berkeley faculty in 1993, and is a Professor in the Law School and in the Goldman School of Public Policy. MacCoun has well over 100 publications, including articles in *Science, Psychological Review,* and other journals. With Peter Reuter, he coauthored the book *Drug War Heresies: Learning from Other Vices, Times, and Places* (Cambridge 2001). His recent work on the deleterious effects of attending sixth grade in a middle school rather than an elementary school received the 2009 Vernon Award of the Association for Public Policy Analysis and Management. He coauthored the now-famous 1993 RAND analysis of the feasibility of lifting the ban on gays and lesbians in the U.S. military, as well as the unit cohesion chapter in the RAND 2010 update study for the department of defense.

Melissa R. Michelson (Ph.D. Yale 1994) is Professor of Political Science at Menlo College. Her two major strands of research include Latino political incorporation and field experiments in voter mobilization of ethnic and racial minorities. From 2006 to 2009, she was principal investigator for the evaluation of the James Irvine Foundation's California Votes Initiative, a multi-year effort to increase voting rates among voters in low-income and ethnic communities in California's San Joaquin Valley and targeted areas in Southern California. She is coauthor of the forthcoming book, *Mobilizing Inclusion: Redefining Citizenship through Get-out-the-vote Campaigns* (Yale University Press 2012).

Paul Musgrave is a Ph.D. student in government at Georgetown University. A George Mitchell Scholar, Musgrave worked as an editor at Foreign Affairs and as special assistant to the director of the nonpartisan Richard Nixon Presidential Library and Museum. He has a B.A. degree in Political Science and History from Indiana University and a Master's degree in Politics from University College Dublin.

Mark Q. Sawyer is Professor of African American Studies and Political Science at UCLA. He is also Director of the Center for the Study of Race, Ethnicity, and Politics. He received his Ph.D. in political science from the University of Chicago. He is the author of the award-winning book, *Racial Politics in Post Revolutionary Cuba* (Cambridge University Press 2006). He is also the co-editor of *Just Neighbors?: Research on African Americans and Latino Relations in the United States* (Russell Sage Foundation 2011). His research focuses on the politics of race and gender in the United States, Cuba, Puerto Rico, and the Dominican Republic.

J. Andrew Sinclair is a Ph.D. Student at the California Institute of Technology. He has a B.A. in mathematics and government from Claremont McKenna College and a Master's degree in Social Science from Caltech. His primary areas of research are California politics, electoral systems, and voting behavior.

Joe Tafoya is a doctoral student at the University of Texas at Austin. He is pursuing his degree in American Politics with emphases in Race and Ethnicity and Latino Politics. Mr. Tafoya has attended the Ralph Bunche Summer Institute and is a 2011–12 Minority Fellow of the American Political Science Association.

Katherine Tate is Professor of Political Science at the University of California, Irvine. Dr. Tate teaches in the fields of American government, public opinion, and race, ethnicity, and urban politics. She is also offering a new political science course on race and ethnicity issues in public policy, focusing on American environmental, agricultural, health, welfare, and crime-control policies for the twenty-first century. She received her bachelor's degree in political science with honors from the University of Chicago, and her doctorate in political science from the University of Michigan. Dr. Tate is the author and coauthor of several books.

James Lance Taylor is Associate Professor and Chair of the Department of Politics at the University of San Francisco. He also teaches in the African American Studies and Legal Studies programs. Dr. Taylor offers courses in the fields of American politics, religion and politics, urban politics, and law and public policy. His primary research interests are religion and politics, political leadership, social movements, and race and ethnic politics. Dr. Taylor served as President of the National Conference of Black Political Scientists (2009–2011). He is the author of *Black Nationalism in the United States: From Malcolm X to Barack Obama* (Lynne Rienner Publishers, 2011).

Clyde Wilcox is Professor of Government at Georgetown University. He has written and edited a number of books and articles on public opinion on social issues such as gender equality, LGBT equality, gun control, and abortion. His most recent books include *Interest Groups in American Elections: The New Face of Electioneering* (3rd edition), *Onward Christian Soldiers, the Christian Right in American Politics* (4th edition), *Religion, Sexuality, and Politics in the U.S. and Canada,* and *New Boundaries of Political Science Fiction.*

Chyvette T. Williams is an Assistant Professor of Epidemiology and Biostatistics at the University of Illinois at Chicago School of Public Health and former Associate Director of the Community Outreach Intervention Projects, a center within the school that provides services and conducts research targeting drug using populations and issues related to drug use. Dr. Williams's research takes an interdisciplinary approach to understanding individual and contextual determinants of health and social behavior among marginalized populations in urban areas, with a focus on social network and geographic contexts on drug and sex behaviors. Dr. Williams served on the policy advisory board for the Disproportionate Justice Impact Study Commission, an Illinois legislative commission investigating racial disparities in incarceration under the drug laws. Dr. Williams is an alumna of the University of Illinois (Urbana and Chicago) and received her doctorate from Johns Hopkins University.

INDEX

Page numbers in *italics* indicate figures or tables. Page numbers followed by "n" indicate notes.

abortion 84, *84*, 91n9
addiction, drug 8–9
adjudication costs 19–21, *20*, 30n5
affect 66, 67, 77
African Americans *see* Blacks
Afrocentric features bias 94
Aguilar Camín, Hector 130–1
AHOJ-G rules 48
Alameda County, California 22, 23, 30n8
Alaska 43–4, *44*
Alexander, Michelle 118, 120
Alpine County, California 64n12
American Indians 6–7
Amsterdam 47–8
Anslinger, Harry 116
arrests: costs 15, 17–19, *18*, 25, *26*, *27*; rates 106, 118, *119*, 145; *see also* marijuana arrests
Australia 44–7, *45*, *46*

bail for marijuana offenders 22, 30n7
banked caseloads 24, 30n11
Banks, Richard 145
Bell, Derrick 9
"Black deviance-White innocence" binary 93–9
Blacks: arrest rates 145; "Black deviance-White innocence" binary 93–9; Blacks, views toward 71–2, *72*, 75–6;

California population statistics 109, 114n11; coercion against 138–41, 145–6, 150–2, 153n4; crime-control policies, attitudes toward 78; criminal justice system, attitudes toward 72, 73–4, 76; death penalty, attitudes toward 67, 73, 78; differential involvement hypothesis 100, 102; disproportionality 99–105; drug use 31–2; drug wars and 102–4, 105–6, 113n3, 118, 120, 150–1; employment, effect of incarceration on 37–8; gay and lesbian rights, attitudes toward 66; incarceration rates 32–3, 144, 145; legalizing marijuana, attitudes toward 67–8, *68*, *69*, 74–8, *75*; legalizing marijuana, effect on 147–9; marijuana use 4, 70, *70*, 106, 110; medical marijuana, attitudes toward 68, *69–70*, 70; "outdoors" corner drug dealer explanation 101–2; police power used against 139–40; political efforts for 7; political views 66, 76; premarital sex, attitudes toward 72, 73; Proposition 19 (California) 59, *59*, 60, *61*; racism against, generally 93–4; racism against, in criminal justice system 95, 100–1, 113n3; religious organizations and leaders 111–12; segregation 9, 151; spanking, attitudes toward 72, 73

Blumstein, Alfred 92, 99–101, 102–4, 114n3, 114n5
booking costs 25, *26, 27*
Broadus, Calvin "Snoop Dogg" 106–7
Brookins, Howard 123
Brown, Michael K. 94
Brown decision (1954) 9
"Building Blocks for Youth" advocacy initiative 95
Bunche, Ralph 152–3
Buscaglia, Edgardo 131
Bush, George H.W. 79, 80, 87
Bush, George W. 123–4, 128
Busted (Frontline episode) 116–17

Calderón, Felipe: drug war 127–8; international legalization policy 135; organized crime, battle against 126, 127; Proposition 19 (California) 121–2, 131, *132–3, 133–4,* 136–7
California: Black population 109, 114n11; Legislative Analyst's Office 16; marijuana arrests 107–9, 110–11, 114nn6–8; Proposition 187 55–6; *see also* costs of prohibiting marijuana in California; Proposition 19 (California)
cannabis *see* marijuana
Cannabis Expiation Notice (CEN) 44–6, *45, 46*
Cannabis Infringement Notice (CIN) 46–7
Cartoon All-Stars to the Rescue (television special) 87
caseloads, banked 24, 30n11
casinos 6–7
Castañeda, Jorge G. 130–1
CEN (Cannabis Expiation Notice) 44–6, *45, 46*
Chicago 123
Chicago Tribune 95
children 7–8, 37
chronic, as term 153n1; *see also* marijuana
CIN (Cannabis Infringement Notice) 46–7
Clinton, Bill 80, 91n4
clubs, buyer/grower 50–1, *52*
CNBC 109–10, 114n12
cocaine 103–4, 105, 128, 142–3
coercion: about 149–50; against Blacks 138–41, 145–6, 150–2, 153n4; push back against 145–6
coffee-shop system, Dutch cannabis 47–50, *52,* 53n5, 148

cohort hypothesis 81–3, *83, 85,* 86, 88–90, *89*
collectives, buyer/grower 50–1, *52*
college education *59,* 60, *61, 85,* 86
Colombia 134
commercialization thesis 49–50, 53n5
community corrections costs 23–4, 25, *26, 27*
community justice model 35
Condemnation of Blackness, The (Muhammad) 95–6
conservatism, political 76; *see also* Republicans
Cope, John 136
Corcoran, Patrick 136–7
correctional supervision statistics 3
corrections costs 15, 16
costs of prohibiting marijuana in California 13–30; about 13; adjudication 19–21, *20,* 30n5; approach toward estimating 16–17, *18;* arrests 15, 17–19, *18,* 25, *26, 27;* calculating 16–25, *18, 20,* 30n5; California Legislative Analyst's Office estimates 16; community corrections 23–4, 25, *26, 27;* corrections costs 15, 16; court and law enforcement costs 16; discussion 28–9, 30n12; estimates, existing 13–16; fines and seizures 24; Gieringer estimate 15, 28; incarceration 25, *26, 27;* interpretation issues 28–9; jail 22–3, 30n8; judicial costs 14–15, 29n3; limitations 28–9; Miron estimates 14–15, *15–16,* 28; parole 23; police costs 14; prison *21,* 21–2, 30n6; probation 23–4; prosecution 25, *26, 27;* sensitivity analysis 25–6, *27,* 28; technical violations 24–5
court and law enforcement costs 16
crack cocaine 103–4, 105
crime: Black attitudes toward 78; media coverage 94–5, 109–10, 114n12; statistics, racial 95–7; White attitudes toward *85,* 86
criminal justice system: attitudes toward 72, 73–4, 76; Blacks, racism against 95, 100–1, 113n3, 146; Latino politics of Proposition 19 (California) 117–18, *119,* 120; racism in, generally 6; *see also* costs of prohibiting marijuana in California; *specific topics*

death penalty 67, 73, 78
democracy 152–3

Democrats: gay and lesbian rights 78;
marijuana legalization, White attitudes
toward *85*, 86, 87–8; medical marijuana,
White attitudes toward *89*, 89–90;
Proposition 19 (California) *57*, 57–8,
58, 60, *61*
deportation from United States 122
differential involvement hypothesis 100,
102
DiIulio, John, Jr. 97
drug addiction 8–9
drug-trafficking organizations, Mexican
121, 122, 127–8, 130–1, 133–4
drug wars: Blacks and 102–4, 105–6,
113n3, 118, 120, 150–1; cycles 153n5;
effects 3–4; history 142–4; HIV and 36;
Latinos and 118, 120; marijuana 143;
Mexico 127–8
Dutch cannabis coffee-shop system 47–50,
52, 53n5, 148

ecological models 34–5
education, college *59*, 60, *61*, *85*, 86
elitism 9–10
employment, effects of incarceration on
37–8
Everingham, Susan 142–3
extramarital sex *84*, 84–5, 91n9

families, incarceration's effects on 37
federal government 5, 42
fines and seizures 24
Fishman, Laura 94
Foucault, Michel 140–1, 149–50, 151
Fox, Vicente 122, 129–30
Frontline 116–17
full-market models 41–2, 51, *52*; *see also*
legalization of marijuana; Proposition 19
(California)

Garcia, Joe 121
gateway theory 31, 47, 50, 71, 112
gay and lesbian rights 66, 78
gay sex *84*, 84–5, 91n9
gender *59*, 60, *61*, 74, *75*, 77
generational explanations 81–3, *83*, *85*, 86,
88–90, *89*
Gieringer, Dale H. 15, 28
Gingrich, Newt 80
Global Commission on Drug Policy
129–30
government coercion *see* coercion

health *see* public-health considerations
heuristics 66, 67
hip-hop rap 106–7
Hispanics *see* Latinos
HIV epidemic 36
home cultivation of marijuana 43–7, *44*,
45, *46*, *52*
homosexual behavior *84*, 84–5, 91n9
hyper incarceration, as term 113n1

Illinois 33–4, *34*
immigrants and immigration 55–6, 120–4
incarceration: children, effects on 37; costs
25, *26*, *27*; employment, effects on 37–8;
families, effects on 37; health risks 36–7;
hyper incarceration, as term 113n1; mass
incarceration, as term 113n1
incarceration rates: Blacks 32–3, 144, 145;
state-level 93; United States 4, 32, 39n5,
93
Independent Party *85*, 86
information costs 55
international legalization of marijuana 133,
134–6

jail costs 22–3, 30n8
judicial costs 14–15, 29n3

knowledge, political *58*, 58–9, *61*
Ku Klux Klan (KKK) 66

Latinos: criminal justice politics 117–18,
119, 120; deportation from United
States 122; drug wars and 118, 120;
immigration politics 120–4; marijuana
arrests 117–18, *119*; marijuana laws
115–17; marijuana use 4; political efforts
for 7; Proposition 19 (California) 59, *59*,
61, 115, 120–4; *see also* Mexico
law enforcement costs 16
legalization of marijuana: alternatives to
full-market legalization, generally 40–1;
benefits 1–2, 3–5, 147; Blacks, attitudes
toward 67–8, *68*, *69*, 74–8, *75*; Blacks,
effect on 147–9; cannabis clubs and
licensing models 50–1, *52*; carceral
system reform and 105–12; drawbacks 2,
5–10, 147; Dutch cannabis coffee-shop
system 47–50, *52*, 53n5, 148; as elitist
9–10; full-market models 41–2, 51, *52*;
home cultivation 43–7, *44*, *45*, *46*, *52*;
international 133, 134–6; marijuana use
and 7; of medical marijuana 1;

opposition to 2, 5–10, 147; political costs of 9; public policy changes 79–80, 83–4; support for 1–2, 3–5, 147; *see also* Proposition 19 (California)
Legislative Analyst's Office (California) 16
legitimacy, political 152–3
lesbian rights 66, 78
liberation hypothesis 98
licensing schemes 50–1, *52*
Los Angeles County, California 22, 23
Loury, Glenn 102

marijuana: clubs and licensing models 50–1, *52*; Dutch coffee-shop system 47–50, *52*, 53n5, 148; home cultivation 43–7, *44, 45, 46, 52*; imports to United States 120; laws, anti-Mexican history of 115–17; medical 1, 68, *69–70*, 70, 80, 123–4; prices 46, *46*, 50; school grounds, sales on 33, 34, *34*; war on 143; *see also* marijuana arrests; marijuana use; *specific topics*
marijuana arrests: California 107–9, 110–11, 114nn6–8; Illinois 33–4, *34*; Latinos, consequences for 117–18; rates 106, 118, *119*
marijuana use: Blacks 4, 70, *70*, 106, 110; health effects 6, 148; Latinos 4; legalization, effect of 7; media coverage 4, 106–7; other illegal drug use compared to 31; racialization of 4; treatment for 49; United States 70, *70*, 106, 110; Whites 4, 107, 110
mass incarceration, as term 113n1
media coverage 4, 94–5, 106–7, 109–10, 114n12
medical marijuana 1, 68, *69–70*, 70, 80, 123–4
Merida Initiative 128
methamphetamine 128
Mexico: as consumer nation 128–9; drug decriminalization, previous 129; drug policy, voices for change in 129–30; drug-trafficking organizations 121, 122, 127–8, 130–1, 133–4; drug war, U.S. cooperation in 127–8; international drug prohibition regime change 134–6; marijuana imports to United States 120; marijuana laws, anti-Mexican history of 115–17; organized crime, battle against 127; Proposition 19, Calderón's statements on 131, *132–3*, 133–4;

Proposition 19, generally 121–2, 126–7, 137–8; Proposition 19, questionable potential of 130–1; *see also* Latinos
minority perspective, generally 3, 12n1
Miron, J. A. 14–15, 15–16, 28, 29n3
moral fabric of community 8
MSNBC 109
Muhammad, Khalil Gibran 95–6, 99–100

National Crime Victimization Survey (NCVS) 98, 104
National Geographic 114n12
Native Americans 6–7
Netherlands 47–50, 51, *52*, 53n5, 148
Newsweek 95
New York City 65, 111
New York state 123
Nixon, Richard 91n8, 105–6
North Carolina 114n5
Noy v. State (Alaska) 43

Oakland, California 1
Obama, Barack 123–4, 135
Oliver, Pamela 144, 145
On the Racial Disproportionality of the United States Prison Populations (Blumstein) 99–101
"outdoors" corner drug dealer explanation 101–2

parole 23, 35; *see also* community corrections costs
partial-market approach 47–50, *52*, 53n5, 148; *see also* legalization of marijuana; Proposition 19 (California)
partisanship 55–6, *85*, 86, 87–8; *see also* Democrats; Republicans
Passage, David 143–4
path-dependence 135, 138n4
Peña Nieto, Enrique 122
Petersilia, J. 95, 113n3
Plessy decision 9
police and policing 14, 100, 139–40
political conservatism 76; *see also* Republicans
political knowledge *58*, 58–9, *61*
political legitimacy 152–3
political tolerance 66
predispositions, nonpolitical 56, 64n8
premarital sex *72*, 73
prices, marijuana 46, *46*, 50
prison costs *21*, 21–2, 30n6

probation 23–4; *see also* community corrections costs
"Prop 19" (documentary) 118
Proposition 19 (California): age as variable
59, *59*, 60, *61*; Calderón, Felipe 121–2,
131, *132–3*, 133–4, 136–7; cost savings
estimates 16; demographic variables
59, 59–60, *61*; education as variable
59, 60, *61*; electoral data 61–2, *62*, *63*;
failure reasons, generally 54–5, 63–4; as
full-market model 41–2, 51, *52*; gender
as variable *59*, 60, *61*; opposition to 2–3;
political knowledge as variable *58*, 58–9,
61; political party as variable *57*, 57–8,
58, 60, *61*; political variables 57–9, *58*,
60, *61*; race/ethnicity as variable 59,
59, 60, *61*; regression, ordered logistic
60, *61*, 64n10; religion as variable *59*,
60, *61*; support for 1–2, 6; survey about
56–60, *57*; theoretical foundations for
study 55–6; *see also* costs of prohibiting
marijuana in California; Mexico
Proposition 187 (California) 55–6
prosecution costs 25, *26*, *27*
prostitution, legalization of 8
public-health considerations 31–9; about
31–2; children and families, effects of
incarceration on 37; drugs, drug laws,
and Blacks 32–3; ecological and community justice models 34–5; employment, effects of incarceration on 37–8;
HIV epidemic 36; incarceration, health
risks of 36–7; marijuana arrests in
Illinois 33–4, *34*; marijuana use health
effects 6, 148; violence 37
public policy changes 79–80, 83–4

racial crime statistics 95–7
racial utility heuristic 66
racism: against Blacks, generally 93–4;
against Blacks, in criminal justice system
95, 100–1, 113n3, 146; in criminal
justice system, generally 6; law and 9; *see
also specific topics*
RAND report 122, 130
Rangel, Charles 3
rap, hip-hop 106–7
Ravin v. State (Alaska) 43
Reagan, Nancy 87
Reagan, Ronald 80, 87
Reed, Adolph, Jr. 98–9
religion *59*, 60, *61*, 74, *75*, 77–8

Republicans: medical marijuana, attitudes
toward *89*, 89–90; Proposition 19 (California) *57*, 57–8, *58*, 60, *61*; Whites *85*,
86, 87, *89*, 89–90
Rydell, Peter 142–3

San Diego County, California 22, 23
schemas 71
school grounds, cannabis sales on 33, 34,
34
school segregation 9
segregation 9, 151
seizures 24
self-interest 56
sex: extramarital *84*, 84–5, 91n9; gay *84*,
84–5, 91n9; premarital 72, *73*
Shirk, David 130
Silver, Nate 131
Snoop Dogg 106–7
social issues, generally 65–7
South Australia 44–6, *45*, *46*
Spain 51
spanking 72, *73*
state coercion *see* coercion
state government 5, 42; *see also specific
states*
State v. McNeil (Alaska) 43
statistics, racial crime 95–7

tax-and-regulate models 41–2, 51, *52*;
see also legalization of marijuana;
Proposition 19 (California)
technical violations 24–5
THC content, taxing by 42
Thernstrom, Abigail 104–5
Thernstrom, Stephan 104–5
Time 95
tolerance, political 66

unemployment and underemployment
6–7
Uniform Crime Reports (UCR) 96, 98,
104
United States: deportation from 122; incarceration rates 4, 32, 39n5, 93; marijuana
imports to 120; Mexico's drug war,
cooperation in 127–8; public policy
changes 79–80, 83–4; *see also specific
states; specific topics*

violations, technical 24–5
violence 37

Wacquant, Loic 102, 113n1
war on drugs *see* drug wars
Weaver, Velsa Mae 94
weight, taxing by 42
Western Australia 46–7
Whites: abortion, attitudes toward 84, *84,* 91n9; "Black deviance-White inno-cence" binary 93–9; cohort hypothesis 81–3, *83, 85,* 86, 88–90, *89;* crime and punishment, attitudes toward *85,* 86; extramarital sex, attitudes toward *84,* 84–5, 91n9; gay sex, attitudes toward *84,* 84–5, 91n9; marijuana arrests 107, 118, *119;* marijuana debate, putting in con-text 83–8, *84, 85;* marijuana use 4, *107,* 110; medical marijuana, attitudes toward 88–90, *89;* Proposition 19 (California) 59, *59, 61*
Wilson, James Q. 104
Wisconsin 145
Wise, Tim 93–4

Zedillo, Ernesto 129
Zuberi, Tukufu 96